THE ARTS AND THE LEGAL ACADEMY

Emerging Legal Education

Emerging Legal Education is a forum for analysing the discourse of legal education and creating innovative ways of learning the law. The series focuses on research, theory and practice within legal education, drawing attention to historical, interdisciplinary and international characteristics, and is based upon imaginative and sophisticated educational thinking. The series takes a broad view of theory and practice. Series books are written for an international audience and are sensitive to the diversity of contexts in which law is taught, learned and practised.

Other titles in this series:

Law and Leadership
Integrating Leadership Studies into the Law School Curriculum
Edited by Paula Monopoli and Susan McCarty

The Moral Imagination and the Legal Life
Beyond Text in Legal Education
Edited by Zenon Bańkowski and Maksymilian Del Mar

Affect and Legal Education
Emotion in Learning and Teaching the Law
Edited by Paul Maharg and Caroline Maughan

The Arts and the Legal Academy

Beyond Text in Legal Education

Edited by

ZENON BAŃKOWSKI
University of Edinburgh, UK

MAKSYMILIAN DEL MAR
Queen Mary, University of London, UK

PAUL MAHARG
Northumbria University, UK

Routledge
Taylor & Francis Group
LONDON AND NEW YORK

First published 2013 by Ashgate Publishing

Published 2016 by Routledge
2 Park Square, Milton Park, Abingdon, Oxfordshire OX14 4RN
711 Third Avenue, New York, NY 10017, USA

First issued in paperback 2016

Routledge is an imprint of the Taylor & Francis Group, an informa business

British Library Cataloguing in Publication Data
The arts and the legal academy : beyond text in legal
education. -- (Emerging legal education)
1. Law--Study and teaching--Methodology. 2. Arts in education.
I. Series II. Bańkowski, Zenon. III. Del Mar, Maksymilian,
1979- IV. Maharg, Paul.
340'.0711-dc23

Library of Congress Cataloging-in-Publication Data
The arts and the legal academy : beyond text in legal education. Vol. 1 / by Zenon Bańkowski, Maksymilian Del Mar and Paul Maharg.
p. cm. -- (Emerging legal education)
Complements the book "The moral imagination and the legal life" by the same editorial team.
Includes bibliographical references and index.
ISBN 978-1-4094-2911-1 (hardback) 1. Law--Study and teaching--Philosophy.
2. Art in education--Philosophy. 3. Law--Study and teaching--Methodology.
4. Law and aesthetics. I. Bańkowski, Zenon. II. Del Mar, Maksymilian,
1979- III. Maharg, Paul. IV. Moral imagination and the legal life.
K100.A88 2012
340.071--dc23

2012027614

ISBN 13: 978-1-138-27725-0 (pbk)
ISBN 13: 978-1-4094-2911-1 (hbk)

Contents

List of Figures

List of Tables

List of Contributors

Bruce Anderson's research and writing has been concerned with legal decision-making and economic theory. Recently, he graduated with a BFA degree (major in sculpture) from the Nova Scotia College of Art and Design. He is a Professor of Business Law at Saint Mary's University, Halifax, Nova Scotia.

Miriam Aziz is a performance artist/musician and composer/film maker/scholar. She is the founder and artistic director of *Artist(s) at Large* based in Italy and in New York.

Zenon Bańkowski is Emeritus Professor of Legal Theory at the School of Law, University of Edinburgh. He was Principal Investigator of the AHRC Beyond Text in Legal Education Project, based at the School of Law in Edinburgh.

Karen Barton is Director of Legal Practice Courses at the University of Strathclyde Law School. She has published widely on many aspects of legal education and professional learning and has been involved in a number of large scale collaborative research projects in these areas including *The Standardised Client Project*, *The Portfolio Pilot Project*, *The SIMPLE Project* and *Simshare: Open Education Resources in Simulation Learning*. She is a member of the British and Irish Law, Education, Technology Association (BILETA) Executive and on the editorial board of the *European Journal of Law and Technology*.

Suzanne Bouclin is an assistant professor at the University of Ottawa's Faculty of Law (French Programme). Her current research is on law and aesthetics and she also writes and teaches on feminist jurisprudence, poverty law, alternative legal methodologies and transformative pedagogy.

James Benedict Brown is Lecturer in Architecture at Norwich University College of the Arts. His doctoral research concerns live projects in architectural education.

Gillian Calder is an associate professor at the Faculty of Law, University of Victoria. Her current research interests include the relationship between women, work and family; the provision of social benefits through Canadian law; feminist, constitutional and equality theories; performance and law, and the intersection of all of these questions with the goal of developing the ethical imagination of today's law student.

Andy Clark is Professor of Logic and Metaphysics in the School of Philosophy, Psychology and Language Sciences, University of Edinburgh. He is the author of *Being There: Putting Brain, Body and World Together Again* (MIT Press, 1997), *Mindware* (Oxford University Press, 2001), *Natural-Born Cyborgs: Minds, Technologies and the Future of Human Intelligence* (Oxford University Press, 2003) and *Supersizing the Mind: Embodiment, Action, and Cognitive Extension* (Oxford University Press, 2008). His research interests include robotics and artificial life, the cognitive role of human-built structures, specialization and interactive dynamics in neural systems, and the interplay between language, thought, socio-technological scaffolding and action.

Sharon Cowan is a senior lecturer in law at the University of Edinburgh. Her research interests include gender, sexuality and the law; law, performance and popular culture, and asylum and immigration law.

Maksymilian Del Mar is Lecturer in Legal and Social Philosophy at the Department of Law, Queen Mary, University of London. He was a key collaborator in the AHRC Beyond Text in Legal Education Project, based at the School of Law, University of Edinburgh.

Valerie Fitch is the Director of Professional Development at Pillsbury Winthrop Shaw Pittman LLP, a US law firm. She became Pillsbury's Director of Professional Development in 1998 after practising in the firm's litigation section for nine years. She is also Adjunct Professor of Law at Brooklyn Law School, teaching Legal Writing and also Fundamentals of Legal Drafting.

John Garvey is Professor of Law and Director of the Daniel Webster Scholar Honors Program at the University of New Hampshire, USA. He is the 2011 recipient of the New Hampshire Bar Association Award for Outstanding Professionalism, based upon his efforts with the Program. He has also been repeatedly selected for inclusion in *Best Lawyers in America* for his expertise as a mediator and arbitrator.

Sophia Lycouris holds a practice-led PhD in improvisational dance performance and is currently Reader in Interdisciplinary Choreography at the University of Edinburgh. She researches the use of interactive technologies in interdisciplinary choreographic projects and the role of movement in the social and public space in relation to issues of architecture, urban planning and social exclusion. She has contributed to *Contemporary Choreography: A Critical Reader*, published by Routledge in 2009, with a chapter on interdisciplinary choreography.

Paul Maharg is Professor of Legal Education at Northumbria University Law School and Adjunct Professor at the Australian National University College of Law. He has written extensively on legal education. He blogs at http://paulmaharg.com.

Kim Morgan is a sculpture/installation artist working in multimedia. For the last six years she has been exploring the process of cross-disciplinary collaborations through the creation of interactive public art projects in partnership with scientists, engineers and other artists. She is an assistant professor at the Nova Scotia School of Art and Design University in Halifax, where she teaches sculpture, installation and public art.

Andreas Philippopoulos-Mihalopoulos is Professor of Law & Theory at the University of Westminster and Director of the Westminster International Law & Theory Centre. His research interests include critical autopoiesis, continental philosophy, law and literature, gender studies, law and art. His edited *Law and the City* (2007) and *Law and Ecology* (2011), and his monographs *Absent Environments* (2007) and *Niklas Luhmann: Law, Justice, Society* (2009) are published by Routledge.

Anne Pirrie is Reader in Education at the University of the West of Scotland. She has wide-ranging and divergent research interests. Her recent work has been on the epistemological bases of social research.

Nancy B. Rapoport is the Gordon Silver Professor of Law at the William S. Boyd School of Law, University of Nevada, Las Vegas. She received her BA in Psychology, *summa cum laude*, from Rice University and her JD from Stanford Law School. Her research involves the intersection of ethics with bankruptcy law, corporate governance and popular culture.

Burkhard Schafer is Professor for Computational Legal Theory and Director of the SCRIPT Centre for IT and IP law at the University of Edinburgh. With a background in theory of science and theoretical philosophy, he has been working in a legal environment for the past 15 years, focusing on the interface between law and the cognitive and natural sciences.

Wendy Timmons is Programme Director for the MSc Dance Science and Education at the University of Edinburgh, where she lectures in Preventive Dance Medicine, Dance Pedagogy and Aesthetics. She is co-author of the book *Basic Principles of Dance Medicine* (2002) and is a member of the Research in Dance Education Editorial Board. Her research activity includes injury prevention and hypermobility in dance and the use of technology to provide sensory feedback for dancers.

Panagia Voyatzis is a Doctoral Researcher in Law at the University of Edinburgh. She researches on precedent-based reasoning and legal education.

Gary Watt is Professor of Law at the University of Warwick and Visiting Professor at the Université René Descartes, Paris. He was named 'Law Teacher of the Year' in 2009 and was made a National Teaching Fellow in 2010 and a fellow of the Higher Education Academy in 2011. He is the co-founder and co-editor of the journal *Law and Humanities* and his books include *Shakespeare and the Law* (with P. Raffield) (Hart Publishing, 2008); *Equity Stirring: The Story of Justice Beyond Law* (Hart, 2009); *Trusts and Equity* (Oxford University Press, 2009); and *How to Moot: A Student Guide to Mooting* (with J. Snape) (Oxford University Press, 2010). He has written for BBC Radio Three and for the *Times Literary Supplement* and he delivers workshops on rhetoric for the Royal Shakespeare Company.

Elaine Webster is Lecturer in Public Law at the University of Strathclyde and Director of the Centre for the Study of Human Rights Law. She is currently undertaking postgraduate studies in academic practice.

Introduction

Zenon Bańkowski, Maksymilian Del Mar and Paul Maharg[1]

General Introduction to the Two Volumes

This present volume is one of two volumes of papers flowing from a project, 'Beyond Text in Legal Education', hosted by the School of Law at the University of Edinburgh. The aim of the two volumes as a whole is to contribute to the reinvigoration of legal education, primarily in law schools but also extending to law firms. We attempt this reinvigoration by introducing the importance and usefulness of pedagogical resources that go beyond text, i.e. resources from the visual and movement arts. Taken as a whole, the two-volume work explores the use of these non-textual resources for legal education and legal scholarship. It is not restricted to any area of law or to any particular form of going beyond text. It includes contributions that explore different ways of visualizing legal knowledge, different ways of designing and interacting with spaces for exploring legal issues, as well as different ways of performing a variety of legal problems. The premise of the work is that the teaching and research of law can be experienced in ways that do not depend exclusively on text, but that have recourse to the full range and diversity of the sensory capacities of teachers, students, professionals and scholars. In that sense, we also recognize that different persons all have different sensory strengths and weakness, that is, that we all experience in different ways and thus also learn via different sensory pathways.

The project that is the subject of this book was part of a UK Arts and Humanities Research Council (AHRC) funding programme called 'Beyond Text'. This funding programme recognized that non-textual material and communication through visual, oral and sensory means were an important part of our culture. We now have the means to reach many quickly and communication becomes rapid and in some cases transitory. The aim was to create a research programme where scholars could study the issues concerning the non-textual dimensions of culture. This would involve, *inter alia,* a study of the material conditions of these non-textual means and also their control and dissemination. Further, it would look at the technology itself and how this impacted upon the culture and tradition. Out of these issues, of particular importance to our project were questions of performativity, of how we transmit multimedia non-textual objects,

---

1 Our thanks to Martin Taggart for assistance with the finalization of the text of both volumes.

and the impact upon traditional methods of cognition in the transmission and remembering of culture. This implied looking at learning and teaching and the way we might be able to use non-textual methods even in areas that are primarily textual. What would be important here would be the mediation between the text and the non-text aspects, the imagination that would be brought into play and the use that imagination could be put to. How do these new modes that use all the bodily senses play on the imagination and what does that imagination do in helping to create an embodied knowledge?

The role of the imagination in teaching and learning, and the way in which these can be enhanced and enriched by the use of non-textual resources, is a key aspect of the 'Beyond Text in Legal Education' project. Although 'imagination' was understood broadly, one of the most important features of the project was to consider how the ethical or moral imagination could be developed through a combination of text-based and (especially) non-text-based resources properly incorporated into tertiary and professional legal education curricula.

Law is very much a text-based discipline, both in its practice and its education. Legal education, both at the tertiary and continuing professional levels, has been and continues to be dominated by recourse to textual resources. Law students and legal professionals are taught to learn and understand general rules and principles, and apply them to pre-manufactured factual scenarios. This is no different when it comes to the education of legal professional ethics, where, typically, moral theories are presented as consisting of general axioms that allow students and professionals to rationally resolve traditional problem cases (pre-articulated factual scenarios that are designed to produce moral dilemmas). The pursuit of professional integrity is dominated by promoting the ability to use complex systems of ethical postulates to justify the making of a certain decision in relation to a pre-determined set of facts.

There is no doubt that the development and use of text-based resources facilitates the exercise of skills that are important to the ethical development of law students and legal professionals. Learning how to better articulate and justify one's reasoning by reference to complex systems of normative languages is important. However, the exclusive emphasis on textual resources, on languages and their manipulation, carries with it significant dangers. Such an exclusive focus can be restrictive in that it can result in law students and legal professionals never acquiring the skill of coming to see and recognize the ethical complexity of any given situation; it places at risk their ability to overcome the limitation of the categories with which they are working, particularly when the particular situation itself puts into question those categories. Coping with this limit requires the exercise of the (ethical) imagination. Such an exercise enables the person to respond to the complexity and particularity of the situation, and to come up with just and imaginative ways of going forward.

There is a considerable amount of work in this context that has been and continues to be conducted by those who emphasize the value of the 'literary imagination' and the use of literature for these purposes. Some of this work has found its way into the post-professional education programmes of major law firms, principally in the USA. While the invocation of the literary imagination in this context is important, it is still too heavily text-based. What the 'Beyond Text in Legal Education' project aimed at was creating a space where the (ethical) imagination can be inculcated and the movement beyond can be experienced in non-textual ways. The project does not wish to suggest that non-textual resources should replace textual ones. It goes beyond text, but does not leave it behind completely. Rather, it seeks to provoke reflection upon the value of non-textual resources in developing imaginative (ethical) perception amongst law students and legal professionals.

In these two volumes, then, it is recognized that legal education and legal practice are both steeped in specific texts and institutions. These texts and institutions define the profession; they orient us; their categories and pathways give us a structure within which we not only participate but also evaluate each other. Yet it is also recognized that the complexity of moral life, and professional life more generally, is not reflected by any one set of texts and institutions. Indeed, it is argued that what is needed, at those moments in which already-existing categories and pathways run out, is the exercise of the (ethical) imagination. However, this (ethical) imagination cannot be understood too cognitively or too rationally; nor can it be said to exist in the manipulation or reorganization of already-existing categories and pathways. This (ethical) imagination is, instead, better understood to be embodied, situated, affective and creative. In constructing this approach to the (ethical) imagination, these two volumes draw on a number of theoretical traditions, including embodied and situated cognition, philosophy of the emotions, theology, aesthetics, and legal and moral theory.

The aim of this volume is to contribute to legal education in a general way, i.e. to the learning and teaching of any area of the law. This volume also includes some chapters that introduce and discuss general resources and issues concerning non-text-based reasoning and non-text-based resources. The remaining chapters in this volume focus on exploring the pedagogical and, to some extent, moral value of non-textual resources in legal education. The companion volume builds on this one and focuses in more detail on the potential contribution of non-text-based resources to moral education in law schools and law firms. The contributors to both volumes include a wide range of theorists and educators, including legal educators in the UK and the USA working in both law schools and law firms, some of whom have used such resources before, and others who did so as a result of the 'Beyond Text in Legal Education' project.

The project started from this thought and this analogy: when people view art objects in galleries, too often they rely on textual explanation, looking for the text in the catalogue to explain it and not letting the object explain itself. Some curators try to get people to engage the art object without text, to use their imagination to let the object speak to them and not be subsumed by the text. Lawyers face an analogous situation when they encounter events that require decisions to be made; too often they look to the text and do not experience the particularity of the situation by letting it speak for itself. Part of the aim, then, practically speaking, was to explore – by working together with an art gallery – this analogy. We wanted to provide a space – literally, a gallery space – where law students and lawyers would be able to experimentally explore legal and ethical skills in unfamiliar ways, precisely by means of non-text-based activities and relying only on non-text-based resources.

Prior to this experiential workshop (about which we will say more below), we held, on 8 November 2008, a one-day workshop, involving a small group of philosophers, theologians and lawyers, who met to discuss the conceptual, ethical and practical implications of this view of law and cognition. These issues were discussed specifically against the backdrop of a provisional programme of activities for the experiential workshop. This initial conference helped us further refine the activities and aims of the experiential workshop.

The experiential workshop itself was the centrepiece of the project. It was held over two days, 7–8 December 2008. The workshop programme and its delivery on the two days was primarily the responsibility of three artists, a visual-based artist (Alicja Rogalska), a movement-based artist (Keren Ben-Dor) and a curator (Zoe Fothergill, who is an artist in her own right). The workshop was held, in large part, in the Talbot Rice Gallery, which is the gallery based at Old College, University of Edinburgh. The participants included legal professionals, legal scholars and legal education (both tertiary and professional) policy makers from the UK and the USA. The artists were all experienced in working with persons who have had no or little exposure to the production and/or appreciation of visual and movement-based art.

The aim of the workshop was in line with the above-described aims of the project, i.e. it aimed to develop non-textually the skills that may enable lawyers to engage the (ethical) imagination, to experience the particularity of the situation and the vulnerability of those in it, and to allow that situation to speak and help them move beyond the law by transforming it, but not destroying it. The experiential workshop, then, delivered on our objective to create a space for legally trained people to explore the production of visually and movement-based art, and also to explore non-textually affective experience and practice in law. It was most certainly a highlight of our project. It was highly risky and experimental. We did things that took us well out of our comfort zones. But the careful planning and skill of the artists made it highly successful both as an event and as a learning experience. The group dynamics that began in this workshop carried over for the whole of the project. We built reflexivity into the workshop so that throughout there was time to reflect together on the exercises and how we felt. The reflexivity included, for instance, randomly placed voice-recorders upon which participants could verbally record their reflections.

The workshop programme has been included as 'Appendix A' of this Introduction. The workshop was also filmed. We hired a film maker, Robert McKillop, who was with us for the entire two days. The film was not a mere record, but was also an artistic outcome in its own right. It also fed into the research itself in that it became part of the research process and interacted with it, and it played an integral role in the succeeding seminars and in our thinking as to how to go forward with the project. In that sense, the film highlighted the 'Beyond Textual' nature of the project and unexpectedly transformed our conception of research method.

After the experiential workshop, we organized two further reflective workshops. The first, held on 6 March 2009, was a small workshop entitled 'Understanding Transformation'. Here, we studied the underlying ethical issues, though more in the context of physical and social processes, bringing together a group of sociologists, philosophers and cognitive scientists with some knowledge of neuroscience to look at the cognitive and sociological processes involved. We looked at the *embodied* nature of what was happening, at the physical and other processes that are involved here, especially legal visualization and what might be called multi-sensory law. We asked: how does the experience of encounter, seeing and vulnerability get played out on the body?

Our second reflective event was a major two-day conference, held on 20–21 June 2009. This conference included some experiential elements, including interactive theatre, but the focus was on the theoretical and practical reflections of participants in the experiential workshop. It is the papers presented at this conference, together with a number of extra specially invited additions, which constitute the chapters published in these two volumes.

Chapters in this Volume

As noted above, the 13 chapters included in this volume are a mix of specially commissioned papers as well as responses from the participants in the 'Beyond Text in Legal Education' project, and especially the experiential workshop organized in December 2008 in Edinburgh. Even the authors of the chapters that were specially commissioned were made aware of the project and its aims and preliminary findings, and so they too can be considered to be responses.

Taken as responses, then, the chapters vary considerably, not so much on a scale of positive or negative but on what one might analogize as a barometric scale of high and low pressure. To a large extent, the participants were selected by the editors or were self-selecting, but given that there was always going to be a community of interests and practices among the participants, what is striking about this collection as a whole is how varied the responses are to the project and how different the individual chapters are. The project seemed to elicit from some participants quite deeply personal responses, though this was not the case with all. Nor was it uniformly so for these participants; instead, the project drew out aspects of legal and educational thinking in which they had already been engaged to some extent. Participants' interpretations of the project were obviously based on their prior personal experiences and their sense of their individual interests, but the main goal of attempting to facilitate legal learning beyond text clearly bound all in a common critical goal.

This volume is divided into three parts. Part I offers chapters that discuss and introduce, from multi-disciplinary and interdisciplinary perspectives, non-text skills and non-text resources. Part II focuses on the uses that can be made of non-text resources in law schools, and Part III on uses of those resources in the context of professional legal education (including professional certificate-level, pre-qualification courses).

Part I: General and Interdisciplinary Perspectives

Many of the issues dealt with later in the volume are raised in Chapter 1 by **Andy Clark**, and in that sense the chapter serves as a signature for what is to come. Moral cognition is Clark's dominant theme and, as he points out, '[r]easoning and inference can now be reconstructed as processes of pattern completion and pattern extension', and much of the chapter is given over to exploring the consequences of this understanding of cognition. For Clark, connectionist approaches reconceive the 'role of linguistically formulated moral rules and principles' precisely because they enable collaboration in the exploration of moral conduct through discussion, argument and dialogue: 'linguistic expression enables a tuning and orchestration of moral response that is vital to moral expertise'. This is true, Clark holds, for the novice as well as the expert (*contra* Dreyfus and Dreyfus); and his example of pattern-recognition in the game Tetris bears this out at the level of manipulation. However, he goes further, and argues that it is the collaborative aspects of linguistic formulations of moral cognition that affect its existence. As he puts it, any persuasive account of moral cognition and moral expertise 'must attend to a variety of thus far neglected, communication-specific, higher-order prototype spaces'.

What might these 'prototype spaces' look like? The rest of the volume provides the answer to this question. Thus, in Chapter 2, **Anne Pirrie** and **James Benedict Brown** explore the space and motion of the professional as wayfarer. Their interdisciplinary chapter, largely architecture and professional education, has direct import for legal education. Exploring two projects that attempted to break out of the architecture design school box, Polyark I (1973) and its successor, Polyark II (2009), they map the challenges of innovative educational practice by adopting the metaphors of wayfaring and travelling. Klee's description of two types of lines is cited: the line that is 'intrinsically dynamic and temporal' and the 'line that is in a hurry', 'more like a series of appointments than a walk'. The first is like the pad sketch: dynamic, fluid, about process and context. The second is equivalent to the formal architectural plan submitted to administrative procedures and other professionals. Each is valuable in its context, but the authors question whether the Polyark initiatives really were profoundly meandering or whether they were a line of appointments. The architectural metaphors are resonant for anyone involved in legal education: which best describes our teaching and our students' learning? How we implicitly accept or attempt to change the architecture and physical space of our curricula affects how much our students can achieve in the way of learning.

Chapter 3 in this part, on the same theme of space, makes the ambitious claim that 'bodily practices such as dance can contribute to the development of ethical and moral reasoning', citing Lakoff and Johnson on 'moral nurturing', as well as Bandura and Vygotsky on the effect of context on learning. **Sophia Lycouris** and **Wendy Timmons** investigate the links between thought and action, and the extent to which 'practical experiences can be used to inform reason' while the concept of embodiment is explored in detail. The authors claim that activities aiming at improving kinaesthetic empathy can help law students in two ways: first, it gives them the 'opportunity to experience viscerally the complexity of exchange between human beings'; and, second, they can 'explore options available for this encounter through experimenting with alterations of its physical parameters'. One of the key options is improvisation, and the authors analyse how physical improvisatory action can affect thought and judgement. For them (and they adduce Clark on this point), dance improvisation can help stimulate the moral imagination of students.

Part II: The Arts and Law Schools

Suzanne Bouclin, **Gillian Calder** and **Sharon Cowan** lead off Part II in Chapter 4 in radical style by clearing not just the books from the library table but the library tables themselves, and substituting card tables where they play card games. As they argue in their introductory remarks, traditional legal pedagogy does not help when we 'confront how we embody performances of raced, classed, gendered and othered selves'. Starting with this central movement away from conventional legal pedagogy, Calder trained in the techniques of Theatre of the Oppressed – an approach to drama that drew upon the work of Freire, Brecht and Augusto Boal. It became clear, however, that the technique itself was not going to be sufficient, and therefore a range of 'performative pedagogies' was developed, one of which is the Card Game. The Game is used with first-year classes. Consisting of repetitions of the game at tables where the rules change at each table (but players are not informed of this), the authors argue that the Game is a non-textual exercise where students 'experience social and legal rules as context-specific'. As they do so, according to the authors, players' interpretations of legal rules are 'complicated by their own normative commitments', while at the same time the rules shift from table to table. The Game, in other words, plunges students into a world where rules begin to seem arbitrary and where they realize how, culturally, negotiation of specific contexts is essential to making sense of the world.

Chapter 5 by **Elaine Webster** focuses, *inter alia*, on the extent to which interpretation of the law is of necessity 'creative as well as bounded'. Much of legal education consists of boundaries: subjects are taught in boxes labelled Contract Law or Public Law; law is often characterized as a discipline centred upon normative rules of interpretation. Webster notes that the experiential workshops, for her, helped to legitimize the interpretive imagination in legal education. In turn, this may help students to develop a foundational and necessary but complex and difficult quality of the law, namely its contingency – as she describes it, 'the coexistence of interdependence and indeterminacy in law'. Drawing upon some of the literature on 'troublesome' knowledge, she then discusses the practicalities of the approach and briefly explores five examples of activities (for instance, asking students to reflect upon an image that contains a 'law-related idea').

At the start of Chapter 6, **Nancy B. Rapoport** points out the primacy of the textual experience for faculty and law students – for example, in parsing cases, identifying the 'holding' or *ratio* and the like. As she points out, however, there is a difference 'between reading a case and using it', and she argues that what would improve students' abilities to think creatively about the law are 'multiple opportunities to use literature, or the visual arts, or even pop culture as a way of teaching the law itself'. She cites examples and describes her own practices in using literature and film, including having students 'write, direct and produce original movies to illustrate ethics rules'. What is striking about this is the student-centred quality of the educational intervention, where student experience is centre stage. To a greater or lesser extent, this is true of every chapter in these two volumes. Rapaport, though, presents a realistic picture of the difficulties of being innovative about the arts in a curriculum where innovation is viewed with suspicion by faculty and students who are socialized into thinking that law can be taught and learned only in specific formalized encounters – the Socratic Method, for instance. In such a culture, the use of Wallace Stevens' poem *Thirteen Ways of Looking at a Blackbird* to help students understand point of view in contract cases can seem to be counter-cultural – which of course it is – but also irrelevant, which it certainly is not.

In the first of two chapters in this part that deal with legal education and physical activity in the world, in Chapter 7, **Andreas Philippopoulos-Mihalopoulos** begins by defining law and its crisis as 'emplaced, corporeal normativity'. His paradoxical aim is to 'create a space in which to think, to traverse disciplines ... and to amble without an objective except for the immanent aim of a walk amidst the law'. The context of this amble is a course entitled 'the Law of the Environment', different from Environmental Law courses. Within this course, students map the city by walking it. By observing movement and immersing themselves in the '*lawscape*', his students are facilitated in their connection of law and urban space and are enabled to remap lawscape in the context of their dynamic experience. Philippopoulos-Mihalopoulos gives us examples of students doing just that, thereby becoming 'nomads', abolishing 'the spatial regulation of the law, the boxing up and locking in and separating and purifying'. In the process they 'establish a *smooth* space ... where new lines of flight, new escape routes, new forms of normative creativity can take place'.

In an intriguing contrast, in Chapter 8, **Gary Watt** draws out what he sees as the essential *stasis* of the legal content in 'legal education' and the kinetic qualities of the educational element of the noun phrase. He describes how his 'Law and

Literature' module tends to the dynamic and embodies movement in its syllabus. In his analysis of the bio-kinetic literature on walking, Watt makes the case for a class to be a dynamic experience, physically as well as intellectually. Following his own practice, in which his 'Law and Literature' module asks for creative writing, he concludes his chapter with an unfinished poem on the walk that is previously described in prose earlier in the chapter. The shift from prose to poetry captures the appreciation of the aesthetic that Watt describes, and in its recursion it mimics the creative repetition of walking as a rhythmic activity, and of walks that are undertaken habitually.

The final chapter in this part, Chapter 9, by **Panagia Voyatzis** and **Burkhard Schafer** addresses problems created for legal practitioners in the Mexican legal system (a civilian system) by the increased use of precedent-based reasoning, and describes how Artificial Intelligence (AI) and visualization tools could 'create teaching tools to address them'. After describing the nature and scale of the problem for practitioners in the first half of the chapter, the authors identify legal education as one solution and legal AI as a useful platform for such educational interventions. They summarize briefly the history of argument expert systems such as CATO and LARGO, and they make the case for reasoning with 'open hypotheticals'. While they point out that the use of diagrammatic reasoning software (often based on Toulmin's work on argument) '*can* have a strongly beneficial effect for solving analytical tasks', they also point out that its use depends on contextual factors such as the organization of the representation and user-centred factors such as prior knowledge. Focusing on the first of these, the authors suggest that such abstract conceptual representations can be improved if visualization tools such as the representation of battles in military history are employed. They suggest that this form of case representation could be developed from static diagrams into animation.

Part III: The Arts and Legal Professionals

The final part of the volume deals with the relation between the arts and legal professionals – largely lawyers. In Chapter 10, **Valerie Fitch** focuses upon her experiences within the law firm. Coming from an arts background, she appreciated the focus of the 'Beyond Text in Legal Education' project but, significantly, when the film of the project was shown to attorneys in her firm in New York, there were mixed reactions: some could see a use for the activities, some not. In her chapter, Fitch shows, *contra* this professional scepticism, how some of the activities in the project can be used to stimulate attorney thinking in client matters.

Chapter 11 by **Miriam Aziz** takes as a case study her project entitled 'Creative Thinking for Lawyers'. After describing the history and aims of the project, Aziz goes on to map her experience of teaching law and working with artists, and to apply this to identify 'best practices regarding pedagogical initiatives' in the 'Beyond Text in Legal Education' project. Her experience of teaching law is unusual in that she taught in a variety of EU Member States. Her experience of working with the arts encompasses music, dance and film making, and she draws on the singular collectivity of this wide range of experience to develop 'a core of universal, transferable skills of problem solving, analysis, negotiation and decision-making' with 'active participation through exercises in creativity'. It is an ambitious programme. Out of the method sprang the project *Were you with me?*, which brought together a group of artists to perform a scripted but improvisatory piece involving music, dance and film. Aziz hopes to 'extrapolate this experience for the purposes of teaching law', taking Wittgenstein on logic and communication as her guide on the journey. In the process, she draws on 'ostensive' teaching theory and practice that 'generate associative habits regarding legal narratives' and that foster the quality of listening to all aspects of the testimony that are given.

In Chapter 12, **Karen Barton**, **John Garvey** and **Paul Maharg** focus on the potential of experiential learning via simulation to move beyond textual relations. At first glance, their chapter describes students mired in text more than ever. The construction of the transactional case they describe is, after all, more textual than other forms of learning. However, as they argue, simulated learning is not just more text but text used in ways that have the capacity to articulate experiences that would otherwise be lost to students. The simulations they describe include the use of 'Standardized Clients' (a heuristic adapted from medical education, and in particular the use of simulated or standardized patients) and of a virtual simulation of a case management system, in which students carry out legal transactions in immersive group work. The simulation environment will entail the splicing of these two simulation approaches such that the clients in the online transaction are the 'Standardized Clients', who can be advised throughout, and from whom the student lawyers need to take instructions. The authors analyse the costs, feasibility and flexibility of the approaches, as well as providing samples of student feedback. In the latter half of the chapter, they look to the future of simulation. They focus on one aspect of the simulation environment, namely online maps, and they extend the locative function of the sim into GPS and geotagged photographs, offering three possible uses in legal education: in learning analytics, in conversation visualization and in participatory and annotative mapping.

In Chapter 13, the final chapter of this part, **Bruce Anderson** and **Kim Morgan** state the problem simply: 'legal education and practice begin and end with texts', and they ask whether visual artists can help students, lawyers and judges to go beyond the discourse of the law. Can art 'expose, reveal, uncover, anything about law'? The authors describe two artworks, *The Acts of Nova Scotia 2009–2010* and *The Crest of the Nova Scotia Supreme Court*. The first, a graphical representation of parliamentary legislation, evokes the ancient trope of law as architecture, but where legal writers often imagine their project as foundation-building, instituting social structures, here the artwork describes 'neglect and decay, obsolescence and irrelevance'. The second artwork is a version of a court crest that is an ironic comment on the quality of justice historically enacted in the courtroom. In the second half of the chapter, the authors draw parallels between the problem solving that is taken to be a benchmark skill of lawyers and the problem solving that artists carry out in their work. Such work, the authors argue, may help the legal profession to appreciate how legal reasoning may be recast as a 'process of discovery' rather than a rhetorical and logical process.

Common Themes

The above claim made by Anderson and Morgan is, in microcosm, the claim of this volume. The place of the arts in legal education is essential, but it has been marginalized and driven to the edge of the curriculum. All the chapters recuperate and legitimate the arts as a learning space that is at the very least capable of improving legal education, often capable of critiquing law itself and sometimes transformative of both the law and legal education.

The themes that link the chapters demonstrate this. Clark's claim for the primacy of collaborative approaches to moral cognitive learning over the individual learning so characteristic of computational cognitive science is reflected in the many chapters that take a collaborative approach to learning the law. Another theme is the extent to which jurisdiction can affect pedagogical approach, but it is also striking that the approaches can be used to good effect across local jurisdictional differences and contexts – the chapters by Schafer and Voyatzis, Bouclin, Calder and Cowan, and Barton, Garvey and Maharg are examples of this. Some authors claim student and lawyer experience undergoes change through use of the arts (Webster, Fitch); all would agree that students are more engaged in the process of learning through the use of the arts in combination with active educational approaches. Some chapters explore the extent to which legal education can become much more embodied in the world – Pirrie and Brown (especially on wayfaring), Aziz (on improvisation), Lycouris and Timmons (on dance), and Watt and Philippopoulos-Mihalopoulos (on walking) are instances. Maps and mapping as alternatives to text appear in at least three chapters. The application of neural nets to linguistic operations is discussed in Clark; digital technologies, stemming from quite different lineages in educational pedagogies, are discussed in Schafer and Voyatzis, and Barton, Garvey and Maharg. And yet even in the latter two chapters, so different in approach, there are approaches that embody the desire to go beyond text – in both chapters' outlines of visualization techniques, for example. All chapters are multi-disciplinary and most of them are genuinely interdisciplinary as well.

A final preliminary point about the chapters in this volume: all authors were encouraged to make use of both visual and multimedia resources, including resources available online, by hyper-linking their text. Some have made more use of this possibility than others. Wherever use has been made of it, those chapters have also included a separate list of those links at the end of the chapter or footnotes in the text containing links for the convenience of those readers who have a print-only version of the volume.

Conclusion

Towards the end of the last chapter, Anderson and Morgan make the ambitious claim that their recasting of legal reasoning as a 'process of discovery' needs to be 'understood as one of the central topics in Jurisprudence courses'. Their claim is in one sense a re-statement of Clark's claim regarding the status of moral cognition and the crucial role that dialogue and discovery plays in that process. In a similar fashion, if this volume, together with the companion volume, has enabled a dialogue and helped to make more visible the place and function of the arts in legal education for you, the reader, it will have fulfilled its purpose – and, in the words of Pirrie and Brown, as a foundation stone it is 'ready for demolition', to free us to 'dance with the law'.

Links

http://www.beyondtext.ac.uk [accessed 25 July 2012].
http://www.ed.ac.uk/about/museums-galleries/talbot-rice [accessed 25 July 2012].
http://alicjarogalska.co.uk [accessed 25 July 2012].
http://www.zoefothergill.com [accessed 25 July 2012].
http://www.robertmckillop.com [accessed 25 July 2012].
mms://law-srv0.law.ed.ac.uk/external/beyondtext.wmv [accessed 25 July 2012].
http://www.law.ed.ac.uk/beyondtext/practiceworkshop.aspx [accessed 25 July 2012].
http://www.research-projects.uzh.ch/p5696.htm [accessed 25 July 2012].
http://www.law.ed.ac.uk/beyondtext/understandingtransformation.aspx [accessed 25 July 2012].

Appendix

DAY 1

11.00 am Welcome
11.10 am Statement from film maker
11.15 am Ice-breakers led by all three facilitators

1) The name game (15 mins)
2) Visual expectations (15 mins)

11.30 am Warm-up activities with Keren Ben-Dor

1) Familiarity with the space, focus and general awareness
2) From self to other

3) Mutuality, trust and non-verbal listening
4) Directionality. Giving and receiving guidance. Promoting trust
5) Movement witness

12.00 pm Drawing activity with Alicja Rogalska – The space in-between
12.30 pm Movement activity with Keren Ben-Dor – The law of the dance
1.00 pm Sculpture/mixed-media activity with Alicja Rogalska – From textual to visual
2.00 pm Responsive activities with Zoë Fothergill

1) Describe and draw (20mins)
2) Viewpoints (40 mins)
3) String theories (30 mins)

3.45 pm Installation art activity with Alicja Rogalska – Mute negotiations
4.15 pm Movement activity with Keren Ben-Dor – The great game of power
5.30 pm Informal discussion

<u>DAY 2</u>

10.00 am Movement activity with Keren Ben-Dor leading – Stop and listen
10.30 am Digital photography activity with Alicja Rogalska leading – Respond and capture
11.30 am Movement activity with Keren Ben-Dor leading – Action/reaction and role reversal
12.00 pm Movement activity with Keren Ben-Dor leading – Group response
1.00 pm Visual activity with Zoë Fothergill leading – Visual essays
2.00 pm Visual activity led by all three facilitators – Drawing movement
2.45 pm Visual activity led by all three facilitators – Display time
3.30 pm Reflective activities led by all three facilitators – Creative reflection

1) Drawing activity led by Alicja Rogalska – Visual reflections
2) Combined visual and movement activity led by Zoë Fothergill – Highlights
3) Performative movement activity led by Keren Ben-Dor – Parting gift

PART I
General and Interdisciplinary Perspectives

Chapter 1
Connectionism, Moral Cognition and Collaborative Problem Solving[1]

Andy Clark[2]

How should linguistically formulated moral principles figure in an account of our moral understanding and practice? Do such principles lie at the very heart of moral reason (Kohlberg 1981)? Or do they constitute only a shallow, distortive gloss on a richer prototype-based moral understanding (Churchland 1989; Dreyfus and Dreyfus 1990)? The latter view has recently gained currency as part of a wider reassessment of the proper cognitive scientific image of human cognition – a reassessment rooted in the successes of a class of computational approaches known as connectionist, parallel distributed processing, or neural network models (McClelland, Rumelhart and the PDP Research Group 1986). In this chapter I will argue that such approaches call not for the marginalization of the role of linguistically formulated moral rules and principles but for a thorough reconception of this role. This reconception reveals such summary maxims as the guides and signposts that enable collaborative moral exploration rather than as failed attempts to capture the rich structure of our individual moral knowledge. The force of this reconception eludes us, however, if we cast public linguistic exchange as primarily a tool for manipulating the moral understanding of other agents (Churchland 1989). Instead, we must focus on the role of such exchanges in attempts to engage in genuinely collaborative moral problem solving. A satisfying connectionist model of moral cognition will need to address the additional inner mechanisms by which such collaborative activity becomes possible and to recognize the ways in which such activity transforms the space of our moral possibilities.

1 This revised chapter first appeared in May, Larry, Andrew Clark, and Marilyn Friedman, eds., Mind and Morals: Essays on Ethics and Cognitive Science, pp. 109–27, © 1996 Massachusetts Institute of Technology, by permission of The MIT Press.

2 I extend special thanks to Margaret Walker, Larry May, Marilyn Friedman Owen Flanagan, Teri Mendelsohn, Peggy DesAutels, the members of the Washington University Ethics Seminar, the Philosophy/Neuroscience/Psychology work-in-progress group and the audience at the 1993 Mind and Morals Conference at Washington University in St Louis.

Connectionism: From Rules to Prototypes

There is a conception of moral reason that informed many classical philosophical treatments but that has recently been called into question. At the heart of this conception lies a vision of informed moral choice as involving the isolation and application of an appropriate law or rule. Thus, to give a simplistic example, we might, on encountering some complex social situation, see it as falling under a rule prohibiting lying and act accordingly. Of course, the body of rules we are supposed (on this conception) to have internalized need not be so simple. Such a moral code could, as Ruth Barcan Marcus points out, be highly elaborate (see Marcus 1987: 190–91). Principles could be hedged by exception clauses or rank ordered to help deal with potential conflicts. The logic of the moral code could be a fuzzy logic,or a non-monotonic logic, or something else. But, however elaborate, the basic vision remains the same. It is a vision in which moral judgements are taken to involve 'the judging of particular cases as falling under a particular moral concept, and thereby being governed by a specific moral rule' (Johnson 1993: 297). Johnson (1993: 4–6) calls such a doctrine 'moral law folk theory'. This doctrine, he claims, permeates our cultural heritage and hence underpins both lay and philosophical conceptions of the moral life. Yet it is a doctrine that, he argues, is radically mistaken and, indeed, morally incorrect. It is, he claims, 'morally irresponsible to think and act as though we possess a universal, disembodied reason that generates absolute rules, decision-making procedures, and universal or categorical laws' (Johnson 1993: 5).

Moral law folk theory is false, Johnson suggests, because it 'presupposes a false account of the nature of human concepts and reason'. This false account depicts concepts (including those that figure in putative moral rules and universals) as possessing classical structure. A concept possesses classical structure if it can be unpacked so as to reveal a set of necessary and sufficient conditions for its application. These necessary and sufficient conditions would effectively define the concept. To grasp the concept on such a model is to know that definition and to rely on it when called upon to deploy the concept. The trouble, as is now well known (Rosch 1973; Smith and Medin 1981) is that most (perhaps all) human concepts do not possess classical structure. Thus, whereas the classical model predicts that instances should fall squarely within or outside the scope of a given concept, according to whether the necessary and sufficient conditions are or are not met, robust experimental results reveal strong so-called typicality effects. Instances are classified as more or less falling under a concept or category according, it seems, to the perceived distance of the instance from prototypical cases. Thus, a dog is considered a better example of a pet than a tortoise and a robin a better example of a bird than a pigeon. Such findings sit uneasily beside the classical image (see Armstrong, Gleitman and Gleitman 1983; Osherson and Smith 1981). It seems we do not simply test for the presence or absence of a neat list of defining features and judge the concept application or inapplicable accordingly. In place of definitions and application rules invoking them, we face a vision of cognition organized around prototypical instances. To bring this vision into focus, we need to say a little more about the very idea of a prototype.

'Prototype' is sometimes used to mean merely a stereotypic example of the membership of some category. Thus understood, the stereotypic pet might be a dog, or the stereotypic crime a robbery. The recent popularity of prototype-invoking accounts in psychology and artificial intelligence, however, depends on a related but importantly different conception. Here, the notion of prototype is not the notion of a real, concrete exemplar; rather, it is the notion of the statistical central tendency of a body of concrete exemplars. Such a central tendency is calculated by treating each concrete example as a set of co-occurring features and generating (as the prototype) a kind of artificial exemplar that combines the statistically most salient features. Thus, the prototypical pet may include both dog and cat features, and the prototypical crime may include both harm to the person and loss of property. Concrete exemplars and rich worldly experience are still crucial, but they act as sources of data from which these artificial prototypes are constructed. Novel cases are then judged to fall under a concept (such as 'pet' or 'crime') according to the distance separating the set of features they exhibit from the prototypical feature complex – hence the typicality effects mentioned earlier (for a full review, see Clark 1993).

Such a vision of prototype-based reason fits very satisfyingly with a particular model of information storage in the brain. This is the model of state-space representation, which draws on both neuroscientific conjecture and recent work with computational simulations of a broadly connectionist type (McClelland, Rumelhart and the PDP Research Group 1986, vols 1 and 2; Churchland 1989; Clark 1989, 1993; Churchland and Sejnowski 1992). The main philosophical proponent of the state-space conception is undoubtedly Paul Churchland (1989), who has also urged its importance for conceptions of moral reason. The flavour of the state-space approach is best conveyed by tracing out a simple example.

Consider the brain's representation of colour. This representation (the example comes from Churchland 1989: 104) is fruitfully conceived as involving a three-dimensional (3D) state space (Land's colour cube; see Land 1977) in which the dimensions (axes) reflect: (1) long-wave reflectance; (2) medium-wave reflectance; and (3) short-wave reflectance. Each such dimension, Churchland conjectures, may correspond to the activity of downstream neural groups tuned to the activity of three different kinds of retinal cone. Within such a 3D space, white and black occupy diametrically opposed locations, while red and orange are quite close together. Our judgements concerning the perceived similarity–difference relations between colours may thus be explained as reflecting distance in this colour-state space. The space thus exhibits what has been termed an inbuilt semantic metric (Clark 1989, 1993).

Connectionist networks constitute one way of both implementing and acquiring representational spaces of this sort. Such networks consist of a complex of units (simple processing elements) and connections. The connections may be positive or negative valued (excitatory or inhibitory). The features of a stimulus are coded as numerical values (corresponding to the intensity of the feature or the degree to which it is present) across a designated group of units. These values are then differentially propagated through the network courtesy of the positive or negative connection weights. A good assignment of weights is one that ensures that activity in designated output units corresponds to some target input-output function.[3] Several layers of units may intervene between input and output. The activity of the units in each such layer will generally correspond to some kind of recoding of the input data that simplifies further processing. It is often fruitful to take each unit of such an intervening ('hidden') layer as one dimension of an acquired representational state space and to investigate the way the system responds to specific inputs by creating patterns of activity that define locations in this space (hidden unit activation space).

The great achievement of connectionism is to have discovered a set of learning rules that enables such systems to find their own assignments of weights to connections. The operation of such learning rules (which I shall not attempt to describe here, but see Clark 1989 and Churchland 1989 for accessible treatments) results in the construction of high-dimensional state spaces with associated semantic metrics. Four important features of this constructive process are that:

1. it is exemplar-driven;
2. it is not bound by the similarity metric on the input vector;
3. it yields prototype-style representations;
4. it treats inference and reasoning as vectorial transformations across state spaces.

The learning process is exemplar-driven in that the tuning of the weights is achieved by exposure to concrete cases. Thus, a network whose target is to transform written text into coding for phonemes (hence speech) does not have its weights changed by exposure to rules of text phoneme conversion. Instead, it must be exposed to textual inputs, allowed to output an attempted coding for phonemes, and then amend its weights according to the difference between the target output and its actual performance.

The weight assignments that a net therefore acquires can exploit hidden layers so as to dilate and compress the input space. Thus, two exemplars whose coding at the input layer is very similar may be pulled apart by the weights leading up the hidden layer. This is useful if, for example, two visual input descriptions are quite similar yet require very different responses. As such, two situations that are visually very similar (such as a person giving money to a beggar versus the same person giving money to a mugger holding a knife) may require very different responses. In such cases, the net can learn to use the hidden layer to recode the inputs in a

3 Not all networks have designated output units, but the basic device of state-space representation characterizes the knowledge acquired even by so-called pattern associator models.

new way such that the pattern of hidden unit activation is radically dissimilar in the cases just described. Correlatively, it may learn to code superficially dissimilar cases (such as giving money to a beggar and posting a cheque to a charity) with very similar hidden unit patterns. The state space defined by the hidden units might thus come to reflect a moral metric, whereas the input space depicted a visual one.

Within such state spaces, the mode of representation will come to exhibit features of prototype-style encodings. The reason is that features common to several training examples will figure in more episodes of weight adjustment than the less common features. As a result, the system will become especially adept at encoding and responding to such features. In addition, the learning regime will ensure that features that commonly occur together in the exemplars become strongly mutually associated. The upshot is that the system extracts the so-called central tendency of the body of exemplars, that is, a complex of common, co-occurring features. Moreover, multiple such complexes can be extracted and stored by a single net. McClelland and Rumelhart (1976) describe a net that: (1) learns to recognize individual dogs by associating visual information with names; (2) extracts the central tendency of the body of dog exemplars and hence exhibits knowledge of a prototypical set of dog features; and (3) can perform this trick for several different categories, simultaneously encoding knowledge about dogs, cats and bagels in a single network. These various prototypes (dog, cat and bagel) are each coded for by distinct patterns of unit activation and hence determine different locations in a general state space whose dimensionality corresponds to the number of processing units. Individual dogs are coded by points relatively close to the dog prototype. Dogs and cats share more features with each other than either do with bagels; thus, the dog and cat prototypes lie relatively close together and at some fair remove from the bagel prototype. The system can use its knowledge of prototypical feature complexes to behave sensibly given novel inputs. To the extent that some new input exhibits several familiar features (for example, a half-dog/half-cat), the system will assign it to an appropriate location (in this case, midway between the dog and cat prototypes) and hence yield suitable outputs.

Reasoning and inference can now be reconstructed as processes of pattern completion and pattern extension. A network exposed to an input depicting the visual features of a red-spotted face may learn to activate a pattern of hidden units corresponding to a diagnosis of measles and a prescription of penicillin. The vector-to-vector transformation involved is of a piece with that by which we perform simple acts of recognition and categorization such as naming a familiar dog. On the face of it, it is a million miles away from the intellectualist artificial intelligence model, which would have us consult a body of rules and principles and issue a medical judgement accordingly (for a variety of similar examples and claims, see Churchland 1989: Chapter 10).

With this rough understanding of vector transformation models in place, we can now begin to address the issues concerning moral knowledge and reason. The primary lessons of the new approach, when applied to the moral domain, look to be twofold. First, the successful acquisition of moral knowledge may be heavily dependent on exposure not to abstractly formulated rules and principles but to concrete examples of moral judgement and behaviour (literature, by depicting complex moral situations, may be seen as another kind of concrete case-virtual moral reality, if you will). Second, our individual moral knowledge and reasoning may not be fully reconstructible in the linguistic space afforded by public language moral dialogue and discussion. This will be the case if, as seems likely, the internal representational space (or spaces) involved has even a fairly modest number of dimensions. Our sense of smell, as Churchland (1989: 106) notes, looks to involve at least a 6D space. If each dimension can take just 10 different values, a space of 10^6 distinct locations is immediately available. Dog olfactory space, Churchland calculates, is of the order of 30^7 (22 billion) possible locations (compare this to a global population of just 3.5 billion). State-space encoding thus allows even limited internal resources of units and weights to support representational spaces of great magnitude. Given the size of the brain's resources, the expressive capacity of biologically realistic inner systems looks unimaginably huge. The attempt to condense the moral expertise encoded by such a system into a set of rules and principles that can be economically expressed by a few sentences of public language may thus be wildly optimistic, akin to trying to reduce a dog's olfactory skills to a small body of prose.

These two implications (concerning the role of exemplars and the resistance of moral knowledge to summary linguistic expression) are remarked on by several recent writers.[4] Goldman (1993) notes the central role of exemplars, Churchland (1989) stresses in addition the general resistance of high-dimensional state-space encoded knowledge to linguistic expression and Johnson (1993) describes how prototype-style encodings take us 'beyond rules'. The rule-based moral vision, according to this emerging consensus, is a doomed attempt to reconstruct the high-dimensional space of moral reason in a fundamentally low-dimensional medium. Such a diagnosis casts valuable light on questions concerning the rationality of moral thought. A well-tuned network, in command of state spaces of great complexity, may issue judgements that are by no means irrational but yet resist quasi-deductive linguistic reconstruction as the conclusion of some moral argument that takes summary expressions of moral rules and principles as its premises. Such a vision is by no means new. Nagel comments that 'the fact that one cannot say why a certain decision is the correct one … does not mean that the claim to correctness is meaningless … What makes this possible is *judgement* [which can] in many cases be relied on to take up the slack that remains beyond the limits of explicit rational argument' (Nagel 1987: 180, emphasis in original), or again, 'We know what is right in a particular case by what we may call an immediate judgement, or an intuitive subsumption … moral judgements

4 'Summary' because extended treatments (such as those of classic literature) may indeed convey detailed information about the structure of moral space. 'Summary linguistic expression' refers instead to attempts to distil moral knowledge into short rules and principles.

are not discursive' (Bradley 1876). As Bradley (1876: 65) points out, phrases like 'judgement' and 'intuitive subsumption' are 'perhaps not very luminous'. The value of the cognitive scientific excursion into state-space representation is just to cast a little light. It helps make concrete sense of a form of rational moral choice that nonetheless outruns what Nagel called 'explicit rational argument'.

The realization that individual moral know-how may resist expression in the form of any set of summary moral rules and principles is important. But it has mistakenly (or so I shall argue) led some writers to marginalize the role of such summary linguistic expressions in our moral life. It is this correlative marginalization that I now set out to resist. Such marginalization, I shall suggest, is the result of a common error: the error of seeing talk in general (and moral talk in particular) as primarily the attempt to reflect the fine-grained contents of individual thought. Such a view seems implicit in, for example, Paul Churchland's general scepticism concerning linguistic renditions. Such scepticism is evidenced in passages such as the following: 'Any declarative sentence to which a speaker would give confident assent is merely a one-dimensional projection – through the compound lens of Wemicke's and Broca's areas onto the idiosyncratic surface of the speaker's language – a one-dimensional projection of a [high] dimensional solid that is an element in his true kinematical state' (Churchland 1989: 18). The high-dimensional solid is, of course, the internalized prototype-style know-how contained in a trained-up neural network. It is this know-how whose linguistic echo is but the flickering shadow on the wall of Plato's cave (Churchland 1989: 18).

More radically still, Dreyfus and Dreyfus (1990) go so far as to demote such low-dimensional linguaform projections to the status of mere tools for the novice-ladders to be kicked away by the true moral expert. Once again, the radical claim has some plausible roots in the observation that (as far as we can tell) truly expert ability (at chess, car driving, philosophy or moral reasoning) is not subserved by a set of compact rules or principles encoded quasi-linguistically by the brain. Instead, it is subserved by the operation of a fast, unreflective, connectionist-style resource or resources whose operation yields 'everyday, intuitive ethical expertise' (Dreyfus and Dreyfus 1990: 246). According to Dreyfus and Dreyfus (1990: 243), the expert, under normal conditions, 'does not deliberate. She does not reason. She does not even act deliberately. She simply spontaneously does what has normally worked and, naturally, it normally works'.

This kind of fluid expertise comes, if it comes at all, only at the end of an extended learning history whose early stages are indeed marked by episodes of linguistic instruction. Dreyfus and Dreyfus in fact distinguish four stages that they claim precede fluid expertise: novice, advanced beginner, competence and proficiency. Linguistic instruction figures prominently (unsurprisingly) in the initial novice stage, while linguistic reflection figures to a degree in all the other non-expert stages: 'The instruction process begins with the instructor decomposing the task environment into context-free features which the beginner can recognize without benefit of experience' (Dreyfus and Dreyfus 1990: 240). These context-free features are then used as components of rough-and-ready rules.

Thus, the would-be chess player is taught the numerical values of pieces (in context-free terms) and told to exchange pieces whenever a profit would accrue. Similarly, the would-be moral agent is told that to say intentionally what is false is to lie and that lying is in general to be avoided (see Flanagan 1991 for a richer and more realistic treatment of this example).

Dreyfus and Dreyfus are surely right to stress the role of language in novice learning. But they go on, wrongly I believe, to marginalize the role of language in truly expert behaviour. They write that 'principles and theories serve only for early stages of learning' and as a result 'the skill development model we are proposing ... demotes rational, post-conventional moral activity to the status of a regression to a pre-expert stage of moral development' (Deyfus and Dreyfus 1990: 252–6).[5] We are thus invited to treat linguistic justification and linguistically couched reflection as mere beginners' tools – rough instruments not to be found in the tool kit of the true moral expert. I do not think this is the case. Rather, linguistic reflection and exchange enables a tuning and orchestration of moral response that is vital to moral expertise. What is needed is not a rejection of the role of summary linguistic expression and linguaform exchange in advanced moral cognition. Instead, we must reconceive that role. Such a reconception will occupy us for the remainder of this treatment.

Language as a Manipulative Tool

As a first move towards such a reconception, consider a question recently raised by Churchland. How, on a connectionist/prototype-based view, does moral knowledge, once achieved, get modified and altered? Churchland bids us distinguish between the kinds of slow, experientially driven adaptive change and learning that configure the weights of individual networks over time and the kinds of fast, flash-of-insight-style 'learning' that seems to occur when we suddenly see that a question with which we have been wrestling is easily solved once we reconceive the domain in the light of some new idea. The question Churchland raises is how (if at all) is slow, connectionist-style learning to cope with fast flash-of-insight-style conceptual change? The answer he develops is that it is able to do so because of the operation of so-called context fixers-additional inputs that are given alongside the regular input and that may cause an input that (alone) could not activate an existing prototype to in fact do so. He terms such a process 'conceptual redeployment' because it often leads to the reinvocation of prototypes developed in one domain in another (superficially very different) one.

Imagine someone trying to solve a problem. To solve it, if the approach outlined in the previous section is correct, is to activate an appropriate explanatory prototype. Sometimes, however, our attempts to access a satisfying (explanatory)

5 'Postconventional' here refers to stage 6 of Kohlberg's hierarchy of moral development (Kohlberg 1981), a stage at which principles are used to generate decisions.

prototype fail. One diagnosis may be that we do not command any appropriate prototype, in which case there is no alternative to slow, experience-based learning. But another possibility is that we do command just such a prototype but have so far not called it up. This is where a good piece of context fixing can help. The idea is that a bare input that previously led to the activation of no fully explanatory prototype may suddenly, in the context of additional information, give rise to the activation of a developed and satisfying prototype by being led to exploit resources originally developed for a different purpose. Huygens, we are told, commanded a powerful wave prototype developed for water and sound media. Once he was led (by luck, scholarship or something else) to combine questions regarding optics with context-fixing inputs concerning light, the optical questions were able to activate the rich and explanatory wave prototypes originally devised for the water domain. The conceptual revolution thus achieved did not involve slow, weight-adjustment-style learning, but rather consisted in 'the unusual deployment of old resources' (Churchland 1999: 23). The context-fixing information thus biases the treatment of an input vector in ways that can radically alter the prototype-invoking response of on-board, trained-up networks.

Now this, as Churchland notes, invites a certain perspective on linguaform debate, for linguistic exchanges can be seen as a means of providing fast, highly focused, context-fixing information. Such information may, as we have seen, induce others to activate prototypes they already command in situations in which those very prototypes would otherwise remain dormant. According to this view, moral debate does not work by attempting to trace out nomological-deductive arguments predicated on neat linguaform axioms. But summary moral rules and linguistic exchanges may nonetheless serve as context-fixing descriptions that prompt others to activate certain stored prototypes in preference to others (see, e.g., comments in Churchland 1989: 300). Applying our story to an example from Johnson (1993), a moral debate may consist in the exchange of context fixers, some of which push us towards activation of an 'invasion of privacy' prototype, while others prompt us to conceptualize the very same situation in terms of a 'prevention of espionage' prototype.

Note that according to such a vision, the linguaform expressions do not aim to embody the reasoning that underlies individual moral judgement. Instead, they figure in exchanges whose goal is simply to prompt another's rich prototype-based knowledge to settle on one existing prototype rather than another. Thus, talk of 'unborn children' may bias prototype activation one way, while talk of 'unwanted pregnancy' may bias it another. Moral rules and principles, on this account, are nothing more than one possible kind of context-fixing input among many. Others could include well-chosen images or non-rule-invoking discourse. Thus understood, language simply provides one fast and flexible means of manipulating activity within already-developed prototype spaces. It is a simple matter, however, to extend this treatment to encompass a special role for summary principles, etc., in individual moral reflection. To see how, consider a non-moral example case.

Kirsh and Maglio (1992, 1994) have investigated the roles of reaction and reflection in expert performance of the computer game Tetris in which the player attempts to accumulate a high score by the compact placement of geometric objects (Tetrazoids, or just Zoids) that fall down from the top of the screen. As a Zoid descends, the player can manipulate its fall by rotating it, moving it to the right or left, or instantly relocating it at the resting point of its current trajectory. When a Zoid comes to rest, a new one appears at the top of the screen. The speed of fall increases with score and (the saving grace) a full row (one in which each screen location is filled by a Zoid) disappears entirely. When the player falls behind in Zoid placement and the screen fills up so that new Zoids cannot enter it, the game ends. Advanced play thus depends crucially on fast decision making. As such, Tetris provides a clear case of a domain in which connectionist, pattern-completion-style reasoning is required for expert performance. If the Dreyfus and Dreyfus model is correct, moreover, such parallel, pattern completion-style reasoning should exhaustively explain expert skill. But, interestingly, this does not seem to be so. Instead, expert play looks to depend on a delicate and non-obvious interaction between a fast, pattern-completing module and a set of explicit, higher-level concerns or normative policies. The results are preliminary and it would be inappropriate to report them in detail. But the key observation is that true Tetris experts report that they do not rely solely on a set of fast, adaptive responses produced by, as it were, a trained-up network but also rely on a set of high-level concerns or policies that they use to monitor the outputs of the skilled network so as to 'discover trends or deviations from … normative policy' (Kirsh and Maglio 1992: 10). Examples of such policies include 'don't cluster in the centre, but try to keep the contour flat' and 'avoid piece dependencies' (Kirsh and Maglio 1992: 8–9). On the face of it, these are just the kind of rough-and-ready maxims that we might (following Dreyfus and Dreyfus) associate with novice players only. Yet attention to these normative policies seems to mark the play of real experts especially. Still, we must wonder how such policies can help at the level of expert play, given the time constraints on responses. There is just no time for reflection on such policies to override online output for a given falling Zoid.

Here Kirsh and Maglio (1992) make a suggestive conjecture. The role of the high-level policies, they suggest, is probably indirect. Instead of using the policy to override the output of a trained-up network, the effect is to alter the focus of attention for subsequent inputs. The idea is that the trained-up network ('reactive module' as they put it) will sometimes make moves that lead to danger situations – situations in which the higher-level policies are not being reflected. The remedy is not to override the reactive module but thereafter to manipulate the inputs it receives so as to present feature vectors that, when processed by the reactive module in the usual way, will yield outputs in line with policy. As they describe it, the normative policies are the business of a distinct planner system that interacts rather indirectly with the online reactive agency: 'It is the job of the planner to formulate a specification of concerns. These concerns are translated into directives for changing the focus of attention. Changes in attention in turn affect the feature vector presented to the [reactive agency]' (Kirsh and Maglio 1992: 10). Just how the shift of attention is accomplished is left uncomfortably vague, but they speculate that it could work by 'biasing certain board regions' or by 'increasing the precision of [certain] values being returned by visual routines' (Kirsh and Maglio 1992: 10).

Despite this vagueness, the general idea is attractive. Effective outputs are always under the control of the trained-up reactive system. But high-level reflection makes a contribution by effectively reconfiguring the input vectors that the reactive agencies receive.

This idea may provide a hint of a solution to the problem of understanding the role of explicitly formulated general commitments (in the form of summary rules or moral maxims) in moral thought.[6] Such commitments – the upshot of individual moral reflection – may help us monitor the outputs of our online, morally reactive agencies. When such outputs depart from those demanded by such policies, we may be led to focus attention on such aspects of input vectors as might help us bring our outputs back into line. Suppose we explicitly commit ourselves to an ideal of acting compassionately in all circumstances. We then see ourselves reacting with anger and frustration at the apparent ingratitude of a sick friend. By spotting the local divergence between our ideal and our current practice, we may be able to bias our own way of taking the person's behaviour – in effect, cancelling out our representation of those aspects of the behaviour rooted in their feelings of pain and impotence. To do so is to allow the natural operation of our on-board reactive agencies to conform more nearly to our guiding policy of compassion. The summary linguistic formulation, on this account, is a rough marker that we use to help monitor the behaviour of our trained-up networks.

The moral of the Tetris example, then, is that advanced pattern recognition is really a double skill. In addition to the basic, fluent pattern-recognition-based responses exemplified by a trained connectionist net, the human expert relies on a second skill. This is the ability to spot cases in which these fluent responses are not serving her well. Such recognition (a kind of second-order pattern recognition) is crucial since it can pave the way for remedial action. And it is especially crucial in the moral domain. Here, surely, it is morally incumbent on us not to be hostage to our own fluent daily responses, no matter how well 'trained we are'. We must be able to spot situations (for example, dealing with sexual politics in a family setting or interacting with certain religious or political groups) in which these fluent responses are failing to serve us. The effect of formulating some explicit maxims and guidelines provides us with a comparative resource in a sense external to our own online behaviours. This resource is neither binding nor a full expression of our moral knowledge, but it can act as a signpost alerting us to possible problems. The advanced moral agent, like the advanced Tetris player, needs to use every means available to sustain successful performance.

---

6 I thank Peggy DesAutels for drawing my attention to the importance of such general normative commitments.

The cases just rehearsed go some way towards correcting the anti-linguistic bias discerned in the previous section. Summary linguistic formulations, it seems, are not just tools for the novice, they are tools for the expert too. But the story remains sadly incomplete, for the image of linguistic tools suggests a merely manipulative role. This manipulative role does not, I claim, do justice to the more primary role of linguistic exchange as a medium of genuinely collaborative problem solving. Yet it is under this collaborative aspect (or so I shall argue) that linguistic formulations make their key contribution to moral cognition. It is to this perspective that we now turn.

Language as a Collaborative Medium

Missing from the discussion so far is any proper appreciation of the special role of language and summary moral maxims within a cooperative moral community. To see this, we can begin by considering the general phenomenon of so-called collaborative learning. The observation here is simply that a procedure of multiple, cooperative perspective taking often allows groups of agents to solve problems that would otherwise defeat them. For example, two children, neither of whom is alone able to come to an understanding of the Piagetian conservation task (understanding how the same quantity of liquid can be manifest in very different ways in differently shaped vessels, such as a long, thin glass and a short, fat one), can often cooperate to solve the problem. The reason is that they 'are often focussing on different aspects of the problem – one saying that the water in the new beaker is higher and the other noting it is thinner, for example … These competing perspectives come to light in the interaction, and in an effort to reach a consensus the children integrate the perspectives, co-constructing, a new perspective' (Tomasello, Kruger and Ratner 1993: 501; see also Perret-Clermont and Brossard 1985).

It is the communal effort to achieve consensus that drives the children to find the solution. Key features of this effort include discussion, joint planning, critiquing of each other's ideas and requests for clarification. Many of these features are transactive in the sense of Kruger (1992). This means that the thinking and perspective of individual members of a group are objects of group attention and discussion. Given the crucial role of such modes of discussion, it is perhaps unsurprising to learn that collaborative learning emerges at about the same developmental moment (age six or seven) as does so-called second-order mental state talk – talk about other people's perspectives on your own and others' mental states. Thus, younger children (age three or four) are capable of seeing others as having a perspective on the world (seeing others as what Tomasello, Kruger and Ratner (1993) call mental agents). But it is only the older children who see others as 'reflective agents' – agents whose perspective includes a perspective on the child's own thought and cognition (see Tomasello, Kruger and Ratner 1993: 501). Collaborative learning, Tomasello, Kruger and Ratner (1993: 501) argue, requires a participant to recognize others as having ideas about each other's thoughts and perspectives. It requires participants to 'understand in an integrated fashion the mental perspectives of two or more reflective agents'.

Such a capacity is plausibly viewed as an essential component of advanced moral cognition. Indeed, many moral problems basically consist in the need to find some practical way of accommodating multiple perspectives, including perspectives on each other's views and interests. Consider a typical moral issue, such as how to accommodate the multiple, and often competing, perspectives and needs of different religions and racial groups in a multicultural society. Attempts to find practical solutions to the kinds of problems thus raised depend crucially on the extent to which representatives of each group are able to engage in what may be termed multiple nested perspective taking. Consider the case of a conflict within a multicultural educational system (an actual case borrowed from Khin Zaw, unpublished). The parents of a Muslim girl requested that she be excused from events involving what (from their perspective) was an unacceptably close physical proximity to boys. The head teacher was inclined to let the child decide. But the likely effect of the child's decision (she did not want to be excluded) would be her total removal from the school. In such a case, the only hope for a practicable solution lies in each party's willingness to try to understand the perspective of the other. It is here, I claim, that the role of linguistic exchange is paramount. The attempts by each party to articulate the basic principles and moral maxims that inform their perspective provide the only real hope of a negotiated solution. Such principles and maxims have their home precisely there: in the attempt to lay out some rough guides and signposts that constrain the space to be explored in the search for a cooperative solution. Of course, such summary rules and principles are themselves negotiable, but they provide the essential starting point of informed moral debate. Their role is to bootstrap us into a kind of simulation of the other's perspectives, which is, as we saw, the essential fodder of genuine collaborative problem-solving activity. No amount of such bootstrapping, of course, can preclude the possibility of genuine conflict between incompatible principles, but it is the exchange of such summary information that helps set the scene for the cooperative attempt to negotiate a practical solution to the problem at hand. Such a solution need not (and generally will not) consist in agreement on any set of general moral rules and principles. Instead, it will be a behavioural option tailored to the specific conflict encountered (see Khin Zaw, unpublished, for just such a defence of 'practical reason').

Thus viewed, the rules and maxims articulated along the way are not themselves the determinants of any solution, nor need we pretend that they reveal the rich structure and nuances of the moral visions of those who articulate them. What they do reveal is, at best, an expertise in constructing the kinds of guides and signposts needed to orchestrate a practical solution sensitive to multiple needs and perspectives. This is not, however, to give such formulations a marginal or novice-bound role, nor is it to depict them as solely tools aimed at manipulating all parties into the activation of a common prototype; rather, it is a matter of negotiating some practical response that accommodates a variety of competing prototypes. (The difference here is perhaps akin to that marked by Habermas' distinction between strategic and communicative action. In strategic action, the goal is to persuade the other, by whatever means, to endorse your viewpoint. In communicative action, the goal is to motivate the other to pursue a dialogue by visibly committing oneself to a negotiated solution: Habermas 1990: 58, 59, 134, 145.)[7]

The successful use of language as a medium of moral cooperation thus requires, it seems, an additional and special kind of knowing how – one not previously recognized in connectionist theorizing.[8] It concerns knowing how to use language so as to convey to others what they need to know to facilitate mutual perspective taking and collaborative problem solving. The true moral expert is often highly proficient at enabling cooperative moral debate. Moral expertise, *pace* Dreyfus and Dreyfus, cannot (for moral reasons) afford to be mute. This additional know-how, like the other expert skills discussed in the first section, may well itself consist in our commanding a certain kind of well-developed prototype space, but it will be a space that is interestingly second-order in that the prototypes populating it will need to concern the informational needs of other beings: beings who themselves can be assumed to command both a rich space of basic prototypes concerning the physical, social and moral world, and a space of second-order prototypes concerning ways to use language to maximize cooperative potential.

To emphasize the psychological reality of the complex of second-order skills, it is perhaps worth remarking that high-functioning autistic children (those with basic linguistic skills) show a marked selective deficit in almost all of the areas I have discussed. It is characteristic of such children to show all of the following: no use of self-regulatory speech or inner rehearsal to help them perform a task (cf. the Tetris example); very limited grasp of how to use language to achieve communicative goals; complete failure to recognize others as having a perspective on the child's own mental states; and no evidence of collaborative learning or any other collaborative activity (Frith 1989: 130–45). These children, Frith suggests, are not able to 'share with the listener a wider context of interaction in which both are actively involved' or to 'gauge the comprehension of listeners' (1989: 126). They will use terms that no one else can understand, such as calling 17–25 year-olds the 'student nurses age group' (Frith 1989: 125), and they 'tend not to

---

7 Habermas often assimilates the idea of strategic action to the idea of the manipulation of others by force or sanctions. Obviously, the idea of manipulation by provision of context-fixing input is importantly different. The question when such provision constitutes genuine manipulation as opposed to collaborative investigation is a delicate and important one. I note in passing that Habermas emphases also echo those of this treatment in other ways, such as the recognition of the importance of multiple perspective taking (Habermas 1990: 138–46) and the conception of norms as practical, flexible aids rather than rigid defenses (1990: 180).

8 This was pointed out to me by Margaret Walker, whose help and comments have improved this chapter in numerous ways.

check whether their speech is actually succeeding and communicating, nor do they show any curiosity as to why a dialogue has broken down' (Baron-Cohen 1993: 512). The linguistic skills of these high-functioning autistics thus leave out all the collaborative dimensions I have been at pains to stress. As a result, Baron-Cohen (1993) raises the possibility that such children are, in a deep sense, acultural: unable to participate in the shared understanding and cooperative action essential to any true cultural group. Oversimplified connectionist models of moral cognition, by marginalizing the collaborative dimensions of moral action, likewise threaten to isolate the moral agent from her proper home, the moral community.

To sum up, it is only in the context of thinking about genuinely collaborative moral activity that the true power and value of principle-invoking moral discourse becomes visible. Summary moral rules and maxims act as flexible and negotiable constraints on collaborative action. Such rules and principles by no means exhaustively reflect our moral knowledge, but they are the expertly constructed guides and signposts that make possible the cooperative exploration of moral space.

Conclusions: Complementary Perspectives on Moral Reason

The kind of exchange between cognitive science and ethics that underlies the present treatment is quite typical. Historically, the bias of computational cognitive science is toward the individual. Ethical theory, by contrast, has concerned itself from the outset with individuals considered as parts of larger social and political wholes. The attempt to formulate a joint image of moral cognition helps correct the historical biases of each tradition. The ethicist is asked to think about the individual mechanisms of moral reason. The cognitive scientist is reminded that moral reason involves crucial collaborative, interpersonal dimensions. Perhaps neither party strictly requires the other to remind it of the neglected dimensions. But in practice, it is often the joint confrontation of the issues that yields progress in the search for an integrated image. In thus striving for a mutually satisfactory vision, we are forced to discover a common vocabulary and to agree on some focal issues, and to the extent that we do so, we prepare the ground for future participants from still other disciplines.

Such long-term benefits aside, the immediate upshot of this discussion is clear: recent connectionist inspired reflections on moral cognition are probably right in asserting both that moral thinking is fruitfully depicted as a case of prototype based reasoning and that summary linguistic principles and maxims can therefore provide only an impoverished gloss on the full complexities of our moral understanding. But the associated tendency to marginalize the role of such principles and maxims (to depict them as mere tools for the moral novice: Dreyfus and Dreyfus 1991) is to be resisted. As we saw, such formulations provide powerful tools for the indirect manipulation of moral cognition both in ourselves and others, and, most importantly, essential signposts and constraints that guide collaborative problem-solving activity. Such collaborative activity is only possible, I argued, courtesy of a special kind of knowing how: a knowing how whose focus is on the informational needs that must be met if others are to participate with us in cooperative problem-solving activity. Such know-how (knowing how to use language to prime the collaborative problem-solving machinery) requires a certain conception of other agents – a conception that recognizes others as already enjoying a particular perspective on the thoughts and viewpoints of their fellows. In the light of all this, we can now see much that is missing from the basic connectionist story. A satisfying story about moral cognition and moral expertise must attend to a variety of thus far neglected, communication-specific, higher-order prototype spaces. To do so will be to recognize that the production and exploitation of summary linguistic rules and principles is not the production and exploitation of mere imperfect mirrors of moral knowledge; rather, it is part and parcel of the very mechanism of moral reason.

References

Armstrong, S., Gleitman, L. and Gleitman, H. 1983. 'On what some concepts might not be'. *Cognition*, 13, 263–308.

Baron-Cohen, S. 1993. 'Are children with autism acultural?' *Behavioral and Brain Sciences*, 16, 512–13.

Bradley, F.H. 1876. 'Collision of duties', in C.W. Gowans (ed.), *Moral Dilemmas*. New York: Oxford University Press, 1987, 62–82.

Churchland, P.M. 1989. *A Neurocomputational Perspective: The Nature of Mind and the Structure of Science*. Cambridge, MA: MIT Press.

Churchland, P.M. 1999. 'Learning and conceptual change: the view from the neurons', in A. Clark and P. Millican (eds), *Connectionism, Concepts, and Folk Psychology: Essays in Honour of Alan Turing*. Oxford: Clarendon Press, 7–44.

Churchland, P.S. and Seinowski, T.J. 1992. *The Computational Brain*. Cambridge, MA: MIT Press.

Clark, A. 1989. *Microcognition: Philosophy, Cognitive Science and Parallel Distributed Processing*. Cambridge, MA: MIT Press.

Clark, A. 1993. *Associative Engines: Connectionism, Concepts and Representational Change*. Cambridge, MA: MIT Press.

Dreyfus, H. and Dreyfus, S. 1990. 'What is morality? A phenomenological account of the development of ethical expertise', in D. Rasmussen (ed.), *Universalism vs. Communitarianism: Contemporary Debates in Ethics*. Cambridge, MA: MIT Press, 237–64.

Flanagan, O. 1991. *Varieties of Moral Personality: Ethics and Psychological Realism*. Cambridge, MA: Harvard University Press.

Frith, U. 1989. *Autism*. Oxford: Blackwell.

Goldman, A. 1993. 'Ethics and cognitive science'. *Ethics*, 103, 337–60.

Habermas, I. 1990. *Moral Consciousness and Communicative Action*, translated by C. Lenhardt and S. Weber Nicholsen. Cambridge, MA: MIT Press.
Johnson, M. 1993. *Moral Imagination: Implications of Cognitive Science for Ethics*. Chicago: University of Chicago Press.
Khin Zaw, S. Unpublished. 'Does practical philosophy rest on a mistake?' Unpublished manuscript.
Kirsh, D. and Maglio, P. 1992. 'Reaction and reflection in Tetris', in J. Hendler (ed.), *Artificial Intelligence Planning Systems: Proceedings of the First Annual International Conference AIPS* 92. San Mateo, CA: Morgan Kaufman.
Kirsh, D. and Maglio, P. 1994. 'On distinguishing epistemic from pragmatic action'. *Cognitive Science*, 18, 513–49.
Kohlberg, L. 1981. *Essays on Moral Development. Vol. 1, The Philosophy of Moral Development*. New York: Harper & Row.
Kruger, A.C. 1992. 'The effect of peer and adult-child transaction discussions on moral reasoning'. *Merill-Palmer Quarterly*, 38, 191–211.
Land, E. 1977. 'The retinex theory of color vision'. *Scientific American*, December, 108–28.
McClelland, I. and Rumelhart, D. 1976. 'A distributed model of human learning and memory', in J. McClelland, D. Rumelhart and the PDP Research Group, *Parallel Distributed Processing: Explorations in the Microstructure of Cognition*, vol. 2. Cambridge, MA: MIT Press, 170–215.
McClelland, J., Rumelhart, D. and the PDP Research Group. 1986. *Parallel Distributed Processing: Explorations in the Microstructure of Cognition*, 2 vols. Cambridge, MA: MIT Press.
Marcus, R.B. 1987. 'Moral dilemmas and consistency', in C.W. Gowans (ed.), *Moral Dilemmas*. New York: Oxford University Press, 271–90.
Nagel, T. 1987. 'The fragmentation of value', in C.W. Gowans (ed.), *Moral Dilemmas*. New York: Oxford University Press, 174–87.
Osherson, D. and Smith, E. 1981. 'On the adequacy of prototype theory as a theory of concepts'. *Cognition*, 9, 35–8.
Perret-Clermont, A.N. and Brossard, A. 1985. 'On the interdigitation of social and cognitive processes', in R.A. Hinde, A.N. Perret-Clermont and J. Stevenson-Hinde (eds), *Social Relationship and Cognitive Development*. Oxford: Clarendon Press, 309–27.
Rosch, E. 1973. 'Natural categories'. *Cognitive Psychology*, 4, 324–50.
Sejnowski, T. and Rosenberg, C. 1987. 'Parallel networks that learn to pronounce English text'. *Complex Systems*, 1, 145–68.
Smith, E. and Medin, D. 1981. *Categories and Concepts*. Cambridge, MA: Harvard University Press.
Tomasello, M., Kruger, A. and Ratner, H. 1993. 'Cultural learning'. *Behavioral and Brain Sciences*, 16, 495–552.

Note added in 2011

Situated Moral Epistemology and Legal Reason[9]

The preceding text is probably best seen as an exploratory foray into 'situated moral epistemology' (Clark 2000) with more than a hint of the embodied and socio-culturally extended mind (Clark 2008; Wheeler and Clark 2008; Wilson and Clark 2008).

A situated moral epistemology will offer an account of moral knowledge and moral reason that is sensitive to the critical roles of a variety of non-individualistic elements. Such elements include the social role of language in collaborative problem solving (as in the preceding text), the scaffolding effects of larger-scale institutional and organizational contexts (see Clark 1997a, 1997b), and the cognitive and developmental benefits conferred by the framework of moral discourse and moral labels through which our neural engines of reason confront the world (Clark 2000, 2006). According to such views, the forces that shape our communal explorations of social and moral space are highly diverse, and include social practices of talking and labelling that act as potent tools that simultaneously shape moral space and make it accessible to pattern-based biological reason. Doing justice to this complex dance is the primary goal of a situated moral epistemology.

A similar goal might now be advanced for the legal domain. Legal argument and understanding would then be best understood by depicting 'legal cognition' as emergent from a web of heterogeneous capacities, scaffolding and forces. These will include the deployment, within individual brains, of connectionist-style (non-text-like) neural encodings and the interaction of those distinctive neural resources with the materiality of externally encoded legal text, the complex constraints imposed by social and institutional structures, and various other forms of socio-technological practice and scaffolding.

This has clear implications for the broader business of understanding legal thought and reason. For such a project cannot then hope to succeed without recognizing that legal reason is a function not simply of our individual psychological profiles, but of the larger social, cultural and linguistic systems in which they participate: larger systems which display a marked historicity and path-dependence, and in which change, progress and evolution are determined as much by their own intrinsic dynamics as by the actions or choices of the individuals 'within' them. In studying and attempting to understand these systems, we should not be tempted to reduce their dynamics to the dynamics of individual biological brains, but nor should we assume that all the interesting work is done by the larger social and organizational structures alone. For the legal machine is genuinely a complex ecology in which there has evolved a fit (for better or worse) between individual agents' practices and expectations, and the social, legal and political

9 Parts of this are adapted from Clark (2000).

institutions and structures in which they are embedded. There has been co-evolution between all the elements of this matrix. Moral and legal debate influences the development of social, political, legal and educational infrastructure. But moral and legal thinking and reasoning *is itself* constantly and profoundly affected and transformed by this web of mutually co-constraining infrastructure.

If this is correct, then our expectation-driven, pattern-completing brains are directed not at some bare, noumenal version of 'legal space' or even at the more mundane space of practical social living. They are directed instead at the (communally constructed) space of local moral and legal infrastructure: a space populated by laws, mutual expectations, constitutions, formal and informal norms and a persistent host of summary moral maxims, as well as by the less visible, but equally constraining, scaffolding structures of commerce, industry and legal and educational practice. Legal cognition thus emerges as a key arena in which to explore the more general topic of the complex relations between language, material culture and mind (see Clark 2006, 2008; Wilson and Clark 2008).

References

Clark, A. 1997a. 'Economic reason: the interplay of individual learning and external structure', in J. Drobak and J. Nye (eds), *The Frontiers of the New Institutional Economics*. London: Academic Press, 269–90.

Clark, A. 1997b. *Being There: Putting Brain, Body and World Together Again*. Cambridge, MA: MIT Press.

Clark, A. 2000. 'Word and action: reconciling rules and know-how in moral cognition', in R. Campbell and B. Hunter (eds), *Moral Epistemology Naturalized: Canadian Journal of Philosophy.* Alberta: University of Calgary Press, 267–90.

Clark, A. 2006. 'Language, embodiment and the cognitive niche'. *Trends in Cognitive Sciences*, 10(8), 370–74.

Clark, A. 2008. *Supersizing the Mind: Embodiment, Action, and Cognitive Extension*. New York: Oxford University Press.

Wheeler, M. and Clark, A. 2008. 'Culture, embodiment, and genes: unravelling the triple helix'. *Philosophical Transactions of the Royal Society*, B 363(1509), 3563–75.

Wilson, R. and Clark, A. 2008. 'Situated cognition: letting nature take its course' (with Rob Wilson), in M. Aydede and P. Robbins (eds), *Cambridge Handbook of Situated Cognition.* New York: Cambridge University Press, 55–77.

Chapter 2

Losing the Plot: Moving Beyond Text in Educational Practice

Anne Pirrie and James Benedict Brown

Introduction

'Losing the plot' may seem an inauspicious title for a chapter that seeks to address the largely undiscovered territory signalled by the words 'Beyond Text in Legal Education'. This is the title of the research project funded by the Arts and Humanities Research Council (AHRC) that gave rise to this volume. Nevertheless, it appears to us that to lose the plot is precisely what is required – if, that is, we are fully to embrace the embodied, situated, affective and creative dimensions of our practice. We use the term 'practice' to refer to activities as diverse as the practice of law, medicine or architecture; to teaching and learning in primary, secondary or tertiary education; and even to the interdisciplinary collaboration between an architect and a social scientist that gave rise to this chapter.

Our aim is to explore the beyond-text dimensions of practice by considering two examples drawn from architectural education. These are intended to illustrate just how difficult it is to move away from packing up and transporting normative practice, even under the banner of 'innovative teaching' that seeks to free itself from the dominion of the text. The examples – Polyark I and Polyark II – provide a framework that will enable us to contribute, albeit in a rather oblique way, to the broader debate on the way knowledge is generated and codified, taught and learned in a range of disciplines, including law. Cedric Price, the architect and educator who was the originator of Polyark (henceforth referred to as Polyark I), was a renowned champion of built-in obsolescence. Notoriously unconcerned about the longevity of his buildings, in the 1970s he was the only qualified architect to be a member of the National Institute of Demolition Contractors. It is thus entirely fitting that we offer a framework for considering education beyond text that can be dismantled when it has served its purpose. It is our intention here to offer a critical perspective on innovative teaching and learning in the professions. We shall attempt to demonstrate that the success of education as a cultural practice rests on a capacity to improvise and to embrace contingency rather than to innovate in the restricted sense of bringing something new into the higher education arena.

The exposition of Polyark I and Polyark II is also the first step in the development of what we might term a 'wayfaring' pedagogy. We shall explore what we mean by wayfaring more fully below. For now it will suffice to point out that the wayfaring researcher or practitioner is one who embraces contingency and uncertainty. She is predisposed to dwell in what the Romantic poet John Keats described as 'negative capability': that is, she is 'capable of being in uncertainties, mysteries, doubts, without any irritable reaching after fact and reason' (Dewey 1934: 33). The wayfarer is prepared to work without a script, to move beyond text and thus to step outside the flow of measured time. She is prepared to improvise, and her 'site thinking', so to speak, 'continually oscillate[s] between material and conceptual, abstract and physical, discursive and experiential, and general and specific points of view' (Burns and Kahn 2005: xxi).

The architect and critic Jeremy Till explained what prompted him to write his book *Architecture Depends* in the following terms: 'first, architecture is a dependent discipline [i.e., it depends on people, time, politics, ethics, mess]. Second, architecture as profession and practice does everything to resist that dependency' (Till 2009: 1). 'Beyond Text in Legal Education' arose from similar concerns. Law, like architecture, is a dependent discipline: it too depends on people, time, politics, ethics, mess and, perhaps first and foremost, upon text. Law also does everything to resist that dependency and to distance itself and its practitioners from contingency, uncertainty and improvisation. Let us begin by unravelling the term 'text', before moving on to consider how text might unravel us.

Coming to Terms

It is of course no small irony that we begin by defining terms. After all, one of the main functions of the units of discourse that we call texts is that they satisfy our need for 'delimiting, ordering and making explicit' diverse aspects of human experience (Ricoeur 1991: 3). This, incidentally, is a task that lawyers and legal educators seem to embrace with particular alacrity. It is evident that narrative modes that use a visual medium such as film or video also serve to illuminate diverse aspects of human experience. Here we are mainly concerned with written texts that have sentences as the base units of analysis, for it is these that predominate in legal education. Suffice it to say that the ability of visual narrative forms to delight or surprise may be related to their novelty value, particularly when used in educational contexts, rather than to their intrinsic properties. The term text here refers both to 'narratives that have a truth claim comparable to the descriptive forms of discourse to be found in the sciences' and to fictional narratives such as epics, essays, dramas, short stories, poems and novels (Ricoeur 1991: 2).

Text is academic discourse relating to the professions, in the form of monographs, journal articles, professional publications, reports, expert opinions, etc. However, it also encompasses official standards relating to professional attributes, knowledge and understanding and professional skills, and the plethora of statutory requirements relating to revalidation and accreditation in law, medicine, dentistry, accountancy and architecture. Many of the arguments advanced below stem from the fact that text has been reduced to an artefact, cut off from an oral storytelling tradition. In professional education, text has become part of the armoury used to delineate and preserve an area of control. The idea of dynamic movement that is so evident in its etymological roots (from the Latin *tessere*, to weave) has largely disappeared.

These various forms of 'storytelling' all have a temporal character. As Ricoeur explains, 'everything that is recounted occurs in time, takes time, unfolds temporally; and what unfolds in time can be recounted' (1991: 2). But what of the moments that seem to fall beyond the flow of time? We are referring here to the small epiphanies or sudden insights that come into being through interaction with others and to which our interprofessional collaboration bears witness.

According to Ricoeur, the core function of narrativity is 'the structuring of incidents, events and experiences that makes us speak of putting-into-the-form-of-a-plot (emplotment) rather than plot' (1991: 3). Although both plot and emplotment may be more readily associated with works of fiction or drama that have a clearly discernible beginning, middle and end, it is possible to conceive of other types of writing in broadly similar ways. For example, although academic articles vary considerably in style according to their base discipline, they generally have a recognizable plot (at least to those operating within the same discipline). The same holds for an account of a legal case, a lesson plan or the design specification for an architectural project. Experienced practitioners in these domains are quick to recognize the plot, as it were, and to apprehend how it unfolds in time. Indeed, they already have in mind a virtual object when they begin to read. Attentive readers can anticipate the pattern and follow the author in the process of construction and assembly of a design or an argument. Indeed the more experienced the reader, the more adept at this enterprise he becomes. It is, as it were, child's play. It is not entirely fanciful to compare such an operation to the completion a child's dot-to-dot puzzle. This is the image used by Ingold in order to convey the essential reduction of the 'trace of a gesture' to 'an assembly of *point-to-point connectors*' (2007: 74). This is in effect a double reduction: from trace to connector; and from an embodied experience that engages the heart and the head in a largely cognitive task. Ingold illustrates this essential reductionism with reference to two related fields: *travel* and *mapping*. It is to an exploration of these that we now turn. We shall then explore the epistemological and ontological consequences of operating within text in professional education.

Wayfaring and Travelling

The first distinction that has a bearing on education beyond text is between *wayfaring* (moving *along* a path) and *travelling* or being transported (moving *across* a surface). Ingold draws on a wealth of ethnographic work, from Inuit hamlets in northern Canada to the Foi people of Papua New Guinea, in order to convey the existential properties of wayfaring. He concludes that 'the wayfarer has to sustain himself, both perceptually and materially, through an active engagement with the country that opens up along his path' (2007: 76). This, we believe, is the hallmark of ethical practice in the professions. It signals a different way of knowing the world. As Smith explains:

> Instead of knowing the world [in terms of *episteme* and *techne*] we might be attuned to it, sensitive to it ... [we] might resonate with it, share its rhythms, the way we might be at one with the natural world if we opened ourselves to it instead of approaching it as scientists. (2008: 186)

The examples from anthropology relate to the way in which people engage with the natural world. The wayfarer might look out for interesting materials to gather or be alert to the traces left by animals. The seafarer might attend to the direction of the wind, the flight of birds or the ebb and flow of the tide. If we extrapolate this notion to legal practice, we can construe the wayfaring researcher or legal professional as one who is attuned to the vagaries of process and open to interactions with others. It appears that some professional practices show greater affinity with wayfaring than others. For example, architects 'draw as they think, and think as they draw, leaving a trace or trail both in memory and on paper' (Ingold 2007: 162). If, to paraphrase Klee (1961), drawing means taking a line for a walk, then architecture is a wayfaring practice *par excellence*.

The education of teachers or lawyers, on the other hand, unfolds along pre-determined plotlines and has its analogue in destination-oriented travel or transport. As we shall see when we come to examine specific examples, architecture education is not immune from such pressures. Unlike wayfaring, travelling 'is not so much a development *along* a way of life as a carrying *across*, from location to location, of people and goods in such a way as to leave their basic natures unaffected' (Ingold 2007: 77). By the same token, the process of following a complex legal argument embedded in a carefully crafted text leaves the basic nature of the lawyer unaffected. Similarly, in a car or train compartment, the 'intimate bond that, in wayfaring, couples locomotion and perception' is dissolved. The traveller (or reader) is disconnected from the world around him, shielded from direct contact with passers-by or (literal and metaphorical) fellow travellers. He becomes a passenger, 'who does not himself move but is rather *moved* from place to place' by the force of an argument (Ingold 2007: 78). Ingold construes travelling as movement through *utopia*, literally a placeless place, as places left behind are obliterated. In contrast, wayfaring is essentially *topian*, as it presupposes continuous engagement with people and places. Let us now consider another distinction that may help us explore the contours of education as ethical practice, namely that between sketch and plan.

Sketch and Plan

Sennett has observed that the craftsman 'understands the importance of the sketch – that is, not quite knowing what you are about when you begin' (2008: 262). Professional education, on the other hand, appears to be about inculcating a sense of knowing *exactly* where you are when you begin. The sketch is active and dynamic. Like its ontological analogue in wayfaring, it represents a process of understanding and engagement, a coming-to-terms. In short, the sketch is the locus of 'creative dialogue between form and error' (Sennett 2008: 258).

In contrast, the plan develops out of the process of aggregating partial views and can be framed in terms of 'getting something generically right' (Sennett 2008: 255). The plan (or course outline) is focused on outcome rather than on process. The result is an artefact that is static, measured and ruled, and delineates clear boundaries between inside and outside. There are evident similarities between text and plan in this respect, although there is not scope to adumbrate these here. The architect and designer Andrea Kahn compares and contrasts the Renaissance plan of Palmanuova (1713) and a sixteenth-century sketch of Milan by Leonardo da Vinci. She describes the Palmanuova Plan as follows:

> [It] depicts the urban site as a clearly bounded place. In this walled enclave intended to be impenetrable to attack, the city is described as a fixed object in an open field. The drawing's centred composition, inset textual inscriptions, and heavy dark lines enclosing fortifications reinforce the reading of a city figure afloat in empty space. The plan strongly delineates inside and outside. (Kahn 2005: 283)

In contrast, the sketch 'swirls with the movements of many trajectories crisscrossing an unbounded space' (Kahn 2005: 284). It comprises 'many overlapping spaces'. The boundaries between inside and outside, above and below become fluid and permeable. The drawing moves across in a way that is dynamic and temporal. The traces of its own making, the movement of the artist's hand across the page, are still clearly visible. Unlike the plan, the sketch is fundamentally concerned 'with what a site "does" in a city rather than what (or where) it "is"' (Kahn 2005: 282). By the same token, professional education that addresses the embodied, situated, affective and creative dimensions of practice addresses the what-does rather than the what-is question. The what-or-where-is question is the preserve of the plan (or the text), in which 'everything sits carefully contained in its proper place' (Kahn 2005: 284). This is resolutely a bird's-eye view, one from which all traces of movement, all gestures of uncertainty have been removed. Think of the ubiquitous city-centre maps that bear the legend 'You Are Here'. This is usually encapsulated in a bright coloured bubble that is intended to draw the viewer's gaze. For now it will suffice to point out that the sense of 'being there' experienced by the reader of these words is generally rather different. Indeed, he is very likely to be standing in front of the map because he feels rather lost and uncertain. In the sketch, site and situation are as one, and in the example considered by Kahn, the drawing appears to spill across the edge of the page towards an infinite regression of other sketches, towards other visions of other sites located in other cities and in other times. It is continuous movement along a path rather than settlement or resolution. The challenge for us as educators is to provide this type of experience for our students. The examples of Polyark I and Polyark II demonstrate the scale of this challenge.

'Getting things in perfect shape' implies a narrow definition of site as an area of control (Burns and Kahn 2005: x). The ability to work with resistance, on the other hand, implies recognition of 'passing forces that act upon the plot without being confined to it ... the area of influence' (Burns and Kahn 2005: x). The plan is the work process that relates to the area of control, the sketch to the area of influence. The sketch (in the context of professional education, read dialogue or interaction) is contingent, provisional and leaves open the doors to the imagination. The plan (or written text) is unconditional, fixed, premised on notions of control and is thus more closed to interpretation. The plan, we suggest, is generally more concerned with delineation or execution than imagining. And so, despite its etymological indications to the contrary, is that ubiquitous form of student assessment, the essay, which is derived from the French *essayer*, to try, to experiment.

There is, of course, a role for both the sketch and the plan in professional education and practice. For example, it is unlikely that an architect would produce a plan of a building after the first meeting with a client. Nor would she submit a sketch to a quantity surveyor in order to receive an estimation of construction costs. The contingency of a sketch is not appropriate for the forms of communication that require a plan. However, it is when the architect and the builder mediate between the sketch and the plan by interacting with each other that things really start to happen. They will talk and scribble on a grubby site plan until a living building begins to take shape...

Occupant and Inhabitant Knowledge

The epistemological analogue of travelling from point to point or remaining within text is *occupant knowledge* (Ingold 2007: 89). This accords primacy to cognition rather than to situated and embodied understanding. Occupancy implies mastery and occupant knowledge is associated with joining up connectors, with moving dot-to-dot, and is 'upwardly integrated'. It is how a surveyor or geographer would construct a cartographic map, or an urban planner might extrude virtual buildings skywards from a digital site plan, seen from an imaginary bird's-eye view that seems to glide effortlessly along a flat surface. It is how a social scientist might synthesize data from various sources in order to produce a research report, intent on presenting 'findings' rather than attending to traces, markings or remains.

Inhabitant knowledge, on the other hand, is associated with locomotion, with going along, with wayfaring rather than travelling, with the experience of 'being there' rather than being told that 'You Are Here'. Inhabitant knowledge is *alongly* integrated. It is quintessentially *topian*, insofar as it engages with the movement from place to place or, to put it in the language of text, from topic to topic. Inhabitant knowledge evolves through continuous and attentive interaction with textures and terrain. It is part of our way of being in the world and is derived from what is at times an uncertain engagement, a place where tripping, slipping and losing the way come with the territory (Pirrie and Macleod 2009, 2010). Inhabitant knowledge therefore demands a capacity to improvise, to explore, to get lost and to correct mistakes – in short to break free from the iron cage of text. In order to explore these ideas further, let us take a look at what happens when we take professional education on the road.

Up, Across and Along: Polyark Revisited

One Wednesday afternoon early in 1973, nine students of architecture boarded a decommissioned London bus and chugged away from the Architectural Association (AA)[1] in London, bound for seven British schools of architecture: Cambridge, Nottingham, Sheffield, Newcastle, Edinburgh, Bath and Kingston. Initially a project of the influential magazine *Architectural Design* (AD), the bus tour was to become better known as an expression of the AA's desire to have a mobile teaching space. Polyark I was an informal organization founded by the architect Cedric Price that developed from his 1966 National School Plan for a network between Britain's schools of architecture. The plan was designed to combat the perceived social and intellectual isolationism of the schools, and would allow them collectively to 'produce a range of architectural education investigation far more comprehensive than that now offered by any single school' (Price 1966a: 1282). Students of architecture would be permitted to switch between schools during the course of their studies in order to benefit from the specialized teaching and research at different institutions. Both the National School Plan and the Polyark bus tour sought to facilitate student mobility and promote interaction between students and the faculty. These initiatives were founded on the belief that through the act of making movement a structural component of an architect's education, students would make connections and draw contrasts between their learning environments in ways that were not entirely predictable at the outset. The organizers of the tour proposed themes (e.g., 'ecology technology' and community action) that they hoped would relate to students' work and interests. Letters sent out before the bus departed explained that 'the success [of the bus tour] will depend on the *enthusiasm and participation* of the schools and students en route' and stressed 'the importance of the two-way exchange of information and ideas' (Murray 1973: 201, emphasis in original).

1 A prestigious independent school of architecture, independent of the state-funded university system, with fees comparable to those of a private school.

The rationale for Polyark I and the way in which it was organized recalls the fundamental connection between wayfaring and the comparative richness of inhabitant over occupant knowledge. As Ingold (2007: 81) observed, 'the inhabitant is … one who participates from within in the very process of the world's continual coming into being and who, in laying a trail of life, contributes to its weave and texture'. This seems a laudable ideal for professional education, and it appears that the Polyark tour had the clear intention of weaving itself through the national scene of architectural education, picking up the pulse of a fragmented student body and carrying impressions of its various activities from one school to another.

Despite the fact that not a great deal of what actually went on in the bus could be described as 'educational' in the restricted sense of the term, the Polyark tour has gained almost mythical status in architectural education and was the inspiration behind Polyark II. It seems that few students from the seven schools accepted the invitation to submit their work to a mobile exhibition on the bus or even to travel onwards with the AA students to the next schools in the tour (Murray 1973: 201). In some respects the Polyark excursion was a pedagogic equivalent of The Beatles' *Magical Mystery Tour*, an hour-long film first aired by the BBC six years earlier. The Beatles had prepared no script. They simply told cast and crew 'to be on the coach on Monday morning'. The Polyark tour was somewhat less glamorous. Things seemed to go wrong from the start and any learning that did take place was, it must be said, rather more incidental than planned (but perhaps this was the point). The students had been unable to complete their ambitious plans to convert the bus, which included rebuilding the sides of the upper deck as downward folding sleeping decks to extend the dormitory space inside. When the students visited Newcastle, they met three architecture students who had bought and were living in a similar decommissioned bus, albeit one that they had made into a watertight, insulated and heated home. *Architectural Design* editor and Polyark participant Peter Murray noted that one envious AA student commented that 'at least it shows the advantages of a good building science course' (1973: 207).

As a more specific response to perceived isolationism in schools of architecture, the tour might be interpreted as an attempt to escape the design studio inherited from the Parisian Ecole des Beaux Arts. Students were not attending to the abstract demands of a project on a blank piece of paper, unrelated to the needs and expectations of clients. Instead, they took to the road to provoke discussions (and reputedly, on one occasion, a punch-up) between their peers, using video equipment to record and replay conversations about the very processes of architecture and education. The Ecole's legacy in architecture education was a predominant mode of design education that celebrated the lone genius, rewarding a student's adherence to his first idea rather than its evolution. This approach emphasized the speed at which a design could be executed and presented (for example, in the short *charette* design competition). With limited exposure to the contingency of the real world, design became a solitary travail, a lone journey to be undertaken in order to reach the hallowed destination of acceptance into the closely guarded profession. The AA students may not have hoped to change the infrastructure of the entire UK university system, but they probably hoped to be able to sow the seeds of a longer-term programme of interactions between students and schools. Murray conceded that the tour had exposed a widespread lack of student and faculty engagement:

> Although we had asked for schools to invite local groups and people from the towns, no one had done so, students did not prepare work … thus all the output came from the bus, the shows were biased in one direction and the show lacked the input of a variety of ideas and viewpoints that would have made it more useful in getting some dialogue going between the various schools. (Murray 1973: 211)

Those frustrated by the current assessment-driven, output-focused and risk-averse environment of academia may romanticize about the freewheeling aspirations of the Polyark tour (for recent critiques, see Grafton 2010; Pirrie, Adamson and Humes 2010). However, to do so would be to downplay the fact that a generously endowed private college was able to subsidize the purchase of a second-hand bus. The National School Plan and the Potteries Thinkbelt, the brainchild of the architect and educator Cedric Price, were the inspiration for Polyark I. The National School Plan was a proposal for an active network between existing schools of architecture across the UK, while the Thinkbelt was a detailed proposal for an itinerant higher education facility. This was a triangular campus of inter-modal base stations and rail-based learning facilities spread over a large ex-industrial area in Staffordshire conceived against the background of the rapid expansion of higher education in the 1960s. The intention was not to append the Thinkbelt to 'the edge of cities that only just avoided having universities back in the fifteenth century' (Hardingham and Rattenbury 2007: 73) (a pointed slight at the creation of the new universities). Rather, it was an attempt to scatter the Thinkbelt through the towns and cities of the Midlands that had been desolated by the collapse of the British ceramics industry. The spaces of learning would move amongst the spaces of manufacture, linking knowledge to craft. This would not only open up higher education, but it would also spread it out into the community and use its resources to regenerate areas that had seen few improvements in residential standards since the nineteenth century. Student housing would be integral to the plan and would 'not just be something grafted onto the Potteries' (Price 1966b: 3). Price proposed that the role of education in a modern society could be one of employment and regeneration: by making the activities of learning itinerant and by interweaving them with the fabric of the communities in which they occurred, interactions between learning and everyday life could occur. Students would not only be removed from the ivory tower, they would become workers in a state-supported knowledge economy:

> It follows from this attempt to unite, rather than separate, student and community that student grants in the Thinkbelt should become, not loans, but straightforward

> salaries. If people are doing a job society wants them to do, they must be paid for it. (Price 1966b: 4)

Polyark I illustrates the pedagogical risk associated with improvisatory practice. The learning gains of that particular initiative were difficult to predict and were certainly difficult to quantify in terms that would satisfy the demands of the contemporary audit-driven culture of higher education. Indeed, this is partly the point. In some respects, Polyark I has to be interpreted in the context of Price's critique of the thinking that lay behind the rapid expansion of the university sector in the 1960s. There is not scope to explore that here, but Price took the view that 'the major justification for the existence of any form of advanced voluntary organised education should be that it enables its users to distort time and location in the learning process' (Price 1990: 6). This may suggest losing the plot and moving beyond text – or certainly beyond the script.

Polyark II

For better or for worse, British students can no longer depend on a government grant to study at university. However, with a nod to the 1973 bus tour and to Price's National School Plan, Polyark II emerged in 2009. Eight schools of architecture were paired for exchanges of sites, projects and teaching. There was no double-decker bus this time: students shuttled between four pairs of schools by train and were given the brief to address vacant or disused land near to the railway terminus in their exchange city. Polyark II did, however, attempt to get conversation and maybe even arguments flowing. The dialogue between students was nurtured through critiques of their respective projects, social events and shared classes. Instead of one group of students visiting seven schools, there were exchanges between eight schools, with students travelling between sites and cities. Neither the original Polyark bus tour nor Price's Thinkbelt had to contend with contemporary public awareness of the environmental impact of personal mobility. In moving its students around the country by train, Polyark II not only suggested a more environmentally sensitive approach to an itinerant academic education, it also went some way towards ensuring that no one school dominated the conversation by being the party that announced its estimated time of arrival and expected an exhibition and buffet to be waiting. In this respect, it was true to Price's original critique of the confining nature of traditional academic education, which he condemned in the following terms:

> While students are at present one of the most mobile social groups of technologically advanced societies the nature of their own particular production plants – schools, colleges, universities, is static, introspective, parochial, inflexible and not very useful. (Price 1990: 6)

Price's involvement in Polyark sought to bring a wayfaring pedagogy to architecture education. However, just like its reincarnation almost 30 years later, it ended up following a pedagogy of packing up and transporting normative practice. In the original Polyark, one of the participants complained about a one-way show of work coming from the bus (Murray 1973). In a Polyark II blog, students from one university are seen discussing work that they will present to students in another institution. The window blind of the Voyager intercity train in which they are travelling has been pulled down in order that they might use it as a screen onto which to project their slides. The liminal space outside the train has been obscured and the focus is entirely on work prepared in one institution that is being transported to another. The sketch as a dialogue between form and error appears to have been harnessed in the service of the overarching plan (or learning outcome). Cedric Price had envisaged a space of collective learning on the tracks through the superfluous intermediate spaces of railway sidings and freight yards. Yet, once again, it appeared that schools of architecture were merely taking their work on tour and that the transformative potential of the experience was systematically underplayed.

Conclusion

The story of these two architectural road trips illustrates the scale of the challenge faced by professional educators when they attempt to move away from normative design practice. Is it enough simply to climb out of the box? Or do we carry the restricted dimensions of that space even when we take to the road?

Through Polyark I and Polyark II, we are reminded of Klee's description of two kinds of lines. There is the line that is 'intrinsically dynamic and temporal' like a sketch that leaves traces of various weights. Then there is the line in a hurry, from which all traces of movement have been removed, the line that is 'more like a series of appointments than a walk' (Klee 1961: 109). Mindful that our own practice oscillates between wayfaring and travelling, we ask whether these two educational initiatives left traces of their meandering through the countryside or whether they merely followed abstracted itineraries between appointments. In retrospect, it appears that neither Polyark I nor Polyark II chose to meander. The first tour took months of preparation and followed a carefully planned itinerary between the schools that responded to the AA's invitation. Exhibitions of varying success were prepared for the students on tour and not all were well attended. The only disruption to the carefully planned itinerary happened when the bus encountered low bridges (one in Nottingham that tore off part of the roof and one on the A1 that almost took the rest). Polyark II had to operate across eight tightly defined curricula and should not be criticized for limiting its students' horizons because of its itineraries. The risk arises in transplanting one's normal patterns of design practice from one location to another: to travel is not enough. The challenge is to identify the means to support intellectual wayfaring, that is, actively to encourage students to engage with the difficulties and problems presented by working outside one's normal frame of reference. It is possible that this might be achieved, at least in part, by encouraging them to move beyond text and thereby increasing their exposure to the unpredictable and unreliable, the contingent and the uncertain.

We recognize that most professional educators will resist the injunction to seek a richer, slower and thicker form of inhabitant knowledge, due to pressure of time and the prevailing culture of accountability in higher education and professional practice. Professional education favours the more certain and seductively blank-canvas character of occupant knowledge. As we saw above, there is nothing particularly wrong with either a sketch or a plan. There is a role for both and being open to the inversion of their traditional roles in design, research, teaching and learning can expose new possibilities. We all have a comfort zone, whether we are design practitioners, researchers or educators. We believe that the key to interrogating the reflexivity and sustainability of one's practice lies in taking uncertain steps and embracing wayfaring practice. This may take us into new and uncertain territory. We hope that we have demonstrated as much by virtue of an interdisciplinary collaboration that has taken us from education and architecture to the fringes of a debate on legal education.

We have explored the notions of wayfaring and travelling, sketch and plan, inhabitant and occupant knowledge in order to illuminate our own practice in our respective fields. The evidence seems to suggest that the dichotomies are not as clear-cut as we initially thought. The irony is that if we had both been architects and had been working on a project relating to the built environment, then we would have generated a series of sketches that preserved the traces of our collaboration. These might have formed the basis for the generation of plans that could have been shared with others. However, like our fellow contributors to this volume, we too are constrained within text. It is through words and in creative dialogue with the editors that we have attempted to retrace our active engagement with the trail.

Rather than seek closure or raise high the roof-beams of a grandiose educational project, it might be politic for us to follow Cedric Price's lead and subscribe to an Institute of Demolition Contractors. After all, if an idea has served its purpose and made us look at the familiar in a different way, then it is ready for demolition. We believe that this is, as it were, the foundation stone for the development of a wayfaring pedagogy in architecture and other professions, one that can help us move both within and beyond text. For 'as in life, what matters is not the final destination, but all the interesting things that occur along the way. For *wherever you are, there is somewhere further you can go*' (Ingold 2007: 170).

References

Burns, C. and Kahn, A. (eds) 2005. *Site Matters. Design Concepts, Histories and Strategies.* London: Routledge.

Dewey, J. 1934. *Art as Experience*. New York: Milton, Balch and Company.

Grafton, A. 2010. 'Britain: the disgrace of the universities'. *New York Review of Books*, http://www.nybooks.com/articles/archives/2010/apr/08/britain-the-disgrace-of-the-universities [accessed 18 July 2012].

Hardingham, S. and Rattenbury, K. 2007. *Supercrit #1: Cedric Price Potteries Thinkbelt*. Abingdon: Routledge.

Ingold, T. 2007. *Lines. A Brief History*. London: Routledge.

Kahn, A. 2005. 'Defining urban sites', in C. Burns and A. Kahn (eds), *Site Matters. Design Concepts, Histories and Strategies*. London: Routledge, 281–96.

Klee, P. 1961. *Notebooks, Vol 1: The Thinking Eye*, translated by K. Mannheim. London: Lund Humphries.

Murray, P. 1973. 'AA/AD/Polyark bus tour'. *Architectural Design*, 43(4), 201–12.

Pirrie, A., Adamson, K. and Humes, W. 2010. 'Flexing academic identities: speaking truth to power'. *Power and Education*, 2(1), 97–106.

Pirrie, A. and Macleod, G. 2009. 'Travels with a donkey: further adventures in social research'. *Power and Education*, 1(3), 270–81.

Pirrie, A. and Macleod, G. 2010. 'Tripping, slipping and losing the way: beyond methodological difficulties in social research'. *British Educational Research Journal*, 36(3), 367–78.

Price, C. 1966a. 'National school plan'. *Architect's Journal*, 145 (May), 1282–4.

Price, C. 1966b. 'Potteries Thinkbelt'. *New Society*, 2 (June), 16–17.

Price, C. 1990. 'The Cedric Price Column'. *Archigram*, 9, 5.

Ricoeur, P. 1991. *From Text to Action*, translated by K. Blamey and J. Thompson. Evanston: Northwestern University Press.

Sennett, R. 2008. *The Craftsman*. London: Allen Lane.

Smith, R.D. 2008. 'Proteus rising: re-imagining educational research'. *Journal of Philosophy of Education*, 42(S1), 183–98.

Till, J. 2009. *Architecture Depends*. Cambridge, MA: MIT Press.

Chapter 3

Physical Literacy in Legal Education: Understanding Physical Bodily Experiences in the Dance Environment to Inform Thinking Processes within Legal Education

Sophia Lycouris and Wendy Timmons

Introduction

In her attempt to develop an appropriate ethical perspective just after the Second World War, French existentialist philosopher and writer Simone de Beauvoir wrote *The Ethics of Ambiguity* (1947). Debra Bergoffen (2010) explains that, in this work, de Beauvoir recognizes the futility of trying to fully understand what happens in the world, as well as fully imposing our ways of understanding it on it. She encourages us to refrain from trying to identify final answers to moral dilemmas of that time and argues for the necessity of 'ethical projects that acknowledge our limits and recognize the future as open … an ethics of existential hope' (Bergoffen 2010). Following a similar principle, this chapter assumes that one of the main purposes of legal education is to equip future legal professionals with good skills in terms of dealing with moral dilemmas and ambiguity, and that one of the ways to achieve this is by encouraging students of law to develop their moral imagination. Indicating the importance of bodily experiences within legal education through references to dance education allows us to discuss how and why certain elements of the latter can contribute to the development of the former. More specifically, this chapter approaches from a dance model perspective the issues discovered and explored during the 'Beyond Text in Legal Education' project about the role of the arts in the development of the moral imagination of students of law. It also points to avenues for development, which truly take on board the physical roots of mental processes, a topic which is currently particularly popular across various academic fields, including philosophy of mind and cognitive science. This debate reconsiders relationships between body and mind and introduces the integration between mental and physical processes emphasizing an overall holistic approach.

Theoretical Perspectives

Reasoning is a distinguishing and defining characteristic of the human condition and is instrumental in the way we decide what is and what is not moral. This viewpoint is used in this chapter to debate the notion that bodily practices such as dance can contribute to the development of ethical and moral reasoning. Lakoff and Johnson (1999: 310) describe these processes as moral nurturance, 'learning how to care for others, to require empathy, concern for the other, responsibility, caring for oneself, and so on'.

Plato, Aristotle and Locke all hypothesized that we learn through associating perception with practical experience. For them, the brain was a tabula rasa. This concept is the basis for what we now understand as metaphysical realism, identifying the connection between the ideas that are in the mind and the essence of things in the physical world. According to Aristotle's concept of phronesis (practical wisdom), learning and understanding are conceived through practical experiences. Stonehouse, Allison and Carr (2009: 35) see phronesis as a 'complicated virtue encompassing the complexity of human moral judgement' and propose that it contextualizes the beginnings of Dewey's pattern of enquiry in which he construes knowledge acquisition as organic, experience-related and evolutionary. This principle of continuity subscribes to a holistic conception of knowledge where experiences past and future interact in the interest of meaningful learning (Carr 2003: 125). Stonehouse, Allison and Carr (2009: 35) also propose that the manipulations of practical experiences and experiential learning are a 'cyclic matter of reflection and experience' that are instrumental in informing judgements.

In some of his earlier work, David Carr suggested that, in philosophy, debates about moral conduct could benefit from a better understanding of the 'relationship between human thought and action', especially by examining this relationship within artistic activities, to understand how aesthetic ideas relate to the action of their materialization through the engagement with (artistic) practical processes (1987: 345). He was particularly intrigued by the idea that in dance 'both the instrument or vehicle of expression of artistic ideas and intentions *and* the physical embodiment of the art work itself are in themselves just forms or modes of human action' and suggested that dance should be considered as a form of human action instead of a form of human movement (1987: 346).

Carr (1981b: 91–2) also discussed the nature of practical knowledge and suggested that it 'depends on an ability to distinguish and identify particular practices and the actions involved in them'. He claimed that to demonstrate practical knowledge, the performing agent should be competent in applying the rules of practical reasoning, a distinct type of logical procedure by means of which practical knowledge is constituted and which differs from theoretical reasoning. More specifically, practical reasoning establishes logical connections 'between specific means and particular ends' (1981a: 60).

Modern psychological theory acknowledges the role of social interaction and environment in establishing behavioural patterns throughout lifespan development, resonating with Dewey's theories of evolutionary knowledge acquisition. The influence that social contexts have on development and learning was also proposed by Bandura (1977) and Vygotsky (1978). The latter also discusses movement within a social context, suggesting that actions and movements that are fundamental to our existence, such as pointing and grasping, can (through interaction with others) develop into meaningful gestures and a complex form of expression and communication. These theories have been applied within a lifespan perspective of human development and the chrono and echo systems proposed by Bronfenbrenner (1979). Bronfenbrenner conceptualizes that within an ecological framework, the context and opportunity for interaction within the environment and the nature and quality of these experiences have a significant effect on our lifespan of physical, mental and moral development.

Recently, ideas suggested by previous philosophical writings have been scientifically explained and the biological basis of human behaviour is now understood at a cellular level. Science tells us that there are synaptic connections established during development that underlie perception, action, emotion and learning (Kandel 2007: 4). The acquisition of knowledge, nurturance of ethical principles and moral actions are now understood to be processes that take place within the complex framework of both our physical or neural and cognitive experiences. Mark Johnson suggested that the sensorimotor system is responsible for the bodily articulation that gives us spatial and temporal perception and awareness, and proposed that the same mechanism that is responsible for the perception of movement within our environment may also be applied to the reasoning of other concepts (1987: xix). Lakoff and Johnson propose the term 'embodiment of the mind' as a new way of understanding reason and the very nature of a person (1999: 7). Thus, embodiment of mind is informed by established evidence provided by cognitive science and it gives empirical confirmation to Aristotle's philosophical notion of *phronesis*, which suggested that practical experiences can be used to inform reason.

Lakoff and Johnson have been exploring the bodily conditions of the production of meaning since 1980, starting with their seminal book *Metaphors We Live By* (1980), in which they discuss the function of conceptual metaphor. Focusing on the interaction between the human body and environment, in some of his own early work, Johnson (1987) proposed that image schemata and metaphorical projections are the means by which imagination links bodily and cognitive structures in how humans make sense of the world around them. More recently, he expanded on these ideas by exploring how feelings, emotions and the visceral relate to bodily processes and the production of meaning, thus drawing attention to the arts, including dance, which deal with these areas (Johnson 2007). Through building on John Dewey's ideas about the role and nature of aesthetic experience and seeking support from cognitive science and neuroscience, he proposed that aesthetics is not just 'the study of art and so-called aesthetic experience [but more generally] the study of everything that goes into the human capacity to make and experience meaning' (Johnson 2007: x). Taking further Dewey's proposition that forms of judgement relating to the aesthetic experience are no different from those operating in ordinary practical matters, he argues that 'art matters because it provides heightened, intensified, and highly integrated experiences of meaning, using all of our ordinary resources for meaning-making' (2007: xiii). In other words, art offers us the opportunity to develop our ability for meaning-making.

Embodiment is also discussed in relation to meaningful existence by Whitehead (1990), who later coined the term 'physical literacy'. Whitehead considers physical and verbal literacy as interconnected forms of human expression that are vital to everyone. Drawing from the work of Nussbaum (2000) and Gardner (1993), she introduces physical literacy as a form of human intelligence and human capability, and a concept that describes the expression of our embodied dimension arising from nurturing our embodied abilities (Whitehead 2010). She discusses the concept of physical literacy as a mechanism whereby the individual develops the ability to 'read the environment' with embodied competencies and a tacit understanding (Whitehead 2010: 51). In this chapter we propose that this same mechanism can be facilitated and developed through a combination of bodily and aesthetic experiences gained through exposure and interaction within a dance improvisation environment. Whitehead (2010: 53) suggests that this mode of reading and responding, which we proposed here through dance improvisation, uses intelligence and imagination common to the kinaesthetic intelligence and intelligent action as discussed by Best (1978: 58) and Arnold (1979: 17). In the second part of this chapter, a number of approaches to movement improvisation are discussed for the specific ways in which they can contribute to the development of physical literacy of students in legal education.

Kinaesthesia is defined as 'awareness of the position and movement of the parts of the body by means of sensory organs (proprioceptors) in the muscles and joints' (*Oxford Dictionary of English* in Reason and Reynolds 2010: 52). The concept of kinaesthetic empathy combines kinaesthesia and empathy to refer to the idea that viewers feel some kind of muscular sympathy for the dance performers through experiencing the movements they watch as if they were physically performing them (Reason and Reynolds 2010: 54). This concept clearly draws attention to the physicality of the viewing experience and begs further dialogue between dance theory and certain current scientific developments, such as mirror neurons in neuroscience (Cross, Hamilton and Grafton 2006; Orgs et al. 2008). Reason and Reynolds, who have researched extensively the character of the viewing experience in dance in their Watching Dance project, criticize this concept for its underlying assumption that all audiences view dances in the same way, irrespective of cultural differences. However, Susan Foster (2011) suggests that a revised version of the original concept of kinaesthetic empathy, in which the cultural specificity of the rapport between the body of the dancer and that of their observer is taken into account, is possible and much more relevant to the present moment.

Focusing on kinaesthetic sensations within the body of the mover is an important aspect of dance training which can be explored by law students for the purposes of developing bodily awareness. Focusing on the effects of kinaesthetic empathy as a result of watching others move can help law students realize how the physicality of other people affects their own physicality and how this relates to their thought process. Engaging with both kinaesthesia and kinaesthetic empathy during improvisational movement exercises can help law students in two ways. First, they can have the opportunity to experience viscerally the complexity of exchange between human beings, as this involves both physical and intellectual elements in highly intricate combinations. Second, they can explore options available for this encounter through experimenting with alterations of its physical parameters.

Movement Improvisation and Imagination

As mentioned in the previous section, Johnson (1987) emphasizes that imagination functions as a link between physical experience and cognitive structures through the use of image schemata and metaphorical projections. He explains that an 'image schema is a recurring, dynamic pattern of our perceptual interactions and motor programs' which leads to metaphorical projection, because it can be 'figuratively developed and extended as a structure around which meaning is organised at abstract levels of cognition' (1987: xiv, xx). In this way, according to him (1987: xx), 'abstract meanings and inferential patterns depend on schemata derived from our bodily experience and problem-solving'. Johnson (1993) has also discussed the crucial role of imagination in moral reasoning in particular.

Philosopher Gilbert Ryle (1979) suggests that processes of 'imagination', 'creativity' and 'originality' are closely connected with improvisational processes and identifies an improvising element in the very mechanism of 'thinking' itself: 'the vast majority of things that happen in the universe are in high or low degree unprecedented, unpredictable, and never to be repeated' and 'innovative thinking is a necessary element in inferring itself' (Ryle 1979: 125, 127). Technically, the way this mechanism operates means it is possible that 'between some premises and some conclusions there are no intermediate steps' (Kolenda in Ryle 1979: 12). Thus, for Ryle, thinking is always creative and involves a degree of improvisation.

This is an unexpected perspective in traditional philosophy, whereby improvisation becomes '*logically* necessary' within the process of human thought (Kolenda in Ryle 1979: 12). Thinking is understood as 'the engaging of partly trained wits in a partly fresh situation' (Ryle 1979: 129) and improvisation becomes the ability to bring together efficiently the partly known with the partly unknown. If it were feasible to devise a general definition of improvisation, this statement would probably be fairly close to it.

From her perspective as a dance educationalist, Barbara Haselbach would probably agree with it, at least as far as movement improvisation in dance education is concerned. Her understanding of the term includes two options: improvisation as 'experience' and improvisation as the 'spontaneous creation of form and content' (1981: 5–6). In the first case, the unknown movement possibilities of the body are explored from the known position of the mover as an individual. This can be accomplished by 'sensitizing experience … focus[ing] not on the creative activity itself, but on the individual perception and its capacity to differentiate' (Haselbach 1981: 5). The second case is a formalization of the human being's need to express her or his 'stored experiences'; it is an 'inside out' process which creates a new (and therefore unknown) vessel (or form) for the already existing (Haselbach 1981: 6), and to apply Ryle's perspective, 'it is the pitting of an acquired competence or skill against unprogrammed opportunity, obstacle or hazard' (1979: 129). Haselbach notices that the distinction between her two notions of improvisation is only a theoretical model, because in reality both types contribute to an actual situation (1981: 7).

British dance artist Miranda Tufnell and architect Chris Crickmay have developed collaboratively an approach to movement improvisation which focuses on the mover's imagination skills. They suggest that the ability of human beings to perceive their environment and respond creatively to it enhances the quality of life and that this depends on their 'capacity to play and imagine with what is there and to meet events with flexibility, curiosity, wonder, humour and passion' (Tufnell and Crickmay 2004: ix). They also suggest that the use of metaphor which results in the creation of images is a key tool towards achieving this aim. In addition to movement explorations, their approach incorporates a variety of additional elements such as writing and making things with materials, typically shifting between different media within the same improvisational session in order to generate the creation of images in various forms (stories, pictures, gestures, etc.).

Elements of movement improvisation have always been present in and are critical to the existence and evolutionary development of folk and social dances. However, during the twentieth century, movement improvisation has been used within the dance profession in three different ways (and of course various combinations between them): first, as a form of self-expression, sometimes specifically aiming at healing and therapy (creative dance as leisure or dance therapy); second, as a form of physical exploration for purely educational purposes (with dance students for example) or choreographic purposes (by choreographers who use it to generate movement phrases or motifs that can be structured in choreographic compositions); and, third, as a form of real-time composition (by dance artists who use improvisation as performance mode) (Lycouris 1996). Tufnell and Crickmay's approach is generic and within certain conditions could be adapted and used in any of the three ways described above. However, it comes under the category of physical exploration more naturally. In this respect, it can be argued that its main benefit is to support those who practise it to increase their pool of available image schemata, as well as enhance those which are already familiar to them by making them sharper and richer. The images created through these improvisations are metaphorical projections, which can be used for self-reflection after the end of the improvisational sessions. They reveal new meanings by offering opportunities to draw connections between previously unconnected elements.

British dance artist and performance improviser Julyen Hamilton, currently based in Spain, is also interested in the creation of images as a way of producing visualizations of stories through movement, text and sound improvisations performed live by professional dancers and musicians. He believes that imagination and physical imagery are strongly interconnected:

> to image your spine puts you in a state which releases a certain imagination … you can deeply be in a story about a horse in a field and you stretch your hand nearly as a joke to yourself to be front of the horse, and you feel the stretch coming up your wrist and then you feel the stretch going down your back. So you lay down on your back and then the next bit is about the horse sleeping at the field … there are memories, there are experiences and histories going on through the whole atoms of the body. (Hamilton in Lycouris 1996: 167)

His method of working with performers focuses on the use of imagination in two ways: the first is to recreate reality and the second is to create 'fantasies':

> We use our imagination also in reality as well as fantasizing what's not real … When you get home and you put the key in the lock and it doesn't quite work maybe you close your eyes to help it work because you know that your body imagines it working, it has the past history … it's just a coordination thing and that coordination is a memory pattern that is re-imagined to help in that very practical situation of turning the lock in the door … The other branch therefore is then fantasy, where you see an apple on the table and you say 'that's my grandmother's dog' … And so you're throwing in another world … making with something that is not real, very real because it's real in its imaginary level right down to somebody killing somebody on stage. (Hamilton in Lycouris 1996: 168)

Hamilton's performers are trained to make images from each other's movements and sounds through using appropriate combinations of 'recreated reality' and 'imagined fantasy' and working together as a group to carry these images to the next stage. They learn how to recognize the moments in which the 'story' can be transformed and collaborate to give birth to the next stage of this journey. Hamilton's work clearly comes under the category of improvisation as a form of real-time composition, which focuses on the performer's ability to exercise choice 'in the moment', through continuously taking into account multiple parameters which evolve simultaneously. With reference to Johnson's ideas about image schemata and metaphorical projections, it can be argued that, in Hamilton's approach, there is a focus on the ability to use highly intricate metaphorical projections 'in the moment', so that meaning is produced to trigger choice, which generates action.

American dance artist Steve Paxton's approach to improvisation also comes under the category of real-time composition, albeit in a very different way, since the parameters to be taken into account in his process of making choices are very different. In his piece *The Goldberg Variations*, Paxton improvises solo frequently against the same recorded musical piece, music written by Johann Sebastian Bach and performed by pianist Glenn Gould (Burt 2002). Paxton works with a 'specified muscle group, specified energy use and line … [his] body rides the music' (Paxton in Benoit 1997: 49) and his choices have to do with 'riding certain images or thoughts and letting others go' (Paxton in Benoit 1997: 51). Due to the various restrictions that Paxton imposes upon himself (energy pattern, identical musical accompaniment, etc.), his work could also be categorized as a form of exploration within strict parameters, the generation of infinite variations. The key to making such tight exploration active seems to be his skill of asking questions and 'accept[ing] temporary answers, and mark[ing] them clearly, so that when they change, they are enlarged' (Paxton in Benoit 1997: 53). It is interesting that in order to describe the nature of the parameters which define his explorations or the domain within which his imagination operates, he uses the term 'thought': 'it's more like a thought form that I have with me, much of the time my movement reflects the thought form' (Paxton in Benoit 1997: 55). There is an interesting inversion here which seems to go beyond Johnson's premise that 'abstract meanings and inferential patterns depend on schemata derived from our bodily experience and problem-solving' (1987: xx). Movement seems to depend on thought and be generated by it. Alternatively, is this still a confirmation of Johnson's position that thought is always determined by bodily conditions since, as Paxton concludes, it is 'a question of what is the movement centre in the thought' (Benoit 1997: 55)?

Like Tufnell and Crickmay, American dance artist Simone Forti's approach to improvisation is a generic one (which can be used for both exploration and compositional purposes and, to a certain extent, for self-expression). It also relates to story; however, this is in the sense of using story as a starting point for the exploration and production of movement rather than for the purposes of producing story, as is the case with Tufnell and Crickmay, and Hamilton. Forti initially studied fine art and then trained with American teacher and choreographer Anna Halprin, who introduced Forti to the use of improvisation as a way of finding solutions to problems – an approach which resonated with Forti's initial training in fine art (Forti in Cooper Albright and Gere 2003: 54). Forti was interested in how problems always exist within given contexts and the importance of good observation skills in working with them. Amongst other elements, she focused on the observation of the movement of animals, the structure and character of natural environments and the experience of processing information coming from daily news. She explains how observation is not only important when one develops work for movement performances but also during the performance event itself:

> The performance is full of discovery. Yet even as it requires an unobstructed carrying through on impulse, it also requires keeping an outside eye: 'A complex of judgements regarding what it is that is evolving, awareness that there is something that you are making. Is it fresh? Is it going somewhere? Is it accessible to the audience?' (Forti in Cooper Albright and Gere 2003: 56)

Forti developed a technique of using various combinations of text with movement, both as preparation for performance and performance mode. In her approach, undertaking automatic writing sessions immediately before a movement improvisation offers an appropriate context for the exploration of the movement that follows. On the other hand, combining movement with spoken text as a way of responding to story-related stimuli during the performance event generates a form of non-linear thinking in relation to the original story: 'It is not illustration. It is not mime … a shift of frame of mind. I have found that we think differently when we are in motion. And this is the thinking I am trying to access' (Forti in Cooper Albright and Gere 2003: 62). A typical exercise that Forti uses in workshops is to ask participants to describe succinctly in words something they remember due to some aspect of movement. As participants narrate their stories, their bodies become animated and produce movement which is later explored improvisationally by other participants.

In Forti's work, observation operates on multiple levels: first, in relation to external elements (other participants, objects or environments); second, in relation to oneself via kinaesthetic awareness; and, third, in relation to the physical responses one has as a result of observing movement performed by other people via kinaesthetic empathy. In her work, movement emerges as a result of problem solving, in the process of which observational skills operating at multiple levels facilitate a shifting of frame of mind, the generation of a different way of thinking, both as a means to an end and as an end in itself. Going back to Johnson's focus on the bodily conditions of the thinking process, it can be argued that in Forti's work, there is a constant interplay between image schemata and metaphorical projections, abstraction and figuration processes continuously morph into each other to produce both thinking and movement which almost vibrates between the two states.

Movement Improvisation and Legal Education

A conference entitled '*Lex Non Scripta, Ars Non Scripta*: Law, Justice and Improvisation', which investigated relationships between law and improvisational practices, was held at the Sala Rossa in Montreal in June 2009 and was later documented in a special issue of *Critical Studies in Improvisation/Études critiques en improvisation*, edited by Tina Piper (2010). Piper suggested that 'thinking about law in terms of improvisation may excite the legal imagination and suggest something instructive about the dynamic nature of the law' (2010: 4). In this conceptual reconsideration of law through the lens of improvisation, it was important to address how both improvisation and law relate to rules available through text (score or script) in terms of restrictions, freedom and room for interpretation. Piper also suggested that 'law and improvisation are both acts and metaphors, and sometimes methods' (2010: 2). She listed a number of concepts that can be relevant to research on both law and improvisation, and which were discussed in the conference and publication and include justice, dialogue, tradition, author(ity), rules and rule-making, norms, responsibility, anarchy, conflict, performance and judgement (Piper 2010: 2). She argued that the 'habits of improvisation: dialogue, sustained listening, widening of community, absence of judgement, and acceptance of a loss of control' (2010: 3) can be instrumental in resolving conflict, which is when reference to law also becomes unavoidable.

Another way of using improvisation as a metaphor to understand how law can be applied most effectively for the resolution of conflict is to refer to improvisation as a form of real-time composition, in particular when improvisation is used as performance mode, as discussed by Lycouris (1996). Successful and exciting composition in any art form relies on the efficient (yet often delicate) balance of all elements involved into a coherent whole which comply with contextual rules and conventions (existing models of composition), or engages in productive dialogue with such models to challenge them and expand them. This would be a perspective to understand why a more imaginative use of legal tools could be beneficial for a more effective resolution of conflict.

However, both of the above approaches are primarily relevant to ways of rethinking law through a different lens more generally, so that legal professionals can be encouraged to develop an overall different relationship with their tools. It is about establishing a new way of understanding law and its function, through 'excit[ing] legal imagination' in Piper's terms (2010: 4). It does not offer anything specific about what can be done better when dealing with ambiguity and moral dilemmas in situations of resolving conflict, where feelings and emotions are an important factor of the equation. Focusing more on the development of the moral imagination of legal professionals (rather than their general ability to use their tools imaginatively) and offering them skills that would allow them to take into account both their own feelings and emotions, as well as those of others, might equip them with better means of addressing moral dilemmas.

Drawing from Johnson's emphasis on the bodily conditions of meaning, the role of emotions, feelings and the visceral in the production of meaning (2007), it becomes clear why a more embodied approach, informed by the approaches of Tufnell and Crickmay, Hamilton, Paxton and Forti (discussed above), would be more beneficial for the development of moral imagination, which is required to address moral dilemmas in situations of conflict. If, as Johnson suggests, 'art matters because it provides heightened, intensified, and highly integrated experiences of meaning' (2007: viii), then of all art forms, dance, which involves the skilful use of the entire body, is the one to offer a more embodied experience of meaning. Goldman (2010: 5) suggests that 'improvised dance involves literally giving shape to oneself by deciding how to move in relation to an unsteady landscape', which is another way of articulating what has been explored in neuroscience and philosophy of mind about the relationship between the human body and environment (Clark 1997: 224). This is why the use of dance improvisation in legal education might offer students of law the perfect context for meaningful, fully embodied experiences that are augmented by the opportunity to also learn how to deal with moral dilemmas more imaginatively. In turn, they would learn how to produce effective innovative 'compositions' as a way of challenging existing models; in other words, finding new ways of achieving a more effective balance between all factors of the equation.

Conclusion

In this chapter we have argued that introducing techniques of movement improvisation in legal education can contribute to the advancement of moral imagination of students of law, in particular with regards to addressing moral dilemmas more effectively. Current developments in neuroscience provide scientific evidence of the connection between bodily and cognitive processes, substantiating in this way philosophical approaches since the Classical Greek period, including the Aristotelian notion of *phronesis*, which emphasized the role of practical experience in the cognitive process of learning. Amongst a number of contemporary philosophers, Mark Johnson (1987) has made important contributions in this field by proposing that image schemata and metaphorical projections function as links between bodily and cognitive structures in human beings. In this chapter we introduced the work of dance artists who use improvisational techniques in their work and explained how each one of these approaches contributes to the function of image schemata and metaphorical projections. From an educational point of view, this chapter emphasizes the need for a holistic approach in legal education which would embrace the concept of physical literacy. If students of law receive an education which targets the development of their physical literacy through engagement with appropriate movement improvisation techniques, they are likely to develop more effective skills of moral imagination and become appropriately equipped to deal with moral dilemmas and ambiguity in their professional lives.

References

Arnold, P.J. 1979. *Meaning and Movement, Sport and Physical Education*. London: Heinemann.

Bandura, A. 1977. *Social Learning Theory*. New York: General Learning Press.

Benoit, A. 1997. *On the Edge: Dialogues on Dance Improvisation in Performance*. Nouvelles de Danse, 32/33. Brussels: Contredanse.

Bergoffen, D. 2010. 'Simone de Beauvoir'. *Stanford Encyclopedia of Philosophy*, http://plato.stanford.edu/entries/beauvoir/ [accessed 18 July 2012].

Best, D. 1978. *Philosophy and Human Movement*. London: Unwin.

Bronfenbrenner, U. 1979. *The Ecology of Human Development*. Cambridge, MA: Harvard University Press.

Burt, R. 2002. 'Steve Paxton's Goldberg Variations and the Angel of History'. *Drama Review*, 46(4), 46–64.

Carr, D. 1981a. 'Knowledge in practice'. *American Philosophical Quarterly*, 18(1), 53–61.

Carr, D. 1981b. 'On mastering a skill'. *Journal of Philosophy of Education*, 1(1), 87–96.

Carr, D. 1987. 'Thought and action in the art of dance'. *British Journal of Aesthetics*, 27(4), 345–57.

Carr, D. 2003. *Making Sense of Education. An Introduction to the Philosophy and Theory of Education and Teaching*. London: RoutledgeFalmer.

Clark, A. 1997. *Being There: Putting Brain, Body and World Together Again*. Cambridge, MA: MIT Press.

Cooper Albright, A. and Gere, D. (eds) 2003. *Taken by Surprise: A Dance Improvisation Reader*. Middletown, CT: Wesleyan University Press.

Cross, E., Hamilton, A. and Grafton, S. 2006. 'Building a motor simulation de novo: observation of dance by dancers'. *NeuroImage*, 31, 1257–67.

De Beauvoir, S. 1947. *The Ethics of Ambiguity*, translated by B. Frechtman. New York: Citadel Press; new edn 1986.

Dewey, J. 1938. *Experience and Education*. New York: Touchstone.

Foster, S. 2011. *Choreographing Empathy: Kinesthesia in Performance*. New York: Routledge.

Gardner, H. 1993. *Frames of Mind: Theory of Multiple Intelligences*. London: Fontana Press.

Goldman, D. 2010. *I Want to be Ready: Improvised Dance as a Practice of Freedom*. Ann Arbor, MI: University of Michigan Press.

Haselbach, B. 1981. *Improvisation – Dance Movement*, translated by M. Murray. St Louis, MO: Magnamusic-Baton (original version 1976).

Johnson, M. 1987. *The Body in the Mind: The Bodily Basis of Meaning, Imagination and Reason*. Chicago: University of Chicago Press.

Johnson, M. 1993. *Moral Imagination*. Chicago: University of Chicago Press.

Johnson, M. 2007. *The Meaning of the Body*. Chicago: University of Chicago Press.

Kandel, E. 2007. *In Search of Memory. The Emergence of a New Science of Mind.* London and New York: W.W. Norton & Company.
Lakoff, G. and Johnson, M. 1980. *Metaphors We Live By*. Chicago: University of Chicago Press.
Lakoff, G. and Johnson, M. 1999. *Philosophy in the Flesh: The Embodied Mind and its Challenge to Western Thought*. New York: Basic Books.
Lycouris, S. 1996. 'Destabilising dancing: tensions between the theory and practice of improvisational performance'. Unpublished PhD thesis, Guildford: University of Surrey.
Nussbaum, M.C. 2000. *Women and Human Development: The Capabilities Approach*. Cambridge: Cambridge University Press.
Orgs, G., Dombrowski, J., Heil, M. and Jansen-Osmann, P. 2008. 'Expertise in dance modulates alpha/beta event-related desynchronization during action observation'. *European Journal of Neuroscience*, 27, 3380–84.
Piper, T. 2010. 'The improvisational flavour of law, the legal taste of improvisation'. *Critical Studies in Improvisation/Études critiques en improvisation*, 6(1). Available at http://journal.lib.uoguelph.ca/index.php/csieci/issue/view/102 [accessed 18 July 2012].
Reason, M. and Reynolds, D. 2010. 'Kinesthesia, empathy, and related pleasures: an inquiry into audience experiences of watching dance'. *Dance Research Journal*, 42(2), 49–75.
Ryle, G. 1979. *On Thinking*. Oxford: Basil Blackwell.
Stonehouse, P., Allison, P. and Carr, D. 2009. 'Aristotle, Plato and Socrates: Ancient Greek perspectives on experiential learning', in T. Smith and C. Knapp (eds), *Beyond Dewey and Hahn: Standing on the Shoulders of Influential Experiential Educators*. Wisconsin: Raccoon Institute Publications, 29–41.
Tufnell, M. and Crickmay, C. 2004. *A Widening Field: Journeys in Body and Imagination*. Alton: Dance Books.
Vygotsky, L.S. 1978. *Mind in Society*. Cambridge, MA: Harvard University Press.
Whitehead, M. 1990. 'Meaningful existence, embodied and physical education'. *Journal of Philosophy and Education*, 24(1), 3–13.
Whitehead, M. 2010. *Physical Literacy: Throughout the Lifecourse*. London: Routledge.

Useful Weblinks (all accessed 18 July 2012)

Documentation of Academic Projects

Beyond Text in Legal Education, http://www.law.ed.ac.uk/beyondtext
Lex Non Scripta, Ars Non Scripta: Law, Justice and Improvisation, http://www.improvcommunity.ca/content/mcgill-colloquium-2009
Watching Dance, http://www.watchingdance.org

Further Information on Academics, Artists, Philosophers and Theorists

Aristotle, http://plato.stanford.edu/entries/aristotle
Bach, Johann Sebastian, http://www.jsbach.org
Bandura, Albert, http://des.emory.edu/mfp/self-efficacy.html#bandura
Bergoffen, Debra, http://philosophy.gmu.edu/people/dbergoff
Bronfenbrenner, Urie, http://pt3.nl.edu/paquetteryanwebquest.pdf
Carr, David, http://www.ed.ac.uk/schools-departments/education/about-us/people/academic-staff?person_id=140&cw_xml=profile.php
De Beauvoir, Simone, http://plato.stanford.edu/entries/beauvoir
Dewey, John (philosophy of education), http://plato.stanford.edu/entries/education-philosophy
Forti, Simone, http://www.independentdance.co.uk/who/teacher.php?teacher_num=80
Forti, Simone (approach), http://www.flashartonline.com/interno.php?pagina=articolo_det&id_art=478&det=ok&title=SIMONE-FORTI
Forti, Simone (observation method), http://www.youtube.com/watch?v=29VCs5TBY5I
Foster, Susan, http://www.wac.ucla.edu/person.php?pid=18
Gould, Glenn, http://www.glenngould.com
Halprin, Anna, http://www.annahalprin.org
Hamilton, Julyen, http://www.julyenhamilton.com
Hamilton, Julyen (method), http://www.gaaraprojects.com/vifgaarae.htm
Haselbach, Barbara, http://www.ancos.org.au/conference/haselbach.htm
Johnson, Mark, http://pages.uoregon.edu/uophil/faculty/profiles/markj
Lakoff and Johnson (embodied cognition), http://plato.stanford.edu/entries/embodied-cognition
Locke, John, http://plato.stanford.edu/entries/locke
Paxton, Steve, http://artsalive.ca/en/dan/meet/bios/artistDetail.asp?artistID=178
Paxton, Steve (approach), http://www.contactquarterly.com/cq/webtext/Paxtontalk.html
Paxton, Steve (*Goldberg Variations*), http://www.youtube.com/watch?v=-8iTMMKtwYQ&playnext=1&list=PL50BD79C6C43B7F8C
Plato, http://plato.stanford.edu/entries/plato
Ryle, Gilbert, http://plato.stanford.edu/entries/ryle
Tufnell, Miranda, http://www.mirandatufnell.co.uk/biography.html
Tufnell, Miranda (approach), http://www.youtube.com/watch?v=IpYC6Tqrlaw
Vygotsky, Lev, http://video.google.com/videoplay?docid=634376752589779456

Terminology

Cognitive science, http://plato.stanford.edu/entries/cognitive-science
Intelligent action, http://mcl.open.ac.uk/Workshop/uploads/GiffordT_BCSHCI2011_Camera.pdf

Kinaesthesia, http://speed.augustboehm.com/kinaesthesia.html
Kinaesthetic empathy, http://www.watchingdance.org/research/kinesthetic_empathy/index.php
Kinaesthetic intelligence, http://www.youtube.com/watch?v=fqh0B82bbBE&feature=related
Metaphor, http://plato.stanford.edu/entries/metaphor
Mirror neurons, http://watchingdance.ning.com/video/part-1-from-mirror-neurons-to
Moral reasoning, http://plato.stanford.edu/entries/reasoning-moral
Philosophy of mind, http://plato.stanford.edu/entries/cognitive-science
Physical literacy, http://www.physical-literacy.org.uk/icsspe2006.php
Phronesis, http://plato.stanford.edu/entries/episteme-techne
Practical knowledge, http://plato.stanford.edu/entries/practical-reason-action
Practical reason, http://plato.stanford.edu/entries/practical-reason
Practical wisdom, http://plato.stanford.edu/entries/wisdom
Tabula rasa (the historical controversies surrounding innateness), http://plato.stanford.edu/entries/innateness-history

PART II
The Arts and Law Schools

Chapter 4
Playing Games with Law

Suzanne Bouclin, Gillian Calder and Sharon Cowan[1]

Shuffling the Deck

> Traditional legal education may actually impair the ability to effectively solve complex problems, particularly those freighted with issues of personal values. (Lerner 2004: 644)[2]

Law is embodied and is organized around embodied concepts. 'Everyday', 'raw' or 'lived' law is performed through the body's movements in social interactions; it is felt in ways that indicate fluid, competing, always-emerging and multiple selves (MacCormick 1994; Holstein and Gubrium 2000; Macdonald 2003: 143–4; Lassonde 2006; Grabham et al. 2009). Our selves-in-process, rather than written texts, are the irreducible sites of law.

Feminist scholars have pointed to the troubled relationship between outsider voices and the dominant racist, classist and gendered conventions surrounding academic practice, including the valorization of text over non-text (Lillis 1997; Feminist Geography Reading Group 2000; Adjin-Tettey et al. 2008; Calder and Cowan 2008). Feminists across disciplines have also critiqued the tendency to favour mind over body, reason over emotion and objectivity over subjectivity, because, as with many dichotomies, the 'weaker' term is associated with 'femaleness' rather than 'maleness' (MacKinnon 1989; Shiva 1989; Harding 1991). We argue that traditional legal pedagogy reinforces such tendencies; it does not aid us in confronting how we embody performances of raced, classed, gendered and othered selves. Rarely do we ask students (or colleagues) to step outside traditional learning techniques, to put their bodies into learning or to attend to the power dynamics of embodying law. When we do, it is done with trepidation and often without the support of our colleagues or institutions.

---

1 We are grateful to the editors for their comments on our chapter and are appreciative to every audience in which we have tried to play the Card Game.

2 We acknowledge with great sadness Alan Lerner's recent untimely death. Alan was an enthusiastic and passionate participant in the 'Beyond Text in Legal Education' project, and his skills, humour and integrity will be much missed.

With attention to these shortcomings in legal pedagogy, the authors have embraced a particular form of non-textual legal pedagogy: 'the Card Game'.[3] In the autumn of 2007, after training in the techniques of *Theatre of the Oppressed* with Victoria's Puente Theatre, Gillian worked with the University of Victoria's Faculty of Law to include a Forum Theatre session as part of its orientation curriculum (Calder 2009). It was anticipated that this non-conventional teaching in an orientation context would elicit a range of reactions from students. It was also assumed that some in the faculty would be apprehensive about such initiatives within a law school. It became clear that for students and faculty to feel comfortable with this approach, a broader range of performative pedagogies would also be required. Of these, the 'Card Game' – which is the centrepiece of this chapter – is now performed as part of the first day of classes for all first-year students.

Gillian has since used the Game with wider audiences. On seeing and feeling the richness of the Game as participants, Suzanne and Sharon also decided to introduce it into their classes (in Quebec and Scotland respectively). This chapter focuses on using the Card Game in law classrooms. We have used it at four different schools, in common law and civil law jurisdictions, and with undergraduate and graduate students. We have, however, also played the Card Game at academic conferences.

This chapter is intended for educators who are interested in thinking about how we teach and learn law, and suggests alternative methodologies for conveying law's multiple and often contradictory messages. First, we describe the Card Game and where and to what ends we have used it. In so doing, we collaboratively reflect on our individual and collective experiences with the exercise. Second, we show the potential of non-textual exercises to foster classroom conditions in which students experience social and legal rules as context-specific. We have found that students come to realize that their experiences of legal rules are complicated by their own normative commitments – commitments that may not be reconcilable with broader and more entrenched group norms and practices. Third, we suggest that this pedagogy is feminist in form and in content. It challenges participants to reflect upon law's hegemonic tendencies (e.g., law's reinforcement of colonialism and imperialism) as well as law's irreducible pluralism. While traditional legal pedagogy often reduces law to authoritative texts, interpreted by authoritative decision makers, the Card Game allows students to see and feel the power of law in an embodied way. We conclude that the Game can guide different and more meaningful empathic responses to law's regulatory power and effects. We hope to leave our readers with the sense that the Game is a 'performative utterance' (Austin 1980: 57): that is, the Game itself enacts embodied law rather than simply describing it.

3 The Card Game is (sometimes loosely, sometimes quite explicitly) inspired by a game entitled Barnga (see http://www.thiagi.com/barnga/). Thanks to Lina de Guevara of Puente Theatre and Chris Downing of Victoria's Multiracial Families Project for introducing us to this important pedagogical tool.

Although the Card Game has clear rules and goals, it works best if participants are unaware of its 'real' objectives.[4] If you are a potential participant and do not want to have this experienced spoiled, stop reading and pick up this chapter after you play the Game. Alternatively, if you are looking for a classroom exercise that is primarily non-textual and will allow students to confront their own assumptions about law, rules, oppression and being 'outsiders' to law's power, then what follows is a brief explanation of what the Card Game entails. Appended to this chapter is a set of materials that describe the playing of the Game in more detail, including questions to aid the debrief and a set of rules that can be used if you want to try this exercise yourselves.

If you are absolutely sure that you want to know, the rules of the Game are, briefly, as follows. The facilitator should set up the room so that it is a series of tables with four or five chairs at each table. The Card Game works best for a group of 20–25 people around five tables.[5] It also works well if the room is rearranged when using the Card Game from either the layout to which the students have become accustomed or to the regular set-up of the room. On each table there should be a set of rules (face down), a deck of cards (28 cards, ace through sevens only, the rest removed and discarded) and a number (the tables should be numbered one, two, three, four, five, etc.). When the students sit down, they should be advised to put all their materials away so that only the rules, the cards and the number are on the table.

The facilitator then will tell all the participants that they are playing a game, one that may be familiar to some, but not to all. When the Game begins, they will have five minutes to turn the rules over and learn them collectively. The facilitator will then tell them that 'the big twist' of this game is that when the five minutes expire, the rules will be taken from each table and the participants will no longer be able to communicate with verbal or written language. If they experience any conflict or confusion, they will have to find some non-textual means for resolving the dispute. The goal of the Game, they are reminded, is 'to get to table five' (or whatever is the highest numbered table).

The Game then begins and the players play a few hands without talking. Once the first round ends, the participants, following the rules, will either move up a table if they have won the most hands, move down a table if they have won the fewest or stay put. Once the movement has settled, the students will then begin another round. What the players do not know is that although they are all playing the same game, each table has learned a slightly different set of rules – for example, at some tables aces are high, at other tables aces are low. This means that when they switch tables or when someone new comes to join them, players at each table will have different understandings of the rules that should apply at that table.

---

4 As Suzanne's experiences show, however, the Card Game can be so rich that even audiences who already know 'the reveal' learn about how they embody and re-embody law.

5 Ideally, there are at least three tables, but we have played the Card Game with as few as two and as many as six.

The more rounds that are played, and the more players that move, the more confusion there will be as to which set of rules are applicable to their table. Although some will realize what has taken place, others will not, and the intrigue of the Game becomes how the students negotiate their confusion and conflict by non-verbal means.

Putting our Cards on the Table

Gillian first played the Game as part of an anti-racist workshop designed to offer insights into oppressive, colonialist and culturally contingent assumptions and behaviours. Her experience was visceral, a lived moment of how law and the body are connected, and in particular the ways in which her privilege manifested itself in the choices she made in how to play. Feeling that the Game was the perfect metaphor for law, she pioneered the Game with law students. In her first endeavour in a law school class, she was amazed by students' honesty and self-reflection, and the ways in which the Game offered them a theoretically rich introduction to law's contingent nature. She has used the Game in three different contexts. Since 2007, it has been an optional exercise as part of the Legal Process curriculum in the University of Victoria's orientation programme. It has also been played by upper-level (second- and third-year) law students in a seminar entitled 'Civil Liberties and the *Charter*' as part of a three-hour session on race and the *Canadian Charter of Rights and Freedoms.* Gillian has also used the Card Game at two conferences. The first (facilitated with Suzanne) was at Carleton University in 2008. Building on the conference theme 'Pedagogical Encounters', the Game was sprung unexpectedly on the participants returning from a break. The second (facilitated with Sharon) was at a socio-legal feminist meeting in Barbados in 2010; for this conference, the Card Game was explicitly on the agenda.

Both Sharon and Suzanne have also been puzzled about law students' attachment to conventional textual ways of learning and a general reticence towards exercises and practices that de-centre the text. Locating these tendencies within a broader critique of disembodied legal pedagogy, Suzanne helped Gillian to facilitate the Card Game in 2008. She realized immediately that this would be an invaluable teaching tool. She has consequently played the Game three years in a row at McGill University. She used the Game in a seminar of undergraduate and graduate students during a class entitled 'Where are Race, Gender and Class?'. The first attempt in 2008 went smoothly; students loved the exercise, which yielded memorable and critical conversations on race, ethnicity, culture and law. In 2009, the reveal was inadvertently leaked when some students (six out of 20) reviewed course materials before class, shifting the dynamic between the students, the facilitator and the rules. In 2010, Suzanne furthered reflection on the Game's potential by delivering it in the same class twice. Used on the first day of class, it generated lines of enquiry into why McGill had a pedagogy course, on the relationship between learning styles, pedagogy and law, and in terms of what students expect (or should expect) from professors. When played again mid-semester, with a reconfigured class, new dynamics arose with respect to the reveal, and new allegiance strategies offered more ways to talk about law and its contingencies.

Encouraged by Gillian's success, Sharon tried the Game in 2008 with a group of 25 Scottish law students. She used the Game in an optional upper-level seminar (third- and fourth-year students) entitled *Criminal Law* and has used it every year since. The Game is played in the first class of the term to introduce questions about law, particularly criminal law. It is also a powerful 'icebreaker' for students who do not all know each other. It tends to prompt discussions on the ways in which similar behaviours are variously labelled 'normal', 'unconventional' or 'criminal', depending on the context. In 2010, Sharon asked students to fill out a short, anonymous questionnaire about their experiences with the Game and to comment especially on its potential as a pedagogical tool for thinking about law. She also asked what embodied learning meant to students and what were some of the benefits and drawbacks of using such exercises in legal education. In answering, students processed their immediate experiences of the Game and some reflected on how they respond to different pedagogical practices in law. Usually one or two students knew about the Game and had played it. None of her students, however, has ever exposed the 'reveal' to the rest of the class.

In each of these contexts, we have relied on similar questions in the debriefing discussions. We tend to begin by asking participants 'easy' questions, to share how the Game made them feel, allowing them space to articulate that it makes them feel frustrated, angry, isolated or powerful. We then ask them directly about their negotiation strategies. The Card Game is revealed as a metaphor for law when students make connections between their strategies for winning (getting to a particular table) and the rules by which they abide (or transgress) in order to achieve that end. We sometimes ask students to juxtapose 'correct' rules with their 'own' rules. These questions usually provide an insight into the ways in which we all work within and outside the law, but also reveal the importance of emotion and values to legal learning.

Every law student is unique. How students respond to the Game is in part dependent upon their own levels of receptivity and what they believe is appropriate learning in a law faculty. In the next section, we discussion how the use of alternative teaching formats such as this game allows us to look afresh at something we take for granted: text-based, content-centred teaching rather than embodied, learning-centred pedagogy.

Play Begins

As described above, participants are divided into groups and are asked to play a simple card game. Many experience the Game as fun, an icebreaker and a novel introduction to the substantive topics of the course or seminar. During the Card Game, participants are positioned in ways that invite identification with people from different social, economic and cultural backgrounds.[6] They gain insight into the dynamics of cross-cultural encounters where people (especially those from more 'dominant' groups) believe they share general norms and rules only to discover that one's perception of those norms and rules is contingent upon their social and cultural location. The Game also allows students to understand how individual subjective interpretations of rules differ and that there is usually more than one set of rules or customs in play in any interaction. It operates as a way for students to experience legal pluralism (the commingling of multiple normative spaces, sites and forms) without an explicit discussion of that concept.

Conflicts occur as participants move from group to group. They arise primarily because participants are not forewarned that each table is playing by different rules. They are heightened because spoken and written communication is prohibited. Consequently, these conflicts are expressed through the body – facial responses and gestures. Participants struggle to understand why others are not playing 'correctly' (according to the rules they know); they also (re-)evaluate their own understanding of the rules. To this end, the Game embodies the legal pluralist assumption that in any interaction there are multiple normative structures at play that may confirm one another, but they may also conflict and collide. Participants demonstrate, to varying degrees, the ability to appraise and adapt to these multiple normative structures during their interactions with other players. Ultimately they behave in ways that confirm or deny what they believe are what Nedelsky calls their 'own laws' or the capacity to develop and sustain relationships that will further autonomy (Nedelsky 1989: 7). In short, each 'plays games with law' according to different rules but within a broader relational context that requires them to be able to reassess those rules in moments of interaction with others. Players learn that they must understand and reconcile these differences if they want to function effectively in their varying and often shifting socio-cultural groups.

Showing our Hands

Legal pedagogues should pay attention to the 'education of affect' in the classroom and in scholarship (Nedelsky 1997). Each of us is concerned about how students respond to the Game and what they think about alternative pedagogies. We have solicited student feedback in various ways, but we note the impact of structural and contextual factors upon our findings. In British Columbia and Quebec, for

6 There are risks to the Game. Educators should plan in advance for an accessible classroom, given the obvious challenges faced by students with visual or mobility impairments, or learning difficulties. For some students, playing cards is not acceptable in their culture or religion because it is associated with gambling. This proviso notwithstanding, the Game can be adapted to suit most student audiences and can prompt a rich discussion on how we approach issues of accessibility and diversity in all of our educational contexts.

instance, law is a graduate degree. In the UK, it is a first degree. Canadian students tend to be older with more 'lived' experience than Scottish students who are, in the main, just out of high school. Edinburgh law students are mainly white, middle class and from the UK. Sharon's classroom may, as a consequence, be less diverse than Gillian's (with a strong indigenous contingent) or Suzanne's (with many international students, at a bijuridical, bilingual school committed to legal pluralism). Suzanne's students are upper-year or graduate level and have chosen to take a course explicitly about legal pedagogy. Sharon's are trained in orthodox legal reasoning and problem solving; evaluations at her school tend to be exam-based and rote-learning is emphasized. Gillian's faculty is known for its innovative approach to legal learning. With these structural differences in mind, we discuss three main findings from using the exercise.

(Resisting) Legal Power and Privilege

Across our game experiences, we have found that students emphasize how it enables them to examine the relationship between formal rule-governed behaviour (for example, actions that are regulated through legal sanctions) and informal rule-governed behaviour (for example, social norms) and to ask new questions about social power. At McGill, this included students relating the ways in which racialized students and new Canadians experience discrimination in law faculties, and how these students' lived experiences are underrepresented in materials taught at law school.[7] Students specifically pointed out that within the current configurations of law schools, these kinds of ('race-conscious') pedagogies remain marginal and marginalized. The exercise worked here on multiple levels: on the one hand, students found that the Game highlighted law's fluidity and contingency, exposing the assumption that there is 'one correct rule' to be applied to every situation; on the other hand, the exercise pushed them to self-reflexively consider whether 'passive' acceptance of rules can be attributed to traditional legal education.[8]

When used in a seminar session focused specifically on the question of formal law's utility in addressing systemic racism, unlike any other pedagogical tool that Gillian has used, the Card Game enables certain students to reflect on their class and race privilege. Used alongside text-based materials, the Game invites explicit connections between negotiating difference and the embodied impacts of racism.

---

7 The students whose views are cited in this paragraph identified, respectively, in the following ways: 'female of Asian heritage living in an Anglo-Saxan [sic] country, and thus as a member of the "unprivileged" group, of adapting to those norms set by the privileged' (2009); 'a Muslim man and a new father' (2010); and 'a male law student' (2010).

8 By her own account, this student, who had given a trick over to another player, felt that she had 'passively accepted a rule which [she] was sure was incorrect'. She reflected further: 'Could I even attribute such submissive behaviour as resonating with my identity as an Australian in a foreign territory?'

For a predominately non-racialized group of students, this is an important set of reflections, shared openly and respectfully with their classmates who have more immediate experiences of being 'other' at law school.

Several participants accepted that 'outsiders' to any system or institution, including a law faculty, may have difficulty comprehending or obeying (dominant) rules, or adapting to life under those rules. When Canadian students are asked to draw parallels between the Game and 'real life', they often raise issues of immigration, colonialism and imperialism, or suggest that moving tables reminds them of class privilege. Some talk about how the Game reproduces their feelings on the first day of law school: 'landing' into a whole new world with special rules that seem obtuse and inaccessible; not knowing how to go about learning those rules and sensing that the rules are tied to privilege.

In questionnaires completed after having played the Game, several Edinburgh students expressed that they wanted more openness to, and respect for, the rules and customs of those whose worldviews do not mirror those of the majority. Majority, to them, meant the 'powerful' law makers during the Game rather than the numerical majority of those at their table who agreed about the rules. Others noted how sometimes one individual could dominate or 'overthrow' all the other players at his or her table. Students were constantly surprised by their own reactions to the Game, amazed to find that they embodied more passive or more dominant ways of playing than expected. Some noted the importance of 'speaking out' against rule-breaking behaviour, while others came to see how people may passively acquiesce to externally imposed rules. As one student put it: 'Now I can understand why people in other countries do not object to laws or customs I do not understand.' Several acknowledged that they attempted to impose in a new environment (at a new table) a set of rules that they have learned elsewhere (at another table) – one student said that next time they would 'fight harder to persuade others of my rules'.

Some of the richest moments occurred when participants felt, saw and learned that these externally imposed rules can be exposed, challenged, reinterpreted and ultimately rejected when they do not meet the exigencies of 'othered' participants. While preliminary conversations often focus on the colonialism metaphor – the effect of outsider rules imposed on an existing table with its own rules – often the conversation is pushed to another level. For example, one University of Victoria student recognized that a table's rules might be problematic – i.e., bad environmental practice – shifting how we might experience a 'dominant' outsider coming in with new, 'better' rules. Working with student responses and motivating them to reflect on the relationship between the Game and systems of law they have seen or studied helps them to process power relationships between insiders and outsiders.

(Unsettling) the Assumed Importance of Law as Rules

The exercise is perhaps most deeply felt when we ask questions that prompt reflection on the relationship between law and rules. These interrogations push students to explore their own assumptions about the relationship between what it means to learn, how to learn law and, importantly, what they assume law to be. What seems especially clear is that law's contextuality and its contingency are felt more powerfully for being bodily experienced rather than conveyed through words on paper. To say there is no 'right set of rules' for this game is not the same thing as to 'feel' that to some students the rules are inaccessible, incomprehensible or arbitrary. Like any other law, the rules for the game are imagined, evaluated, given strength or dismissed by the people who practise, challenge or defer to them.

Students seem aware that they have internalized a desire for consistent rules and that this desire informs the way they play the Game – regardless of which table they play at. They are also acutely aware of the conflict and confusion that arises when rules are interpreted differently by different people. The Game helps them to reflect on the importance of expressing their views when trying to resolve disagreements; it also highlights the range of social mechanisms available for dealing with confusion and 'rule-breaking behaviour'. Finding appropriate ways to deal with rule-conflict becomes all the more significant when comparing those who seem to sit back and allow others to resolve the confusion with people who try to 'control' the Game or particular players. One Edinburgh student applauded the exercise for foregrounding our eagerness to follow rules, and thereby the central role of legal rules in maintaining social cohesion. Another rejected the need for rigid rules, suggesting that the Game showed the law to be flexible, porous and 'plastic', stating that 'it can be difficult to stick to one set of rules when you experienced many different sets of rules'. Others still felt that it is too complicated to establish one set of clear rules for everyone to follow. Indeed, one Edinburgh student despaired that 'the world will never unite in its views and laws'.

The contingency of 'the rules' was perhaps most transparent in Suzanne's 2009 seminar, when a group of students discovered the 'reveal' in advance of the class. On one level, the 'aha!' moment – when students confront the reality that they are playing by different rules – was somewhat stifled. On another, students used their advantage and knowledge in ways that were surprising and offered much scope for critical reflection during debrief. One group of students took over table one for the entire game because they preferred to play cards together than to deal with conflict and competition. Another student 'jumped the queue', going directly from table two to five and staying there throughout the Game. On another level still, the reveal dynamic shifted as Suzanne was the one who was not 'in' on the Game's 'twist'. She only found out at the end of the exercise that some people had accessed the explanatory documents before class. It was momentarily destabilizing for her and in many ways simulated in her the very response she was trying to get from students.

The Card Game can therefore also be used to reflect on the importance of trust between rule-makers and participants, and the place of resistance. In one iteration of the Game, a participant was overtly resistant. At the start of each hand she would lay out her cards face up for all to see and let others play her cards, while she sat back and watched, not playing as the others or the rules dictated. While some of the participants struggled with the discomfort of what seemed like a challenge to the facilitators, for us this kind of response is a gift, allowing us to explore explicitly how much agency our students employ in their encounters with law. Why, within an exercise that was pushing boundaries of acceptable behaviour, do students not more frequently draw on pure active resistance as a strategy? It was not lost on us that there is a huge privilege in being able to withdraw from a card game with little to no consequence. The same cannot be said of the 'real' legal system. This is perhaps most obvious in the comment from a Canadian student who suggested that the Game is not analogous with law because the Game 'does not carry penalties for those who break the rules'.

Alternative Pedagogies Matter

Legal education should not focus 'with laser-like singularity of purpose, on the students' cognitive powers' if the result is to exclude 'their values and emotional systems' (Lerner and Talati 2006: 97). Our experiences with the Card Game have reinforced our beliefs that unconventional forms of pedagogy are ethically meaningful in the legal classroom (Calder 2010; Lerner and Talati 2006). When students discuss the role that these exercises should have in legal education, some welcomed such pedagogy (though often combined with traditional learning). One Edinburgh student stated that 'alternate methods of teaching keep learning interesting and probably make it more effective'. Another reinforced the value of any teaching that avoids the 'tedious' tendency of having students 'just listening'. Others see such exercises as having a 'minor' or 'slight' role (in an introductory, scene-setting, team-building or ice-breaking capacity) either because they do not invite reflection of 'complex legal ideas', according to one Edinburgh student, or because they are simply 'too much fun', according to a McGill student. Students nonetheless appreciated how the exercise facilitates discussion and the opportunity to challenge their conceptions of self as law students but also as people leading their everyday lives.

One of the effects of the Card Game is that it gets law students 'out of their heads' and 'into their bodies'. The main skills they have learned to value are those considered intellectual in the strictest sense. Consequently, knowledge that comes from experiential learning and embodied experience is lost or devalued. When asked what they consider 'learning law in an embodied way' to mean, few Edinburgh students understood the term. Nevertheless, their answers exhibited an awareness of, and openness to, learning law more 'reflectively', 'comparatively', 'contextually', 'practically', 'fully' or 'conceptually'. The Card Game, as a result, also invites students to feel 'reflectively', 'conceptually', etc. about law.

Students do not expect to use their bodies to learn law. While some participants have embraced the idea of using more physical, embodied and experiential learning techniques, it is clear that few students understand the importance of feeling in your body what it means to be a subject of law, within and outwith the classroom. A few Edinburgh students did highlight the importance of experiential learning – that they could better understand law not just through text but also by actually 'experiencing and seeing it'. Even though many of them were open about their feelings of discomfort in playing the Game, particularly around moments of recognition of power imbalance and their own reactions to that, students did not translate this experience across to examine the power dynamics that they experience when actually learning law in the classroom or when they go out to practise law in the 'real' world. When taken alongside responses suggesting that the role of such exercises in legal education is introductory or marginal, it seems that students who have been taught by the Socratic method and mainly through text are either not aware of, not open to or judge as peripheral alternative forms of teaching that try to shift the legal privileging of mind over body or reason over emotion.

Many students struggle to accept formal law's inability to deal with issues of systemic racism, sexism, ableism and homophobia; teaching them about the unevenness of law's power is a complex task. It is also difficult to reach a generation of students whose technologically advanced styles of learning differ so greatly from those we were exposed to in the 1980s and 1990s. But it is the role of today's legal educator to cross unfamiliar terrain and find new and engaging ways to communicate with our students. If some of our students' responses indicate a lack of understanding or acceptance of alternative pedagogies, or the importance of non-textual methods of learning, we as law teachers have only ourselves to blame. Using the Card Game that is *in itself* a 'performative utterance' can help to move us towards a more transformative approach to legal learning.

It is challenging to teach students that law's intrusion into one's life can be messy and uncomfortable. Demonstrating that law's moments and sites of tension and discomfort require creativity, imagination and empathy is even more demanding. The most common downside to the Game, as reported by students, was feeling confused and frustrated throughout the exercise. The inability to communicate orally requires that they find new or somewhat atrophied ways of expressing their bewilderment, their dissent, their outrage or their desire for clarification. To some, this frustration led to apathy, submission and a sense that they had to 'go along with other people's rules'. Students in all three jurisdiction in which the Game has been played have felt disappointment or inadequacy when they did not understand what was going on or thought that they were 'losing' the Game, or when they realized afterwards that the rules were different at each table. The Card Game is therefore a unique opportunity to experience discomfort in a (relatively!) safe classroom environment and then learn from one's own strategies and the strategies of others.

The Cards are Reshuffled, Ready for Another Hand …

> In truth, a session of Theatre of the Oppressed has no end, because everything which happens in it must extend into life. Theatre shall have no end! Theatre of the Oppressed is located precisely on the frontier between fiction and reality – and the border must be crossed. If the show starts in fiction, its objective is to become integrated into reality, into life. (Boal 2002: 276)

Law is 'beyond text'. It is the messy stuff of human existence. It inherently involves the exercise of power. The Card Game brings these features of law into the foreground as players become aware of their expectation of (and desire for) fundamental rules and principles that can settle all disputes. When participants experience the incompatibility of conflicting rules and norms, they are better positioned to feel, and consequently to understand, that to avoid oppression, law's authoritative power must be mediated through dialogue, negotiation and empathy.

Notwithstanding the Card Game's initial reliance on textual 'rules' as part of an approach to pedagogy that pushes students to experience the power of law using experiential, non-textual learning, it is an excellent tool. It also provides an opportunity to remind ourselves, as Lerner and Talati (2006) write, how infrequently we bring to the surface questions of the value and emotional systems of our students. It allows for an engaging way to think differently about law, but it does not work for everyone, thus illustrating a critical point: neither does law when instantiated in rigid rules.

Creating space within the exercise for self-reflection and criticism of the tool itself opens up opportunities for even more enlightenment. Ensuring space within the debrief for reflection on the Card Game as legal pedagogy also reinforces the complex and continual interaction and negotiation of power, participation, communication and compassion. Our shared experiences have showed that many students appreciate the opportunity to come to law, and legal education, through embodied experience rather than text. The Card Game de-centres text. In the process, it offers participants the chance to approach key questions of power, control and decision making in a more open, empathic and sensitive way.

These empirical assessments of classroom experiences with unorthodox non-textual performances are part of an ongoing conversation about the practice of embodied legal pedagogy. Our understanding of embodied legal practices is in turn grounded in the theoretical heritage of feminist theories, post- and anti-colonial theory, and critical race theory. These frameworks help us dismantle the myth that learning law is fundamentally about learning texts. We believe that what the Card Game shows is how law engages our full range of perceptual, sensory and imaginative human experiences. It helps us and our students think about how law is experienced intersensorily. Consequently, the Game helps us get at how different bodies 'live and feel through' law (Goodrich 1990: 259).

References

Adjin-Tettey, E. et al. 2008. 'Postcard from the edge (of empire)'. *Social and Legal Studies*, 17(1), 5–38.

Austin, J.L. 1980. *How to Do Things with Words.* Oxford: Oxford University Press.

Boal, A. 2002. *Games for Actors and Non-Actors*, 2nd edn. London and New York: Routledge.

Calder, G. 2009. 'Embodied law: theatre of the oppressed in the law school classroom'. *Masks*, 1, 1–35.

Calder, G. 2010. 'Guantanamo: using a play-reading to teach law'. *Canadian Theatre Review*, 142, 44–9.

Calder, G. and Cowan, S. 2008. 'Re-imagining equality: meaning and movement'. *Australian Feminist Law Journal*, 29, 109–30.

Feminist Geography Reading Group. 2000. '(Un)doing academic practice: notes from a Feminist Geography Workshop'. *Gender, Place and Culture*, 7(4), 435–9.

Goodrich, P. 1990. *The Languages of Law: From Logics of Memory to Nomadic Masks.* London: Weidenfield & Nicolson.

Grabham, E. et al. 2009. *Intersectionality and Beyond Law, Power and the Politics of Location.* London: Routledge-Cavendish.

Harding, S. 1991. *Whose Science? Whose Knowledge? Thinking from Women's Lives.* Milton Keynes: Open University Press.

Holstein, J. and Gubrium, J. 2000. *The Self We Live By: Narrative Identity in a Postmodern World.* New York: Oxford University Press.

Lassonde, J. 2006. 'Performing law'. LLM thesis, University of Victoria. Available at: https://dspace.library.uvic.ca:8443/bitstream/handle/1828/117/LassondeFinal2.pdf?sequence=3 [accessed 18 July 2012].

Lerner, A. 2004. 'Using our brains: what cognitive science and social psychology teach us about teaching law students to make ethical, professionally responsible, choices'. *Quinnipiac Law Review*, 23, 643–707.

Lerner, A. and Talati, E. 2006. 'Teaching law and educating lawyers: closing the gap through multidisciplinary experiential learning'. *International Journal of Clinical Legal Education*, 9, 96–133.

Lillis, T. 1997. 'New voices in academia? The regulative nature of academic writing conventions'. *Language and Education*, 11(3), 182–99.

MacCormick, N. 1994. 'Four quadrants of jurisprudence', in W. Kravitz, G.H. von Wright and D.N. MacCormick (eds), *Prescriptive Formality and Normative Rationality: Essays in Honour of R S Summers*. Berlin: Duncker and Humbolt, 53–70.

Macdonald, R.A. 2003. 'L'hypothèse du pluralisme juridique dans les sociétés démocratiques avancées'. *Revue de droit de l'Université de Sherbrooke*, 33, 133–52.

MacKinnon, C. 1989. *Towards a Feminist Theory of the State.* Cambridge, MA: Harvard University Press.

Nedelsky, J. 1989. 'Preconceiving autonomy: sources, thoughts, and possibilities'. *Yale Journal of Law and Feminism*, 1(7), 7–36.
Nedelsky, J. 1997. 'Embodied diversity and the challenges of law'. *McGill Law Journal*, 42(9), 91–117.
Shiva, V. 1989. *Staying Alive: Women Ecology and Development.* London: Zed Books.

Appendix: The Card Game

Learning Objectives

- To experience, in a very tangible yet safe manner, the impact of being in, or arriving in, a place in which the rules are different from the ones that you know and where you have no effective means of communicating.
- To explore, in a preliminary way, the experienced differences with the goal of functioning effectively and respectively in a group with whom you may not share a culture or a common set of understandings.
- To articulate as a group, again in a preliminary way, a set of mutual expectations, understandings and commitments with respect to classroom and institutional climates.

Introduction

In this card game (often called Barnga), participants experience the shock of realizing that despite many similarities, people of differing cultures perceive things differently or play by different rules. Players learn that they must understand and reconcile these differences if they want to function effectively in a cross-cultural group.

Overview

Participants play a simple card game in small groups, where conflicts begin to occur as participants move from group to group. This simulates real cross-cultural encounters, where people initially believe they share the same understanding of the basic rules. In discovering that the rules are different, players experience a form of shock that attempts to re-create the actual experience of entering a different culture. They then must struggle to understand and reconcile these differences to play the game effectively in their 'cross-cultural' groups. Difficulties are magnified by the fact that players may not speak to each other but can communicate only through gestures. Participants are not forewarned that each is playing by different rules; in struggling to understand why other players do not seem to be playing correctly, they gain insight into the dynamics of cross-cultural encounters.

Instructions for Instructors

The Room

- The room should be set up with a series of tables each with space for four or five students at each table.
- On each table should be a pack of cards, a set of instructions turned upside down and a table number (one through five, or however many tables there are).
- The pack of cards will only include the cards ace through seven (the other cards have been removed).
- Students should be encouraged to choose and sit at a table without their paper, pencils, laptops and not to turn over the instructions until instructed to do so.

Playing the Game

Time requirement: 40–60 minutes.

Set-up

Set up (approximately) six tables (about four people per table), depending on the number of people participating. On each table there should be a copy of the rules for that table per player plus a deck of cards (use only ace to seven – no picture cards or other cards). To start with, the tables are given a set amount of time to learn the rules collectively with the warning that after a certain (short) period of time, the rules will be taken away and they will no longer be able to use spoken or written language to communicate. Next, EVERYTHING is removed from the playing tables and the participants are informed that they can no longer speak.

After allowing a few rounds without talking at the home table, participants must switch tables – the person who won the most tricks moves up a table, the person who loses the most tricks moves down a table. *What the players do not know is that each table has learned a different set of rules (see below).*

The Rules

Depending on the number of players, rule sheets can be altered or discarded for the number of tables being used. A website with sample rule sheets can be found here: http://yeoresources.org/Documents/Files/Barnga.pdf. Some samples of rules are as follows:

- Table 1: ace high, no trump.
- Table 2: ace low, diamonds trump.
- Table 3: ace low, clubs trump.

- Table 4: ace high, hearts trump.
- Table 5: ace high, spades trump.
- Table 6: ace low, no trump.

Each table shares the following rules:

- The deck is dealt.
- The dealer can be anyone at the table and the person who plays first will be to the left of the dealer.
- The first player for each trick may play ANY suit. All other players must follow suit (play a card of the same suit). For each round, each player plays one card.
- If a player does not have that suit, a card of any suit must be played. The trick is won by the person with the HIGHEST card of the ORIGINAL suit (players will begin to become confused when some players believe their card is a trump and others disagree or contradict this).
- Whoever wins the most tricks will move up a table.
- Whoever loses the most tricks will move down a table.
- Everyone else stays at the same table.
- Ties are resolved by rock-paper-scissors.
- Each round will be about five minutes long (longer if time allows) and each round will consist of as many games as time allows.
- After the initial round, players will not be allowed to see the rules or speak to each other. Gestures are allowed, but players are not allowed to use words.
- The goal of the game is set out explicitly – that of getting to (or staying at) the highest-numbered table. In this sense, the game 'winners' will be the persons who end up at the highest-numbered table (of course, once game play starts, winning will likely take a back seat to trying to figure out what everyone else is doing, as they are playing by different rules).

Instructions (These are the Instructions to Give to the Students Orally)

- You are going to play a card game at your table.
- The rules for the game are on the red piece of paper on your table.
- When I say start, you are going to read the rules and ensure that everyone understands them.
- This will be important because in about five minutes, I am going to yell 'stop' and then take the rules away from you.
- *The twist is this*: after I have done that, you will no longer be able to communicate through words, either oral or written.
- You will then play the game.
- Each round of the game will be timed.

- If you have any questions in the first five minutes, call me to your table, otherwise you need to find some way to ensure you all know the rules of the game before the rules disappear and you can no longer communicate orally.
- OK, go.

Keep time on the rounds and enforce the movement between tables every five minutes; play until there has been some considerable movement and mixing between the tables and the effect of the game can be seen visually.

Note: what you want to avoid is having to answer the question, in front of the whole group, about whether the rules are the same at each table; give some thought to how to manage this question if it arises.

Debriefing

- How did being in this game make you feel?
- If you could describe the game in one word, what would it be?
- What did you expect at the beginning of the game?
- When did you realize that something was wrong?
- How did you deal with it?
- How did not being able to speak contribute to what you were feeling?
- What impeded your ability to function in the group?
- What did you learn in struggling to understand why other players did not seem to be playing correctly?
- What *specific* real-life situations does this game remind you of?
- Choose *one* of these real-life situations. What are the underlying causes of the problems or difficulties?
- What does the game suggest about what to do when you are in a similar situation in the real world? *What did you do during the game that 'worked' for you?*
- How did the individual goal of winning impact on the collectivity experience of finding a solution to each table's dilemma?
- Based on our experience of the card game, what mutual expectations, understandings or commitments can we articulate as a group with respect social interactions in the classroom and in the law school?

Chapter 5

From Interpretive Imagination to Contingency in Law: An Argument for Moving Beyond Text[1]

Elaine Webster

Introduction

The 'Beyond Text in Legal Education' project's practical workshop was an opportunity to experience moving beyond text. There was sketching, sticking, moulding, movement, observation – all in the service of reflecting upon the potential of beyond-textual resources to enrich legal education. Questioning the value of going beyond text involves considering the unique contribution that beyond-textual resources can make.[2] This concerns the difference in experience of interacting with text to interacting with non-textual communicative forms. This is a fundamental question into which, it is expected, the 'Beyond Text' programme will aim more widely to provide insight. Questioning the value of going beyond text equally involves asking what a rationale might be for using non-textual resources. We might simply assume that a greater variety of sources to draw upon within a teaching and learning programme can only be positive, in order to maintain the interest and engagement of learners. More specifically, however, how might the integration of beyond-textual resources be positioned and justified? The contribution that this chapter aims to make is to explore one approach to situating the potential contribution of non-textual resources within legal education.

The point of departure is my experience of beyond-textual resources during the practical workshop: what was the principal insight gained from my experience of going beyond text and in what sense did I understand this as relevant to education in law? The principal insight concerned interpretation in law. More precisely, participation in the workshop acted as a reminder that interpretation is creative as well as bounded. The *imaginative investment* required in interpretation stood out in certain exercises during the workshop. These exercises emphasized the necessary

1 I would like to thank my colleague Claire McDiarmid for discussions on the idea of contingency in law, and my colleague Peter Robson for pointing me towards helpful literature on popular perceptions of law.

2 Reference to 'beyond-textual resources' is intended to encapsulate beyond-textual materials and objects as well as activities and interactions.

investment of one's imagination in order to derive meaning within the limits constituted by the object of interpretation. This resonated with law – working with the law requires the exercise of imagination as well as reason, an integral part of arriving at possible interpretations. This in turn resonated with legal education. It is suggested herein that if learners accept the place of interpretive imagination, this can help them to understand a foundational idea central to their grasp of the discipline. This foundational idea is labelled 'contingency'. Contingency refers to the coexistence of interdependence and indeterminacy in law, and it is suggested that this is a challenging concept for learners to accept and an important objective of legal education. It will be argued that beyond-textual resources have the potential to help students grasp the concept of contingency. This is due to the ability of such resources to emphasize interpretive imagination – a core aspect of the contingent nature of law.

The discussion will begin with reflections upon the practical workshop. From this, the idea of interpretive imagination will emerge. The following section will explain what I understand by the idea of contingency. This section will then focus on the relationship between interpretive imagination and understanding law as essentially characterized by contingency. In light of this, we shall return to beyond text in practice, where suggestions will be put forward as to the form that beyond-textual resources might take. It will be argued that situating the value of moving beyond text as contributing to an area that students may find particularly difficult is a potentially fruitful approach for the academy.

Reflections on the Beyond Text Practical Workshop: Realizing Interpretive Imagination

The backdrop to participation in the workshop was consideration of the potential relevance of beyond-textual resources in legal education. In reflecting upon the range of activities undertaken and the overall experience of participating, the element that stands out most strikingly is the creative interpretive engagement that was triggered in certain of the exercises – the dimension of *interpretive imagination.* As shall be explained below, this resonated with the study of law.

The 'Beyond Text in Legal Education' practical workshop[3] explored many aspects of engaging in non-text-based interactions. Participants engaged in a wide range of activities that presented different forms of experiencing, responding and communicating. I perceived the activities undertaken during the workshop to fall into three principal categories: activities concerning perception, trust and interpretation. Activities that urged consideration of perspective included, for example, the paired drawing of silhouettes, viewing artworks from changing vantage points and drawing with a part of the body that one does not usually draw

3 Practical workshop, 7–8 December 2008. See also the workshop film by Robert McKillop: http://www.law.ed.ac.uk/beyondtext/film.aspx [accessed 18 July 2012].

with. Such activities encouraged participants to reflect upon different points of view. An activity that explored trust, for example, involved being guided around the space by a partner whilst unable to see. The physicality of one-to-one and group interactions was a prominent theme.

The activities that involved interpretation resonated most strongly for me. These activities were about seeing and imagining different possible meanings. They centred upon understanding an object (or objects) of interpretation. They also involved consideration of, and responses to, the understandings of others; investing one's own meaning in interpretations put forward. Words or themes were visualized and represented in unique ways by different participants. One exercise that stood out was the 'power' game. This involved a changing configuration of chairs, a table and a bottle to represent different participants' understandings of the meaning of 'power'. The broad range of understandings expressed in the changing positions was striking. There were many possible ways in which to interpret the word 'power' and many ways to interpret each new configuration. Other stand-out activities included a word-interpretation exercise of representing a single word in an artwork using a range of materials; a respond-and-capture exercise, which involved taking photographs in the local environment based on prompts given in the form of images, colours and textures; and collage-making. The meaning that could be attributed in these exercises was not unrestrained; this did not involve pure creativity. Limits were provided by the objects themselves – the word 'balance' in my case in the word-interpretation exercise; a red square in respond-and-capture. The creativity involved was thereby not unrestrained. These were exercises in interpretation rather than pure imagination. To observe that such exercises involved the attribution of meaning to different stimuli is not surprising; it is based upon a broad view of interpretation, which encompasses all understanding (see, for example, Barak 2005: 38). The remarkable thing, however, was the extent to which the limits to interpretation seemed to take second place behind the creativity involved in attributing meaning. In other words, a certain dimension of interpretation stood out: when expressing understanding of objects in the alternative non-textual forms that the workshop involved, the *imaginative* side of interpretation was palpable. Imagination is an integral part of all interpretation, which can be described as a form of bounded creativity – creating meaning within limits provided by the object of interpretation. The attribution of meaning to an object of interpretation requires a creative input of imagining possible meanings. For me, beyond-text activities brought this personal, imaginative input to the fore. I was highly conscious of the creativity required in order to attribute meaning to the different stimuli.

Why might this have been the case? Were the limits to interpretation less visible in non-textual form, giving the impression of greater imaginative freedom? Were the limits less rigid, allowing for a vast range of possible, legitimate interpretations? It is difficult to say *why* my experience was that creativity was promoted via such beyond-textual exercises. Yet this was the case. It is interesting that not only was I required to be consciously imaginative, I also found this easy.

The form of stimulus and/or form of expression involved seemed to demand and facilitate imaginative, inventive and interpretive engagement. It is possible that this experience of heightened creativity was simply due to the fact that I was doing something different. An explanation for the reaction provoked by this form of activity is perhaps a central question into which the wider Beyond Text project will provide insights. I can only observe that my impression was that the inescapable creativity seemed to stem from the form of the objects of interpretation or the form of expression elicited, since my reaction to the exercises felt unusual in a positive sense. This is what stood out from my experience of the beyond-textual activities.

As noted above, the backdrop to participation in the practical workshop was consideration of the potential relevance of beyond-textual resources in legal education. The relevance of interpretation in itself strongly resonated with law and legal education for obvious reasons. Interestingly, the imaginative dimension of interpretation that stood out in the beyond-textual activities was at once clearly familiar yet seemed somehow underlying in the context of legal education, particularly when I considered the point of view of the learner. Interpretation in law, like all interpretation, is bounded creativity – a combination of reason and imagination. It is probably unnecessary to provide an example as disciplinary experts will surely find this to be a simple and basic observation. I shall give just one example nevertheless. In the field of human rights research, I am interested in judicial interpretation of the right not to be subjected to torture, inhuman or degrading treatment. For example, I am interested in whether self-inflicted ill-treatment might fall within the scope of this rule in light of the judicial development of this right to date. The activities during the practical workshop were reminders that interpretation in law is not only about the logical steps in reasoning, but is equally about the creativity that is an integral part of arriving at new meanings. When reflecting upon my experience of legal education in juxtaposition to the obvious imaginative engagement in the beyond-text exercises, the 'bounded' dimension of interpretation seemed to be most prominent. It seemed that legal education emphasized reasoning within the limits of texts whilst personal investment of one's imagination was often only implicit. I recognized a stronger focus on the boundaries rather than the creativity. If we take the chain novel metaphor for legal interpretation, for example, we would say that the importance of the chain seems to be emphasized in legal education over the content of new chapters. This is perhaps because the creativity is deemed to come naturally, whilst the special nature of the limits within legal interpretation need greater emphasis in learning. Or it is perhaps because law does not tend to highlight the intangible, fluid, imaginative dimension of its constitution. Whatever the explanation, this creative dimension is integral to interpretation in law and students who do well are able to put forward imaginative readings, suggesting content for grey areas within doctrine.

This chapter draws upon this insight concerning interpretive imagination and explores one approach to situating the potential contribution of non-textual resources within legal education. It is suggested that learners must be taught to respect boundaries in interpretation but also to exercise creativity. Non-textual resources have the potential to support learners by cultivating confidence in the relevance of being creative in interpretive engagement with law. This is important, it is argued, because familiarity with and acceptance of the need to exercise interpretive imagination encourages learners to confront a concept that is central to the discipline. This is the concept of contingency, which, it will be suggested, has a special importance. The relationship between interpretive imagination and contingency in law will be further explored below. I understand the idea of contingency to be a foundational feature of law that learners must grasp in order to 'get' how law works. It is foundational and at the same time can be seen as a potentially difficult idea for learners to grasp. This learning process may be facilitated by exposing learners to the legitimacy of interpretive imagination.

From Interpretive Imagination to Contingency in Law

The concept of contingency is tied to the essentially interpretive nature of law. Simply stated, law's operation and development through interpretation involves a web of related, pre-existing interpretations of legal texts (written and oral) upon which legal actors project new legal meanings. The idea of contingency in this context encompasses two coexisting aspects: interconnectedness in law and indeterminacy in law. It points to interrelations and dependence, and at the same time openness, possibility and uncertainty. Therefore, on the one hand, contingency suggests relationships of conditionality. Something is contingent when its existence is dependent on prior, existing conditions. On the other hand, contingency also invokes a lack of certainty. If something is contingent, it is open to different influences. It has no pre-determined outcome. The combination of these features can be seen to constitute a fundamental characteristic of law, so much so that becoming a successful student of law requires one to confront and accept this.

Yet, I believe that confronting and accepting this idea may prove challenging for students of law. It follows that it is of special importance for educators to find ways of supporting students to grasp this foundational idea, which is where beyond-textual resources may come into play. In what sense might the idea of contingency in law prove conceptually challenging? I think this is an idea that can be seen as 'troublesome', to use Perkins' term – 'troublesome' as a consequence of being alien or contradictory (Perkins 2006: 37–41).[4] The contingent character

4 Meyer and Land draw upon Perkins' notion of 'troublesome knowledge' in their discussion of disciplinary threshold concepts (2003: 417–20). These are concepts that may be particularly challenging to grasp, but once mastered allow for a transformed view of the discipline to emerge. Meyer and Land summarize a threshold concept as 'akin to a portal, opening up a new and previously inaccessible way of thinking about something' (2003: 412). Understanding of a threshold concept may require a challenging shift in perspective

of law might appear to students as counterintuitive. At the same time, however, it might appear familiar. Ambiguity in this respect may be exacerbated by preconceptions that many students may hold. Students may arrive at their study with preconceptions of the law that do not present a one-dimensional picture – for example, preconceptions stemming from personal encounters with the legal system and popular culture.[5] Personal encounters with the legal system, directly or indirectly, may serve to reinforce or break down any conceptions of law's 'greatness'. Portrayal of law in popular culture may bolster a perception of law as a vehicle of justice (think *Erin Brockovitch*) and/or as nothing more than a game to be played (the example that springs to mind is *Chicago, The Musical*). It is generally accepted that popular cultural portrayals influence the views of laypersons and new legal learners (Salzmann and Dunwoody 2005: 414–20; Sharp 2005: 233–4). Students will not necessarily have this kind of consciousness, but such mixed preconceptions, if they are held, may contribute to the challenge faced by students to accept contingency. Regardless of pre-existing mixed consciousness, all students must 'negotiate' their transition to becoming legal insiders. Sharp (2005: 235) writes of first-year law students taking 'a step away from the culture of the public and into the domain of the legal'.

Coming from 'the culture of the public', the concept of contingency in law is understandably an untidy idea. Law's official public discourse, to which all learners have been exposed simply by virtue of their membership of society, invokes impartiality and personal detachment: the rule of law institutionalized. An expectation of neutrality and objectivity may translate into an expectation of an 'equation-oriented' approach to learning law (McDiarmid and Webster 2010), i.e., that a body of legal rules must simply be learned and applied. Legal educators will likely recognize this as a familiar expectation of students. The skill of a lawyer may be expected to lie in knowledge of the rules and principles, knowledge of previous interpretations of relevant texts and application to the facts at hand. This speaks to the conditionality dimension of contingency in law, which evokes interconnectedness in interpretation, and consequently dependency upon existing rules and previous interpretations. Interconnectedness in interpretation, however, lies alongside uncertainty, indeterminacy and freedom of interpretation – the second dimension of contingency. Salzmann and Dunwoody (2005: 415) refer to the law as 'a fluid circular process, constantly changing as its content is created, challenged and abandoned', which highlights shifting interpretations rather than

---

for learners – an ontological shift in how the learner sees the world and her or his place within it (Land et al. 2005: 58; Meyer and Land 2003: 415). I have elsewhere described contingency as a 'threshold concept' in law (McDiarmid and Webster 2010), highlighting both the special importance of the idea of contingency and why it might be conceptually challenging.

5 Asimow et al. list seven sources upon which first-year law students may build perceptions of lawyers, including news coverage, jury service and having friends or family members who are lawyers (2005: 424).

constancy and clarity. Students may justifiably see this combined picture of interdependence and indeterminacy as a contradictory or counterintuitive one: a lack of determinacy may appear ill at ease with law's public face of neutrality and objectivity. Furthermore, accepting the concept of contingency may entail unsettling realizations. It becomes impossible to see the role of a lawyer as the mechanical application of neutral rules. Personal investment in the business of constructing legal meaning is unavoidable. For students, such 'freedom of choice' (Levinson 1996: 189) may be a daunting prospect. Gewirtz (1996: 11–12) notes that court judgments (which must inspire confidence in terms of 'legitimacy and authority') often remind us that 'each account contains the shaping mind of its describer, and that judges come to different understandings about what the law means'. Furthermore, students must simultaneously accept that 'stories' created by legal actors have very real consequences. It becomes inescapable, for example, that ultimately individuals are punished (or not) on the basis of the 'well-formedness and force of the winning story' (Brooks 1996: 18). Ultimately, students must accept that different interpretations must legitimately be invented by legal actors.

It is here that a link is visible between the troublesome concept of contingency and interpretive imagination. The dimension of indeterminacy in law invites imaginative interpretations by individual actors within the legal system. The need for legal actors to exercise interpretive imagination is therefore one consequence of the contingent nature of law, in the sense that uncertainty and indeterminacy imply space to creatively derive possible meanings from an object of interpretation. Engaging in activities that encourage the exercise of interpretive imagination as part of a course or curriculum would promote the legitimacy of this form of interaction with law. This would potentially provoke learners to reflect upon the implications of interpretive imagination. A focus on the creative dimension of interpretation would thereby provide opportunities for learners to confront the concept of contingency.

As educators, we are perhaps less accustomed to openly promoting creativity in interpretation than schooling learners in the limits of their own investment in engagement with law. Consider the centrality we give to legal authority in teaching and the importance placed upon evidence-based argument. Yet the ability to inject creativity and imagination is clearly valued: we identify as the strongest students those who demonstrate an ability to manipulate facts and to construct arguments in a creative way. Law schools encourage students to engage in legal role play, which is one of the clearest examples of asking students to imaginatively construct arguments within the constraints of existing doctrinal positions. In assessment, we expose students to discussion of the most persuasive argument or ask for problems to be solved in ways that are at once reasoned and imaginative. When students grasp this combination of reason and imagination in light of the contingent nature of law, they are able to authentically progress. However, directly and explicitly exposing students to this integral element of interpretive imagination is, in my experience, not something that legal education habitually involves. An opportunity is available for beyond-textual resources to act as a support mechanism for this if such resources can indeed be seen to promote acceptance of, and confidence in, interpretive imagination.

Moving Beyond Text: Towards Understanding Contingency in Law

Cassandra Sharp (2005: 249–50) writes that the 'process of becoming a lawyer is a fascinating transitional phase in which students use all legal texts at their disposal … to make sense of legal culture and to contribute to it'. Non-textual resources can be positioned as part of a concrete response to an area of conceptual difficulty, thereby supporting successful learning. In this vein, the inclusion of non-textual resources within teaching repertoires has the potential to contribute to supporting students in the transition from learner to lawyer by helping to illuminate the fundamental idea of contingency in law. The next step is to consider what the inclusion of beyond-textual resources might look like in practical terms by returning to reflection upon the Beyond Text workshop. What form might beyond-textual resources take within a teaching and learning programme? This section will consider some practicalities that would have to be addressed upon the introduction of non-textual resources and will suggest five examples.

The examples put forward here aim to meet the objective of creating opportunities for learners to confront the concept of contingency in law. These activities should encourage learners to consider the place of creativity in legal interpretation and should be feasible in practice. The activities noted above, which stood out as provoking the exercise of interpretive imagination during the practical workshop, could all potentially be useful. Some would be easier to put into practice than others in a teaching setting, but activities would be modified to suit the context, taking into account any practical constraints. And, of course, such activities were only examples themselves; educators could create activities and resources tailored to their own contexts and could find support through the sharing of a bank of activities and case studies.

There are likely to be a number of practical concerns faced by educators who are contemplating the use of beyond-textual activities. These may include concerns such as subject matter, timing, group size, motivating students and resource demands. In terms of subject matter, should resources/activities be obviously law-related? This was not the case for the majority of activities during the workshop from which insight into law and legal education was nevertheless drawn. 'Respond and capture', for example, was based on a range of 'random' prompts in the form of colours, textures, etc. An activity with no obvious legal link may indeed be particularly provocative, leading to discussion of the relevance of, and rationale behind, asking learners to engage in this way. This could encourage reflection upon the experience of engagement rather than the subject matter. In activities that aim to highlight interpretive imagination, an object of interpretation that is not an obviously legal term may be shown to have a legal meaning, as may be the case with ordinary, everyday words. If the focus of an activity could be shaped to include direct reference to law, this may have the benefit of being more easily digestible to a student audience. Within a higher education learning programme, beyond-textual activities would be well placed in an induction context for new students, but also within specific modules. The examples below reflect both options.

Group size must be taken into account. Smaller groups, with a less anonymous audience and closer interaction with students, would likely be the optimal setting for inclusion of beyond-textual resources. This would undoubtedly be less challenging, but activities can be designed so as to be equally feasible in large groups. The examples below that are deemed to be suitable for large groups have been configured on the premise that activities would not necessarily require students to individually and directly exercise their own interpretive imaginations. The principal requirement is that the activity should aim to provoke reflection upon the role and legitimacy of creativity in interpretation. This could involve observation of, working with and/or discussing beyond-textual representations of particular ideas. It would indeed be valuable to aim to give learners the opportunity to directly exercise imagination when engaging in an interpretation, but the possibility of both approaches widens the range of activities that would be feasible from an organizational point of view for large groups. A related concern is how to motivate students to participate on a voluntary basis. Very large group sizes would perhaps magnify this issue. In such groups, nevertheless, one could hope that even the participation of a minority would give sufficient material for discussion. It would be possible to resort to a competitive approach, seeking the most imaginative interpretation. In the first year of using an exercise, this may be a good way to build a bank of examples for subsequent students. When students perceive something to be 'just the way it is done', they often seem less ready to question whether they should participate or not. Concerns about voluntary participation presume that many students might feel inhibited by the non-textual format if perceived as novel. Conversely, however, many might find the format liberating (as was my experience in the Beyond Text practical workshop). Either way, the activity could be expected to get students talking – questioning why they are being asked to participate in such an exercise is clearly a step in the right direction. Some activities may lend themselves to a potential link to assessment; for example, a non-textual piece and related written reflection, or reflection upon a non-textual stimulus. Finally, how resource-intensive might such activities be? Clearly, moving beyond text would open up the possibility of using a wide range of sources, some of which may require access to particular objects, artworks and materials, and certain activities would require a suitable space. It would be possible to tailor an activity to the resources that are available, even where such resources are scarce. The examples suggested below deliberately demand few resources in order to facilitate incorporation.

The examples are of activities that aim to confront students with the use of imagination in interpretation and the relevance of this to their studies. They include different forms of engaging with beyond-textual resources: as in the practical workshop, activities include interpretation of non-textual objects expressed in non-textual form (e.g., as in 'respond and capture') and interpretation of text expressed in non-textual form (e.g., the artistic word-interpretation). In each, students would be asked to express their understanding and would be exposed to several understandings of the same object of interpretation. In the first example of an activity that I would adopt, students would be asked to observe, reflect upon and discuss an image portraying a law-related idea, for example, from the collection reproduced in Morris L. Cohen's *Law: The Art of Justice* (1992). This would be a gentle introductory option that I would incorporate into an induction programme for new students. What do they see in the image? What appears to be going on here? What might this image represent? This simple activity would prepare students from the outset for reflection upon non-textual sources.

I would base a further induction activity upon the 'power' exercise used in the practical workshop (the group activity involving physical interpretation of the theme by creating a changing configuration of objects). In the workshop, my experience was that the need to continually adapt the configuration prompted spontaneous creativity in interpretation. It is important that this activity be based on a theme that would not inhibit new students. 'Power' was an ideal choice as a familiar yet rich concept. A potential theme that I would use is 'family' – this has scope for various interpretations and students should not find it difficult or inhibiting to participate and to suggest their own understandings of this term. I would follow this exercise with a demonstration of the word as it occurs in diverse legal contexts, with the intention of highlighting the multiplicity of possible interpretations and of provoking discussion of the impact that interpretations expressed by the group would have on the meaning of a wider text. To give an example from my own teaching area, I would invoke the meaning of 'family' in Article 8 of the European Convention on Human Rights, the right to respect for private and family life, home and correspondence, alongside a case law example, such as the European Court of Human Rights' understanding of 'family' in cases concerning disappeared persons. Discussion examples from a number of areas of law could be used in order to encourage students to identify insights gained from this beyond-textual activity as relevant discipline-wide.

If small group work was possible in an induction setting, I would use a collage-making exercise. This would require provision of sufficient space and materials to work with, which would be manageable in small group format. Again, students would be prompted to imagine a unique interpretation on the basis of a shared, limited pool of materials. This activity would work well based on interpretation of a term that is deliberately challenging to define, the complexity of which could be expressed in the collage format of overlapping images, such as 'responsibility' or 'reason'.

In the module-specific context of public law and/or human rights teaching, I would ask students to observe and suggest links between non-textual representations of particular human rights and controversial or borderline issues. Both would be in non-textual form to encourage openness in interpretation of the rights as well as the issues. I would ask: 'What do you see in these sets of images and how might they be related?' I would use images representing the right not to be subjected to inhuman or degrading treatment or punishment, the prohibition of slavery, the right to liberty, the right to respect for private life, the right to marry and found a family, and so on. Alongside this would be representations of diverse issues, such as anti-terrorism measures, divorce, trafficking, prostitution and destitution. There are not unambiguous relationships between such issues and rights protections. It is hoped that participants would consider the breadth, and see the importance of, the scope of interpretation of the rights as well as different ways in which the issues themselves might be understood.

In the context of human rights teaching, an interesting and feasible beyond-text activity would be a photographic 'respond and capture' exercise on the subject of human dignity. This would be well suited to large or small groups. It would be resource-light, given the ready availability of digital cameras/mobile phones. I would accompany this activity with an online exhibition and subsequent group discussion in the whole group or in related seminars. Students would be asked to capture images of what human dignity means to them. Looking for visual representations of dignity in the everyday environment would aim to encourage a freedom of interpretation and promote an understanding of the myriad ways in which we might individually interpret the concept of human dignity. Interpretation of the concept of human dignity would be considered in light of the principle of respect for human dignity as itself a principle of human rights interpretation. This beyond textual exercise would, it is hoped, prompt students to imagine possible meanings of dignity and to contemplate the impact of interpretations accorded to this fluid term on the scope of meaning of legal rules.

All of these activities would aim to provoke reflection upon the place of personal imaginative input within the system of legal rules that students will come to learn and, in turn, reflection upon the concept of contingency. The objective of moving beyond text would be to encourage students to view the exercise of imagination as legitimate and necessary in working with law.

Concluding Thoughts

The argument put forward in this chapter is rooted in my experience of engaging with beyond-textual resources in the project workshop. As to the capacity of beyond-textual interactions to stimulate interpretive imagination, there remains an inevitable gap in this respect. I have articulated my experience of moving beyond text without giving an explanation of why these resources had this effect. As noted above, perhaps the wider Beyond Text project will provide such explanation. I have instead proceeded to suggest, in a practical vein, a rationale for introducing beyond-textual resources into legal education.

As project participant Valerie Fitch described it, law is ‘innately creative’. Fellow participant Tom Mayo referred to the difficulty in encouraging students to ‘unleash their creativity’.[6] If beyond-textual activities are indeed able to bring to the fore the necessary investment of one’s imagination, used in a teaching context such resources can encourage learners to view the exercise of imagination as relevant to their interaction with law. Accepting that legal actors must be imaginative and inventive when working with law can encourage learners to grapple with the fundamental nature of law as free from pre-determined outcomes – seen as one important objective of legal education. ‘Good lawyers’, practising or academic, understand that law is not pre-determined but nevertheless rooted in legal doctrine, and strive to creatively exploit indeterminacy within limits.

It has been argued that this is one sense in which beyond-textual resources have the potential to make a valuable contribution to legal education. It is not suggested that moving beyond text is limited to confronting imagination in interpretation. As noted at the outset, the meanings that could be drawn from the experience of interacting in non-textual ways, even from the short workshop, were potentially rich (notably, there seems to be a relationship between the dimension of perception in beyond-textual activities, the ethical development of legal practitioners and the realizations that may accompany acceptance of the idea of contingency. It would be interesting to explore this further). This contribution has focused on just one approach to considering and justifying the value of moving beyond text in legal education. The use of beyond-textual resources has been placed not simply as a bonus in legal education, but as a potential response to an existing area of conceptual difficulty, helping students to make sense of the ‘mysterious process known as the law’ (Salzmann and Dunwoody 2005: 412).

References

Asimow, M. et al. 2005. ‘Perceptions of lawyers – a transnational study of student views on the image of law and lawyers’. *International Journal of the Legal Profession*, 12(3), 407–36.

Barak, A. 2005. *Purposive Interpretation in Law*. Princeton: Princeton University Press.

Brooks, P. 1996. ‘The law as narrative and rhetoric’, in P. Brooks and P. Gewirtz (eds), *Law’s Stories: Narrative and Rhetoric in the Law*. New Haven and London: Yale University Press, 14–22.

Cohen, M.L. 1992. *Law: The Art of Justice*. New York: Hugh Lauter Levin Associates/Macmillan.

Gewirtz, P. 1996. ‘Narrative and rhetoric in the law’, in P. Brooks and P. Gewirtz (eds), *Law’s Stories: Narrative and Rhetoric in the Law*. New Haven and London: Yale University Press, 2–13.

6 See workshop film: http://www.law.ed.ac.uk/beyondtext/film.aspx.

Land, R., Cousin, G., Meyer, J.H.F. and Davies, P. 2005. 'Threshold concepts and troublesome knowledge (3): implications for course design', in C. Rust (ed.), *Improving Student Learning: Diversity and Inclusivity*. Oxford: Oxford Centre for Staff and Learning Development/Alden Press, 53–64.

Levinson, S. 1996. 'The rhetoric of the judicial opinion', in P. Brooks and P. Gewirtz (eds), *Law's Stories: Narrative and Rhetoric in the Law*. New Haven and London: Yale University Press, 187–205.

McDiarmid, C. and Webster, E. 2010. 'Contingency and contested narrative: a threshold concept in legal education'. *UKCLE Directions in Legal Education Newsletter*, Spring edition, 8–9.

Meyer, J.H.F. and Land, R. 2003. 'Threshold concepts and troublesome knowledge: linkages to ways of thinking and practising within the disciplines', in C. Rust (ed.), *Improving Student Learning: Theory and Practice – 10 Years On*. Oxford: Oxford Centre for Staff and Learning Development/Oxonian Rewley Press, 412–24.

Perkins, D. 2006. 'Constructivism and troublesome knowledge', in J.H.F. Meyer and R. Land (eds), *Overcoming Barriers to Student Understanding: Threshold Concepts and Troublesome Knowledge*. Abingdon and New York: Routledge, 33–47.

Salzmann, V.S. and Dunwoody, P.T. 2005. 'Prime-time lies: do portrayals of lawyers influence how people think about the legal profession?' *SMU Law Review*, 58, 411–52.

Sharp, C. 2005. 'The "extreme makeover" effect of law school: students being transformed by stories'. *Texas Wesleyan Law Review*, 12, 233–50.

Useful Links

'Beyond Text in Legal Education' practical workshop: http://www.law.ed.ac.uk/beyondtext/practiceworkshop.aspx [accessed 18 July 2012].

'Beyond Text in Legal Education' workshop film: http://www.law.ed.ac.uk/beyondtext/film.aspx [accessed 18 July 2012].

Chapter 6
Analysis and the Arts

Nancy B. Rapoport[1]

Introduction

The legal job market in the USA has changed dramatically in the last few years. Few believe that the job market will ever go back to the possibly easier days, when law firms brought in large entering classes of new lawyers and when clients paid for the training of those new lawyers (see Burk and McGowan 2011). More clients are pressing their lawyers to reduce their legal bills, and lawyers have discovered that outsourcing certain repetitive tasks – for example, by outsourcing legal research to India – keeps their profit margins reasonably secure. Firms that haven't figured out ways to cut costs are closing.

Graduates of the classes of 2009, 2010 and 2011 are finding it harder to secure employment as associates than at any time since the mid-1990s. They might get jobs as contract attorneys if they're lucky, or they might not find legal employment at all. They have had the misfortune of graduating at a time when the legal market is saturated. Moreover, they are all graduating with roughly the same skill sets. Some are graduates of more elite schools and some are graduates of less elite schools. But they all have had roughly the same type of legal education. What graduates need is a way to differentiate themselves, especially because they are now competing with laid-off lawyers for jobs. The laid-off lawyers can, at least, demonstrate some job skills. This situation begs the following question: what can we do for law students now to give them an edge in this changing world?

In a recent *Sunday New York Times Magazine* piece, Bill Keller (2011) described some management training he received at the Wharton School. This training covered all of the usual things that business schools teach, but it also included a three-hour poetry session. I've had some of the same training myself from the Harvard Institutes for Higher Education. Both of the two programs that I attended had a session that used poetry.

Law school presupposes that matriculating students like to read, or at least that they have the *sitzfleisch* to endure reading hundreds of densely packed pages a day. Law professors teach first years how to parse a case, how to sift the holding from

---

1 Many thanks to the University of Edinburgh and its conference, *Beyond Text in Legal Education* (20–21 June 2009) and to Zenon Bańkowski, Bernie Burk, Maksymilian Del Mar, Randy Gordon, Jennifer Gross, Paul Maharg, Nettie Mann, Morris Rapoport and Jeff Van Niel.

any dicta and how to reconcile seemingly contradictory results in multiple cases. At the end of that first year, every law student who has paid attention in class can read a case.

There is a difference, though, between reading a case and using it. We rediscover that difference every time we grade exams. Most students can figure out when to cite to a case, many students can apply a case to a hypothetical in our exams and a few students can understand how the nuances of a case might affect their analysis of the hypothetical. The problem is that lawyers trained in other countries have the same range of abilities with respect to cases that US-trained lawyers do. If those non-US lawyers are less expensive to use, then US graduates can find themselves unemployed (or underemployed).

We have a chance to build better law students through the arts. One way is to find avenues to introduce some cultural references. Although few lawyers need to cite to William Butler Yeats in their daily activities, it is safe to say that some of the better lawyers have Yeats or other literary references in their arsenal. The power of a brief that contends that ‘the centre cannot hold’[2] is multiplied if the judge reading that brief shares the same type of educational background. Recently, the United States Supreme Court began an opinion with *Bleak House*[3] *and the United States Court of Appeals for the District of Columbia Circuit referred to Forrest Gump.*[4] One simple fix for law schools, then, is to add courses in Law and Pop Culture or Law and Literature (if they do not already offer them).[5]

But what we really need to do is to provide law students with multiple opportunities to use literature, or the visual arts, or even pop culture as a way of teaching the law itself. Some law schools are already doing that. Professor Russell Murphy of Suffolk Law School argues that:

---

2 This classic line comes from William Butler Yeats, *The Second Coming* (1919), available at http://www.potw.org/archive/potw351.html [accessed 22 July 2012].

3 *Stern v. Marshall, United States Supreme Court*, Case No. 10-179 (23 June 2011) at 1: ‘This “suit has, in course of time, become so complicated, that no two lawyers can talk about it for five minutes, without coming to a total disagreement as to all the premises. Innumerable children have been born into the cause: innumerable young people have married into it”; and sadly, the original parties “have died out of it.” A “long procession of [judges] has come in and gone out” during that time, and still the suit “drags its weary length before the Court”.’

4 *Uthman v. Obama, United States Court of Appeals for the District of Columbia*, Case No. 10-5235 (29 March 2011), at 13: ‘Uthman’s account piles coincidence upon coincidence upon coincidence. Here, as with the liable or guilty party in any civil or criminal case, it remains possible that Uthman was innocently going about his business and just happened to show up in a variety of extraordinary places—a kind of Forrest Gump in the war against al Qaeda.’

5 Students who can demonstrate that they write creatively (and well) should have an edge in interviews.

> My experience with using film and storytelling in a first-year Criminal Law course provides an illustration of what can be done in the classroom by an individual faculty member. My approach addresses the following question: can the existing disconnect between a law student's substantive analytical work and matters of justice, morality, human experience, and social good be remedied, in part, by the use of documentaries, movies, non-legal narratives, and 'real world' stories of the people involved in appellate cases? I believe it can. (Day and Murphy 2009)

Murphy shows his Criminal Law students documentaries and other films (including *The Exonerated*) that personalize the names in the cases that the students are reading. Professor Judith Maute has made the key characters in the *Peevyhouse* contracts case come alive with original documents (and even a song) (Maute 1995).[6] By bringing out the 'human' in cases, efforts like these let law students understand that there are more perspectives to law than just legal rules. Part of the problem is that legal education tends to emphasize pragmatic goals and neglect the imagination that is a vital component of law. In a sense, legal education has a tendency to strip away things from students and leave them with only one way of approaching a problem.

The 'Beyond Text in Legal Education' conference certainly opened my eyes to these types of possibilities and the possibilities of developing the imagination through the arts. In the first half of the conference, we experienced the arts in ways that I had never done before, even in college. Not only did I enjoy the experience as an art-lover, but the experience reminded me of how the arts, quite literally, open people's minds to new viewpoints, which was of course the point of the exercises in which we engaged and the point of the project as a whole. We participated in a variety of exercises with the help of artists in the plastic and movement disciplines. The exercises have been described elsewhere but, amongst others, we looked at artwork from a variety of unusual physical perspectives (close up, on my back on the floor, with a magnifying glass); I sketched a description of someone else's art while my back was to it, after my colleague Randy Gordon narrated what he saw in the art; we took photographs based on trigger words; and, at one point, I play-acted a pram.[7] These experiences also led me to brainstorm about how I could bring this experience back to our law students: to look at what I have been doing and what I might do.

6 Professor Maute's research developed into a documentary film: *The Ballad of Willie & Lucille: Disappointed Expectations of Contract Law and the Legal System* (2008).

7 Giving the lie to the assertion that I cannot do a 'wheelbarrow' movement.

Teaching and the Arts

Professional Responsibility

Law schools are already experimenting with incorporating the arts (see Adamson et al. 2008; Day and Murphy 2009; Higdon 2007; Levit 2009; Schulze Jr. 2006). I have done so myself in my Professional Responsibility course. If ever there were a course that lends itself to teaching through the arts, professional responsibility is it. I could quite easily teach Professional Responsibility entirely with film clips. In fact, for years, I have taught mini-PR courses (continuing legal education sessions, Law and Pop Culture) using film clips. The advantage of using films is that most characters are developed well enough for law students to be able to identify with them.[8]

Take *My Cousin Vinny*, which is, in many ways, the perfect law film. It covers everything from competency to decorum in the court to unauthorized practice of law to barratry – and it is a wonderful example of the problems caused by cascading lies. Although the film is obviously a comedy and obviously fiction, several scenes smack of real-life lawyering. Some lawyers have problems understanding a court's order, and this brief scene captures their thick-headedness:

> JUDGE: I'm setting this matter for trial this Monday, February 2nd, 10 a.m. Mr. Gambone, stand up.
> (Vinny stands) Now didn't I tell you the next time you appear in my court that you dress appropriately?

8 Here is just a partial list of films that I have used to teach PR: *Adam's Rib* (MGM, 1949); *A Civil Action* (Buena Vista Pictures, 1998); *A Fish Called Wanda* (MGM Home Entertainment, 1988); *All of Me* (Lions Gate Films, 2003); *Anatomy of a Murder* (Columbia Pictures, 1959); *... And Justice For All* (Columbia Pictures, 1979); *Bananas* (United Artists, 1971); *Caddyshack II* (Warner Bros., 1988); *Cars* (Walt Disney Pictures, 2006); *Chicago* (Miramax, 2002); *The Client* (Warner Bros., 1994); *Clueless* (Paramount Home Video, 1999); *The Devil's Advocate* (Warner Bros., 1997); *Defending Your Life* (Warner Home Video, 1991); *Down Periscope* (20th Century Fox, 1996); *Double Jeopardy* (Paramount, 1999); *Erin Brockovich* (Columbia TriStar, 2000); *A Few Good Men* (Columbia TriStar, 1992); *15 Minutes* (New Line Home Video, 2001); *The Firm* (Paramount, 1993); *Flash of Genius* (Universal Studios Home Entertainment, 2009); *Henry V* (Samuel Goldwyn Co., 1989); *The Informant!* (Warner Home Video, 2010); *Inherit the Wind* (MGM/UA Home Entertainment, 1960); *Legal Eagles* (Universal Pictures, 1986); *Legally Blonde* (MGM, 2001); *Liar Liar* (Universal Pictures, 1997); *The Life and Times of Judge Roy Bean* (1972; Warner Home Video, 2000); *The Man Who Shot Liberty Valance* (Paramount, 1962); *Masterpiece Theatre: Bleak House* (BBC Video, 2005); *Matlock: The First Season* (Paramount, 2008); *Michael Clayton* (Warner Home Video, 2008); *Murder in the First* (Warner Bros., 1995); and, of course, *My Cousin Vinny* (20th Century Fox, 1992). And that's just part of my list from the first half of the alphabet.

VINNY: (incredulously) You were serious about that?[9]

I probably could teach the entire Professional Responsibility course with two films: *My Cousin Vinny* and *The Verdict*. I could also use songs, such as 'Rock and Roll Lawyer' by the Austin Lounge Lizards or Warren Zevon's 'Lawyers, Guns, and Money'. Would students pay attention? You bet. Would I get my points across? I think so.

What makes my Professional Responsibility course so much fun, though, isn't the films that I show. It's the films, the songs and the games that the students themselves develop as part of the course. I require our students to work in teams to teach the ethics rules to their colleagues, and each semester, students outdo themselves with original work. I have seen film students write, direct and produce original films to illustrate ethics rules. I have seen students develop games for their classmates to play. I have heard them sing.[10] What makes this type of teaching different from most other law teaching is the measure of control that the students regain. They are not just learning from the podium, they teach from it.

This is not to say that students universally welcome this idea of teaching. My teaching evaluations always include some comments that are some variant of 'we pay her to teach; why are we doing it?'. But most of the students understand my reasons. For one thing, I want to demystify the law by showing them that they can teach themselves. (I would never do this to first-year law students or to students in complicated courses, but Professional Responsibility is uniquely accessible as a field.) For another, I want them to learn some other skills that they will need as lawyers: the ability to present material to people clearly and the ability to work in teams. Most of all, though, I want them to reclaim some of what they lose in law school. Law school seems to teach law students that what they learned before – what they majored in as undergraduates – is of no use. I need them to realize that being a legal counsellor means more than just applying law to facts. It means reaching clients in a variety of verbal and non-verbal ways. When I see my Professional Responsibility students reclaim their 'former' selves as they develop their presentations, I can visualize them as lawyers, years later, using their non-legal knowledge as well as their legal knowledge to better advise their clients.

Professional Responsibility is not the only way I could incorporate the arts in teaching substantive courses. Many other courses lend themselves to an arts-inclusive approach.

Contract Law

Although first-year law students present a clean slate, they quickly react when a professor deviates from how a course 'should' be taught. If professors in other sections are using the traditional Socratic Method, students will get very nervous

9 Launer 1992: 55.

10 Some of them well.

if their professor uses group work or other teaching methods. Therefore, for any first-year course, it is important that the professor creates a strong climate of trust before branching out to more non-traditional teaching methods.

There are all sorts of ways to use literature in a Contracts course. Ambiguity is a difficult concept for first-year students to grasp, in part because they are focusing so hard on mastering the vocabulary of law that they often assume that the way that they read a passage in a case or a clause in a contract is the way that everyone else would read that language. Take the classic case of *Sherwood v. Walker* (1887), in which the issue was whether the cow being sold was sold as a barren cow (sold for beef) or as a cow that might be barren, but might not. When the cow turned up pregnant, the seller refused to convey her to the buyer on the theory that, had he known that the cow could conceive, he would not have sold her for such a low price. In sorting through the issue of whether the mistake of the cow's barrenness was a mutual mistake or a unilateral one, the majority opinion provided the following less-than-elucidating test:

> If there is a difference or misapprehension as to the substance of the thing bargained for; if the thing actually delivered or received is different in substance from the thing bargained for, and intended to be sold, then there is no contract; but if it be only a difference in some quality or accident, even though the mistake may have been the actuating motive to the purchaser or seller, or both of them, yet the contract remains binding. (1887: 576–7)

The majority found that the parties had mutually been mistaken over the 'very nature' of the cow; the dissent was sceptical:

> There is no question but that the defendants sold the cow representing her of the breed and quality they believed the cow to be, and that the purchaser so understood it. And the buyer purchased her believing her to be of the breed represented by the sellers, and possessing all the qualities stated, and even more. He believed she would breed. There is no pretense that the plaintiff bought the cow for beef, and there is nothing in the record indicating that he would have bought her at all only that he thought she might be made to breed. Under the foregoing facts, and these are all that are contained in the record material to the contract, it is held that because it turned out that the plaintiff was more correct in his judgment as to one quality of the cow than the defendants, and a quality, too, which could not by any possibility be positively known at the time by either party to exist, the contract may be annulled by the defendants at their pleasure. I know of no law, and have not been referred to any, which will justify any such holding, and I think the circuit judge was right in his construction of the contract between the parties. (1887: 925)

One could teach this case in a variety of ways. I normally have the students make a list of the facts favouring the conclusion that there was mutual mistake and a list of the facts that would weigh against such a conclusion. Then we discuss how the parties are supposed to be able to figure out what goes to the 'very nature' of the contract and, finally, we discuss how lawyers might emphasize certain already-existing facts and de-emphasize others – and what the ethics considerations would be in crafting an argument. There is nothing wrong with walking through the case this way.

But here is what might happen if we tied in Anne Tyler's (2001) opening line in *Back When We Were Grownups: A Novel*: 'Once upon a time, there was a woman who discovered she had turned into the wrong person.' We could work backwards from that line to discuss how the 'barren' cow turned into a fertile one, or even how lawyers can 'turn' facts in favour of their client. Or, what if, before the students read *Sherwood v. Walker*, they read Wallace Stevens' *Thirteen Ways of Looking at a Blackbird*?[11] This poem provides an excellent introduction to the topic of point of view and thus to the subject of mutual mistake.

Using Wallace Stevens' poem, we could explore how someone's perspective would affect how he or she defined the subject of a contract. We could even use some art, such as M.C. Escher's *Relativity*, to describe how differently two people can see the world.

Bankruptcy Law or Client Counselling

Bankruptcy law is difficult to teach because, in order to understand any of it, a student has to slog through the entire course. It is only in the last week of a basic bankruptcy course that students start to see how the various Bankruptcy Code provisions fit together. It is all well and good to tell students, for example, that bankruptcy involves three stages: figuring out who owns what and who owes what (the 'estate' and 'claims'), increasing the size of the estate (executory contracts and avoidance powers) and the fresh start (reorganization and liquidation; discharge). But until they get to the topics of discharge or reorganization, they have only learned a string of disjointed concepts.

One of the concepts involves increasing the size of the estate by unwinding certain pre-petition actions. One pre-petition action that begs for unwinding involves fraudulent transfers: did the debtor hide or transfer any of her property before she filed for bankruptcy? The Bankruptcy Code uses this definition of a fraudulent transfer:

> (a)(1) The trustee may avoid any transfer (including any transfer to or for the benefit of an insider under an employment contract) of an interest of the debtor in property, or any obligation (including any obligation to or for the benefit of an insider under an employment contract) incurred by the debtor, that was made or

11 This poem is available at http://www.writing.upenn.edu/~afilreis/88/stevens-13ways.html [accessed 22 July 2012].

> incurred on or within 2 years before the date of the filing of the petition, if the debtor voluntarily or involuntarily –
>
> (A) made such transfer or incurred such obligation with actual intent to hinder, delay, or defraud any entity to which the debtor was or became, on or after the date that such transfer was made or such obligation was incurred, indebted; or
>
> (B)
>
> (i) received less than a reasonably equivalent value in exchange for such transfer or obligation; and
>
> (ii)
>
> (I) was insolvent on the date that such transfer was made or such obligation was incurred, or became insolvent as a result of such transfer or obligation;
>
> (II) was engaged in business or a transaction, or was about to engage in business or a transaction, for which any property remaining with the debtor was an unreasonably small capital;
>
> (III) intended to incur, or believed that the debtor would incur, debts that would be beyond the debtor's ability to pay as such debts matured; or
>
> (IV) made such transfer to or for the benefit of an insider, or incurred such obligation to or for the benefit of an insider, under an employment contract and not in the ordinary course of business.[12]

Actual fraud is not very common, but getting rid of assets before a bankruptcy – either deliberately or unintentionally – is quite common. A debtor might not realize that giving a friend a set of vintage baseball cards a year before bankruptcy might create a problem in the bankruptcy itself, or that giving a fiancée an heirloom engagement ring might not be a good move.

During this part of the course, I ask one student to play a debtor who is meeting with her lawyer, played by another student. I ask the lawyer-student to interview the debtor-student to get a feel for whether the debtor-student made any questionable transfers before filing for bankruptcy protection. Almost always, the lawyer-student uses legal terminology to ask the debtor-student whether she has transferred any property 'with intent to defraud' or 'for less than reasonably equivalent value'. What the lawyer-student fails to do is put her questions in a

12 11 U.S.C. § 548; see also § 544(b) (incorporating state law causes of action, which would include state fraudulent transfer laws).

vernacular that a non-law-trained person might actually understand – and a scared, stressed-out non-law-trained person, to boot. It usually takes a while before the lawyer-student starts to ask questions like: 'Did you give anyone any birthday gifts this year? Did you get engaged?'

Law students could benefit from a dose of understanding that different people experience the world differently. For those students who have not yet read Ralph Ellison's *Invisible Man*, this book provides an excellent starting point for a discussion of how people might feel disenfranchised:

> I am an invisible man. No, I am not a spook like those who haunted Edgar Allan Poe; nor am I one of your Hollywood-movie ectoplasms. I am a man of substance, of flesh and bone, fiber and liquids – and I might even be said to possess a mind. I am invisible, understand, simply because people refuse to see me. Like the bodiless heads you see sometimes in circus sideshows, it is as though I have been surrounded by mirrors of hard, distorting glass. When they approach me they see only my surroundings, themselves, or figments of their imagination – indeed, everything and anything except me. (Ellison 1995: 3)

Among the lessons of *Invisible Man* is the lesson that a person's point of view stems from a variety of life experiences. This lesson works as well in a bankruptcy course as it does in any client counselling course. Students need to get out of their law-trained heads once in a while.

One way to get students out of their law-trained heads is by using pop culture, and there are a variety of films and TV shows that can help convey the realities of bankruptcy to students. One of the best is the film *A Civil Action* (Buena Vista Pictures, 1998), based on a real story. Not only does the protagonist actually file for bankruptcy protection – and the film shows a hearing that is not too far away from the reality of a section 341 meeting of creditors[13] – but the film also shows what it is like to have one's goods repossessed and the power turned off. Slightly less glum versions of pop culture also show the creditor–debtor dynamic. *Confessions of a Shopaholic* (Touchstone Home Video, 2009) covers how easy it is for a smart person to find herself in massive debt, as well as demonstrating why collection harassment is an unfair debt collection practice. The cartoon series *The Simpsons* (20th Century Fox Home Entertainment, 2009), in a Season 20 episode called *No Loan Again, Naturally*, demonstrates the link between adjustable-rate mortgages and home foreclosures. The film *Despicable Me* (Universal Studios, 2010) has a wonderful visual of the 'Bank of Evil' with the slogan 'Formerly Lehman Brothers' and a series of visuals of crushing debt. It also demonstrates how banks determine the worth of collateral. And the classic visual of bankruptcy law and debt problems is the US version of *The Office* (NBC/Universal Home Entertainment, 2005), Season 4, in the episode called *Money*. In this episode, Michael Scott walks into

13 11 U.S.C. § 341 provides creditors with the opportunity to ask questions of the debtor near the beginning of the bankruptcy case.

the main office area and screams: 'I declare … bankruptcy!' In the next scene,[14] Oscar, one of his employees, knocks on his office door and explains:

> OSCAR: Hey, I just wanted you to know that you can't just say the word 'bankruptcy' and expect anything to happen.
>
> MICHAEL: I didn't say it. I *declared* it.
>
> OSCAR: Still, that's … that's not anything.

The scene in which Oscar shows Michael a spreadsheet of the components of his debt is a good illustration of debt counselling:

> OSCAR: OK, the green bar is what you spend every month on stuff you need, like a car and a house.
>
> MICHAEL (pointing to the spreadsheet on the computer screen): That's so cool, how you have my name at the top.
>
> OSCAR: The red bar is what you spend on non-essentials, like magazines, entertainment, things like that. This scary black bar is what you spend on things that no one ever, ever needs, like multiple magic sets, professional bass-fishing equipment.
>
> MICHAEL (pointing to the screen again): How do you do this so fast? Is this PowerPoint?[15]

The episode is light-hearted, but it illustrates the problem of out-of-control debt quite nicely.

Trial or Appellate Advocacy: Legal Writing Course

Many law students cannot write well. They are not stupid, but somewhere between first grade and law school, too many of them missed the rules of grammar and precious few of them have developed an ear for good writing. Even for those law students who can write well, there is a disconnect between most of the legal writing that they have to read in school – mostly cases and statutes, with some articles thrown in – and the type of writing that creates a compelling narrative. Their first attempts are wooden, possibly because they mistakenly believe that legal writing has to sound the way that legal opinions do.

14 I transcribed this scene.

15 I transcribed this one too.

Aside from requiring law students to read some literature each semester, it is difficult to help them make the transition from stilted descriptive writing to the type of writing that guides the reader towards an intended conclusion. In their daily reading assignments, students receive countless examples of passive voice, impenetrable prose (like the prose in *Sherwood v. Walker*) and flawed reasoning. What they need is a dose of 'Call me Ishmael' (Melville 2003).

Well, maybe not 'Call me Ishmael'. But they need to read some powerful narrative in order to avoid a *Dragnet*-ish 'just the facts' narrative. A professor would not have to bring in classic literature to demonstrate the power of good descriptions – Harry Potter would do just fine. So would this excerpt from Dorothy Parker's *Such a Pretty Little Picture*:

> Mr. Wheelock was clipping the hedge. He did not dislike doing it. If it had not been for the faintly sickish odor of the privet bloom, he would definitely have enjoyed it. The new shears were so sharp and bright, there was such a gratifying sense of something done as the young green stems snapped off and the expanse of tidy, square hedge-top lengthened. (Adams et al. 2010: 67–8)

There is a world of difference between 'Defendant was clipping a hedge' and Dorothy Parker's description of the sounds and smells involved in clipping a hedge. Unless we show students excerpts like this one, we should not expect them to know the difference.

For the give-and-take of good examinations and cross-examinations, though, nothing beats the films. There are two classic films that I use, although several others could fit the bill as well.[16] *A Few Good Men* (Columbia TriStar, 1992) contains a masterful, if briefly unethical,[17] examination that ends with the iconic line: 'You can't handle the truth!' Lieutenant Kaffee sets the logical trap for Colonel Jessep by first asking him to confirm that Marines obey orders. After Jessep explains that Marines always follows orders, then – and only then – does Kaffee ask why, if Marines always follow orders, and if Jessep had ordered that Santiago was never to be harmed by other Marines, there was ever a need to transfer Santiago off the base. This cross-examination, with the questions in this order, completely boxes Jessep in.

This scene is rich with teaching opportunities: the importance of planning an examination so that the witness does not see what is coming; the ability to 'read'

---

16 That list includes *Adam's Rib* (MGM, 1949), *A Fish Called Wanda* (MGM Home Entertainment, 2001), *All of Me* (Lions Gate Films, 2003), *Bananas* (United Artists, 1971), *Chicago* (Miramax, 2002), *The Client* (Warner Bros, 1994), *Flash of Genius* (Universal Studios Home Entertainment, 2009), *Inherit the Wind* (MGM/UA Home Entertainment, 1960), *The People v. Larry Flynt* (Columbia Pictures, 1996), *To Kill a Mockingbird* (Universal International Pictures, 1962) and *The Verdict* (20th Century Fox, 1982).

17 During the examination, Lieutenant Kaffee misleads the court about potential testimony.

the witness' body language (such as the long pauses as Jessep recalculates what to say); the importance of rhythm, tone, pace and even volume to the questions; and the ability to exercise restraint. For this last point, the class could discuss why Kaffee did not interrupt Jessep when Jessep was asking questions instead of answering them.

My Cousin Vinny (20th Century Fox, 1992) offers almost too many good trial scenes to count, including this one, which comes after the 'two youts'[18] exchange between Vinny and the judge:

> VINNY: Let me rephrase the question. Is it possible that the two defendants entered the store, picked out twenty-two specific items off the shelves, heated up a burrito, had the clerk pour a slush drink, take money, make change then … <u>leave, then,</u> two DIFFERENT men drive up in a similar looking car, go in, tie up the clerk, rob him, shoot him and leave?
>
> TIPTON (shakes head): No. They didn't have enough time.
>
> VINNY: How much time were they in the store?
>
> TIPTON: Five minutes.
>
> VINNY: Are you sure it was five minutes? Did you look at your watch?
>
> TIPTON: No.
>
> VINNY: In five minutes, you made breakfast?
>
> TIPTON: That's right.
>
> VINNY: Can you remember what you had?
>
> TIPTON: Eggs and grits.

---

18 VINNY: Is it possible the two youts who entered the store were …
JUDGE (interrupting): Two what? What was that word?
VINNY: What word?
JUDGE: Two what?
VINNY: What?
JUDGE: Did you say 'youts'?
VINNY: Yes, two youts.
JUDGE: What is a yout?
VINNY: I'm so sorry, your honor, two you<u>th</u>s. Is it possible the two you<u>th</u>s who entered the store were not the same you<u>th</u>s you saw leaving the store? (Launer 1992: 96, stage directions omitted).

VINNY: How do you make your grits? Regular, creamy or al dente?

TIPTON: Uh … just … regular, I guess.

VINNY: Instant grits?

TIPTON: No self-respecting southerner uses instant grits. I take pride in my grits.

VINNY: So Mr Tipton, how could it take you only five minutes to cook your grits – <u>when it takes the entire grit-eating world TWENTY minutes</u>? . …

TIPTON: I dunno … I'm a fast cook, I guess.

VINNY: A fast cook? That's it? Are we to believe that boiling water soaks into a grit[19] quicker in your kitchen than any other place on the face of the earth?

TIPTON: (humiliated) I dunno.

VINNY: Perhaps the laws of physics cease to exist on your stove?

VINNY: [Were] these 'magic grits'? Did you buy them from the guy who sold Jack his beanstalk beans?

TROTTER: Objection, your honor …

JUDGE: Objection sustained. Mr Tipton, you can ignore the question. Mr. Gambino, you've made your point.

VINNY (to Tipton): You sure about that five minutes?

TIPTON: I … may have been mistaken …

VINNY (turning away): Thank you. I got no more use for this guy. (Launer 1992: 96–8)

Although the draft script for *My Cousin Vinny* is not quite the same as the final dialogue, even the script indicates some teachable moments. For one thing, this scene – like the one in *A Few Good Men* – indicates the importance of listening carefully to the testimony of the witness. For another, it illustrates the risk of using irony in questioning: irony might not always play well with a jury. Finally, it voices

19 The word 'grit' cracks me up, just as it does every other Southerner. 'Grits' are never singular.

what many of us think (but dare not say) when we have finished questioning a witness.

Not all law schools have the luxury of teaching trial advocacy as a practicum, using small groups, individual exercises and one-on-one critiques. Using films to illustrate advocacy techniques is another way to provide virtual hands-on training.

Conclusion

What I have tried to do here, in reacting to the 'Beyond Text' project, is to see how one can find a space in law teaching for the 'Beyond Text' method. Ironically, the present legal job market makes it important to be able to differentiate the training of lawyers to show how they have something extra and valuable to give them an edge in the market. We are at the right time to go 'Beyond Text' even if we didn't plan it. But what are the benefits and risks?

Benefits of Integrating the Arts into Legal Education

The single most difficult transition that a law student must make upon becoming a lawyer involves understanding a lawyer's role as a problem-solver. Law students are trained to describe. They do legal research and report on what the current law says about a subject. Only if they enrol in a clinic do they realize that clients do not simply want to know what the law is – they want to know what to do.[20] Clinic students learn how to diagnose the problem(s) that a client's case might present, how to relate those problems to the current law and how other, non-law issues will factor into their decisions.

Law students who only know how to find and describe the law are, at best, half-trained. They need to be able to step out of their own perspective and into a client's perspective, and they need to be able to draw on all sorts of ways of approaching a problem. The lawyer who can out-think the other side's lawyers by using 'law-plus' (law plus other perspectives) is at much less risk of being outsourced. More important, the fully trained lawyer has a broader variety of career options. Lawyers who merely think like lawyers are a dime a dozen these days. Lawyers who think like doctors or teachers or (yes) artists can use their legal skills to represent their clients or can become entrepreneurs (and someone else's client). Having the ability to tap into the arts is, like being bilingual, an 'extra' that can distinguish the good lawyer from the journeyman lawyer. This approach gives back other parts of the human experience so that students can see more than one way to interpret something – more than one way to approach a problem.

20 The more value a lawyer can provide to his or her client, the more likely it is that the lawyer will retain the client over time. A lawyer who only finds cases is not nearly as valuable as a lawyer who can reconceptualize an issue in a unique and productive way.

It is a way of giving students the sense that they can have their whole life back. They will be better lawyers and probably better people.

Risks

A course's syllabus will invariably expand to fill the hours allotted to the course and, once the syllabus has been around for a few years, deciding what to cut is difficult. Therefore, convincing a professor that he or she should reduce some course coverage in order to add in some non-law perspectives will be a hard sell. Although the arts are for everybody, teaching the arts in a law school course is not. Schools that are rightly concerned with their graduates' ability to pass the bar exam are not going to be comfortable with adding 'fluff' at the expense of substantive law coverage. (Schools with a high bar passage rate may have less concern about adding in the arts.) Moreover, adding in some literature or some visual arts only works when a professor has some familiarity with examples that might tie into the course. Some professors are not good with technology, so showing film clips or playing songs might not be easy for them. A school might not have the technology for audio-visual work of this kind. Then there is the matter of taste and judgement. I could teach Yeats' *Leda and the Swan* (1924) as an example of powerful language, but I am likely to find myself the subject of student protests because the poem involves sexuality. Once students are shocked or offended, they will stop listening – and then the whole point of using the arts to make a point has been lost.

Worse, the payoff for introducing the arts into a course can come years after the course itself. Maybe a student will not understand the purpose of reading good non-law writing during law school. Maybe he or she will not understand it for several years afterwards, especially if he or she is doing the type of repetitive work that beginning lawyers seem to attract. If we are lucky, though, at some point in his or her career, he or she will be casting about for a way to describe something or a new way to approach a problem, and he or she will remember that there are ways of thinking about issues that have nothing to do with judicial precedent or statutory construction. That is where the arts and 'Beyond Text' come in.

References

Adams, F.P., Benchley, R., Parker, D., Ferber, E., Hale, R., Broun, H., Stewart, D.O. and Bonds, L. 2010. *Bon Bons, Bourbon and Bon Mots: Stories from the Algonquin Round Table.* El Paso, TX: Travelling Press.

Adamson, B., Brodoff, L., Berger, M., Enquist, A. Lustbader, P. and Mitchell, J.B. 2008. 'Can the professor come out and play? – Scholarship, teaching, and theories of play'. *Journal of Legal Education*, 58, 481.

Burk, B.A. and McGowan, D. 2011. 'Big but brittle: economic perspectives on the future of the law firm in the new economy'. *Columbia Business Law Review*, 1, 1–117.

Day, K.N. and Murphy, R.G. 2009. '"Just trying to be human in this place": storytelling and film in the first-year law school classroom'. *Stetson Law Review*, 39, 247.

Ellison, R. 1995. *Invisible Man*. New York: Random House, Inc.

Higdon, M.J. 2007. 'From Simon Cowell to Tim Gunn: what reality television can teach us about how to critique our students' work effectively'. *Perspectives*, 15, 169.

Keller, B. 2011. 'I Yield My Time to the Gentleman From Stratford-Upon-Avon', *New York Times Magazine*: http://www.nytimes.com/2011/08/14/magazine/giving-washington-a-lesson-in-meter-and-verse.html?_r=1&ref=magazine [accessed 22 July 2012].

Launer, D. 1992. *My Cousin Vinny*. New York: Twentieth Century Fox.

Levit, N. 2009. 'Legal storytelling: the theory and the practice – reflective writing across the curriculum'. *Journal of the Legal Writing Institute*, 15, 259.

Maute, J.L. 1995. '*Peevyhouse v. Garland Coal & Mining Co.* revisited: the ballad of Willie and Lucille'. *North-Western University Law Review*, 89, 1341.

Melville, H. 2003. *Moby-Dick, or, The Whale*, edited by Thomas Crawford. New York: Dover Publications Inc.

Schulze Jr., L.N. 2006. 'Homer Simpson meets the rule against perpetuities: the controversial use of pop culture in legal writing pedagogy'. *Perspectives*, 15, 1.

Stevens, W. 1917. *Thirteen Ways of Looking at a Blackbird*: http://writing.upenn.edu/~afilreis/88/stevens-13ways.html [accessed 22 July 2012].

Tyler, A. 2001. *Back When We Were Grownups: A Novel*. New York: A.A. Knopf.

Films and Television Shows

15 Minutes (New Line Home Video, 2001).
Adam's Rib (MGM, 1949).
All of Me (Lions Gate Films, 2003).
Anatomy of a Murder (Columbia Pictures, 1959).
... And Justice For All (Columbia Pictures, 1979).
Bananas (United Artists, 1971).
Caddyshack II (Warner Bros, 1988).
Cars (Walt Disney Pictures, 2006).
Chicago (Miramax, 2002).
A Civil Action (Buena Vista Pictures, 1998).
The Client (Warner Bros, 1994).
Clueless (Paramount Home Video, 1999).
Confessions of a Shopaholic (Touchstone Home Video, 2009).
Despicable Me (Universal Studios, 2010).

The Devil's Advocate (Warner Bros, 1997).
Defending Your Life (Warner Home Video, 1991).
Down Periscope (20th Century Fox, 1996).
Double Jeopardy (Paramount, 1999).
Erin Brockovich (Columbia TriStar, 2000).
A Few Good Men (Columbia TriStar, 1992).
A Fish Called Wanda (MGM Home Entertainment, 1988).
The Firm (Paramount, 1993).
Flash of Genius (Universal Studios Home Entertainment, 2009).
Henry V (Samuel Goldwyn Co, 1989).
The Informant! (Warner Home Video, 2010).
Inherit the Wind (MGM/UA Home Entertainment, 1960).
Legal Eagles (Universal Pictures, 1986).
Legally Blonde (MGM, 2001).
Liar Liar (Universal Pictures, 1997).
The Ballad of Willie & Lucille: Disappointed Expectations of Contract Law and the Legal System (University of Oklahoma College of Law: Zone IV Productions, 2008).
The Life and Times of Judge Roy Bean (1972; Warner Home Video, 2000).
The Man Who Shot Liberty Valance (Paramount, 1962).
Masterpiece Theatre: Bleak House (BBC Video, 2005).
Matlock: The First Season (Paramount, 2008).
Michael Clayton (Warner Home Video, 2008).
Murder in the First (Warner Bros, 1995).
My Cousin Vinny (20th Century Fox, 1992).
The Office, Season 4 (NBC/Universal Home Entertainment, 2005).
The People v. Larry Flynt (Columbia Pictures, 1996).
The Simpsons, Season 20, Episode 12 (20th Century Fox Home Entertainment, 2009).
To Kill a Mockingbird (Universal International Pictures, 1962).
The Verdict (20th Century Fox, 1982).

Links

Austin Lounge Lizards, 'Rock and Roll Lawyer, Lizard Vision', available at http://www.artistdirect.com/nad/window/media/page/0,,46116-2533534,00.html [accessed 19 September 2012].
The Ballad of Willie & Lucille: http://www.worldcat.org/title/ballad-of-willie-lucille-disappointed-expectations-of-contract-law-and-the-legal-system/oclc/213816030 [accessed 22 July 2012].
Bankruptcy Code definition of fraudulent transfer: http://www.law.cornell.edu/uscode/11/usc_sec_11_00000548----000-.html [accessed 22 July 2012].

Dragnet: http://en.wikipedia.org/wiki/Dragnet_%28series%29#.22Just_the_facts.2C_ma.27am.22 [accessed 22 July 2012].

Escher, M.C. *Relativity*: http://en.wikipedia.org/wiki/Relativity_%28M._C._Escher%29 [accessed 22 July 2012].

Harvard Institutes for Higher Education: http://www.gse.harvard.edu/ppe/programs/higher-education/index.html [accessed 22 July 2012].

Yeats, W.B. 'The Second Coming': http://www.potw.org/archive/potw351.html [accessed 22 July 2012].

Yeats, W.B. 'Leda and the Swan': http://www.online-literature.com/yeats/865/ [accessed 22 July 2012].

Zevon, Warren, *Lawyers, Guns and Money, A Quiet Normal Life: The Best of Warren Zevon*: http://www.last.fm/music/Warren+Zevon/A+Quiet+Normal+Life%3A+The+Best+of+Warren+Zevon [accessed 22 July 2012].

Chapter 7
Mapping the Lawscape: Spatial Law and the Body

Andreas Philippopoulos-Mihalopoulos[1]

Turning Outwards

What can one do when the air is thick with crisis, when signals of decay are rehearsed constantly in rhetorical and other forms, when we are made to feel grateful for still being here, alive, employed, thinking? What is the teacher's response to the crisis? What is more, what is the student's performance of crisis? How is crisis to be internalized in the curriculum, ingested in the classroom and felt by the thinking process that takes place in the space between student and teacher? The obvious way is to analyse it and look for causal links, harm done and liabilities attributed. The less obvious way, at least in the context of the curriculum, is to take to the streets. Hit the road, spread bodies on the bitumen, hang brains from observatories, smell and hear and feel the crisis. Equally: bring the streets in, open the walls for the smell of exhaust to come in, make room for the frantic movement of an outside-in-crisis to come and dance in the centre of the classroom. Become Naples: enable 'the inexhaustible law of the life of this city, reappearing everywhere' (Benjamin 1985: 171) to flood through the windows of the classroom and reverberate with its urban spleen. Take your class out and bring the out in. Confound. And map.

When faced with crisis, our one act of resistance as teachers is to become better teachers. Facetious as it may sound, crisis enables and urges a return to the basics. This does not simply mean imparting the kind of knowledge that will enable students to fend better for themselves, but significantly engaging different avenues for dealing with reality, providing them with an understanding of embodied, spatialized ethics that deal with reality in an unmediated way. There is something apocalyptic in crisis – both 'revealing' and awe-inspiring. Crisis unveils the urgency of different realities while dragging one violently aground, to the elements of earth and its connection to the body – is it a coincidence that

1 I am grateful to my Law of the Environment class 2010–2011 for taking the walk, for being so enthusiastic about it and for allowing me to share their findings here. Above all, I am grateful to them for remaining such an inexhaustible source of inspiration.

we are told to grow our own vegetables?[2] Crisis forces one to rely on one's body and find ways in which these bodies address reality – and this includes constructing an alternative reality. Law has a particularly pivotal role in this: law *is* crisis, *krinein*, deciding, judging, cutting. As Douzinas and Gearey (2005: 38) write, law as *krinein* 'is a diacritical or cutting force, a critical separation and demarcation.' Law (and its crisis) is both instrumental in thinking about crisis, as well as resisting it and denuding it from its rhetoric. Perhaps not the law as *laws*, namely as existing banking regulations or redundancy agreements, but the law as the emplaced, corporeal normativity that might, under adequate conditions, give rise to justice, in its turn an emplaced, material, *spatial* justice (Philippopoulos-Mihalopoulos 2010).

No doubt, it is in the interests of every era to describe itself as in crisis, and our era is far from original in this. To mention two rather famous examples, Hegel (1979: 6) has talked about 'the gradual crumbling' before the 'indeterminate apprehension of something unknown' and the 'frivolity and boredom that open up in the establishment' – all harbingers of forthcoming change. Husserl's *The Crisis of European Sciences* (1970), on the other hand, offered an escape route from crisis in the form of a return to the European spiritual birthplace of the ancient Greek nation (safe in the knowledge that their crisis was less dependent on international monetary measures than the present one). Crisis is the plane on which critique can operate most successfully, erecting new edifices on the ruins of the previous ones. To some extent, critique augurs crisis (Koselleck 1998), builds itself on it, indeed, constructs the crisis. Our present crisis is another spasm in an uninterrupted chain of critical convulsions. In that sense, every era needs its critique, as it would also seem that it needs its crisis. As such, crisis is both exceptional and unexceptional.

Nevertheless, this is not a text on crisis. I will leave crisis as an introductory remark, a gesture of context as it were, which, however, intends to underline the text that follows. Indeed, the performance of crisis is the reason why what follows is not just relevant but urgent. In some obvious ways, what follows is a gesture of critique and of critical resistance to the supposed urgency of crisis. This critique, however, intends to present us with the real urgency: not that of crisis, but that of a material critique to the law. In the remaining text, I focus on a recent whirling of the law, that of *spatial turn*. The materiality that this turn entails (both spatial and corporeal) is echoed in the need to introduce concepts and practices of embodied, spatial and generally material ethics into the curriculum. I would like to contextualize my position as a contribution towards this move, indeed a move of resistance to the rhetoric of crisis that demands quick results and as close to fully-fledged practitioners as possible, and instead the urgency of another, altogether

2 'Offices urged to set up a vegetable patch in drive to boost grow your own', *Daily Telegraph*, 19 February 2009: http://www.telegraph.co.uk/earth/earthnews/4690207/Offices-urged-to-set-up-a-vegetable-patch-in-drive-to-boost-grow-your-own.html [accessed 22 July 2012].

more important realization: namely, and especially amidst all this crisis talk, the need to create a space in which to think, to traverse disciplines, to feel the law through one's body and to amble without an objective except for the immanent aim of a walk amidst the law.

After a brief analysis of what the spatial turn entails, I share some practices of spatial understanding of the law inspired by the wholehearted embracing by my class of mapping the city by walking and observing their movement. This experience is contextualized in a broadly Deleuzian/Guattarian methodology, namely a theoretical approach that confounds limits and generates alternative lines on which bodies move. Finally, this allows me to present the case for what I have called the *lawscape*, namely a connection of reciprocal invisibility between law and the urban space, and to enable my students to remap it by throwing themselves into the middle of its folds.

I will start with a few words on the context of the course, part of which is the exercise that follows. The course is called Law of the Environment, deliberately distinguishing itself from a generic Environmental Law course and examining the connection between the human, the natural and the legal through an often performative, generally theoretical and always solidly interdisciplinary way. The class discusses in equal measure concepts like sustainable development, the precautionary principle or atmospheric pollution (all more or less typical environmental legal issues); deconstruction, radical ethics, ecofeminism, phenomenology and autopoiesis; and ideas borrowed from legal theory, philosophy of science, geography, literature, music theory, art theory, economics and biology. In the process, such standard distinctions as that between natural and human/artificial/technological are questioned, alongside the ability of the law to deal with such collapsed distinctions. Initially the students are uncertain about how to go about the class, but they quickly take to it in earnest, fully immersing themselves in a performativity that involves their body, the space of the classroom and, in some ways, the world at large, and start pushing their limits and those of the class as a whole. They are fundamentally encouraged to pursue their own interest in composing a reflective log midway through the class and a final project that emphatically does not have to be textual on a topic of their own choosing in consultation with me. There is no lecture as such, but we are all required to read a text, find information or complete a small project in advance of every week's meeting. The discussion is student-led but teacher-channelled, taking risks every single week by flirting with unpredictability originating in boredom, tiredness, lack of preparation or simply the wrong mood. Still, the course offers continuous stimulation with a full electronic environment that complements the class (discussion boards, Google Docs, Camtasia and so on) and the structure is modular in that after the first basic classes, the students organically determine the topics to come. The hope (largely granted) is to ensure that students attend the class and come prepared, with a good measure of energy and intellectual appetite.

Spatially Turning

Law's discovering its spatiality is perhaps the single most important theoretical development in law since the linguistic turn in its fully deconstructive form. The spatial turn relies on the linguistic turn in that both movements forced the law away from its closure and into transdisciplinary self-critique. However, the spatial turn treats the law a little more roughly than the linguistic turn. It grounds the law on the material, the spatial, the *here*, and demands a certain distance from the more traditional abstract, historical and *future* understandings of the law. Ever since Nicholas Blomley's (1994) powerful invitation to put law and space together on a solid philosophical and socio-legal footing, several attempts to respond to the challenge have emerged. Yet, and rather unexpectedly, resistance to spatiality did not come from the traditional positivist front (largely because to that front, spatiality remains invisible), but from the majority of the subsequent literature working on the conjunction. Surprisingly, space and law have quickly fallen into a few rather too comfortable patterns, all of which end up banalizing and rendering innocuous the confluence of law and space. I will schematically list three types of confluence in full consciousness of the unjust violence of such a categorization (drawing on Philippopoulos-Mihalopoulos 2011a).

The first and most obvious way, because of its relatively unproblematic acceptance, is spatial law as jurisdiction (Blacksell, Watkins and Economides 1986). By following existing legal principles of applicability, space remains fixed, 'static' and simply following its traditionally more alluring antipodes of time (however, see Ford's definition of jurisdiction as 'simultaneously a material technology, a built environment and a discursive intervention' (2001: 201)). A surprising amount of literature is still characterized by what I have called 'the parochial turn', namely the turning towards a convenient empirical canvas that confirms theoretical hypotheses, barricading itself behind the specific of a geographical emplacement. In so doing, it fails to deal with two issues: the progressive erosion of the concept of jurisdiction in view of globalization; and the absence of a theorization that would adequately address the complexity of the confluence between law and space.

The second approach constructs space as a fluid, dynamic process. Space is idealized as an ever-changing hotpot of difference, thus succumbing to what Henri Lefebvre (1991) had called the fetishization of space. The law clings onto this new 'ideal' space and delivers itself from its normative obsession by allowing the spatial influx to operate as law's new clothes. While this is arguably preferable to the aforementioned parochial turn, it can work against the potential of spatial turn for the law. Counterintuitively, the greatest problem with the approach is its spatial idealization. Idealization renders space a panacea to social problems, in the process marginalizing the disorder, fragmentation and unpredictability that come with it in favour of a limpid and linear geometrical construction. As a result, the potentially radical nature of space becomes institutionalized, co-opted as part of the institutional discourse, streamlined to serve the purpose of the system.

Finally, the third category of space and law literature can perhaps be a little harshly summarized as 'add space and stir' (Ellem and Shields 1999). Space becomes simply 'another' social factor, 'another' perspective that does not offer anything more than at best a context and at worst a background. This is probably what Lefebvre wanted to avoid when he wrote that 'space is not a thing among other things, nor a product among other products: rather, it subsumes things produced and encompasses their interrelationships in their coexistence and simultaneity – their (relative) order and/or (relative) disorder' (1991: 73). If the spatial turn exhausts itself in considerations of background, thus failing to function as the ground on which such 'coexistence and simultaneity' can be demonstrated, then the spatial turn denotes business as usual for the law.

The radical potential of space for law is both alluring and dangerous. Once turned, the law cannot regard space as simply yet another parameter in the sense of a jurisdictional, property or planning background. The law is expected to deal with a decisive influx of materiality. Materiality, and more specifically spatial materiality, affects first and foremost the disciplinary closure of the law; second, it affects the process of legal production in general, by bringing bodies (and with them movement, unpredictability and fragility) closer to the law; and, third, it affects the way in which law is understood, no longer as an abstract force but concretely, as a ruler that determines distance and propinquity, spaces between and limits of places, human/animal/technological connections and interactions. Spatial materiality reveals law's frequently insidious ways of controlling bodily movement or pause, often making one feel lost and directionless. But, equally often, law dons the bodies that move into space with a certitude of destination, a safety of limits. Spatiality in law does not upset these functions. It merely makes them more visible and thus more open to critique. In some respects, law responds to the crisis of space, as manifested in geopolitics, environmental scarcity, transboundary pollution and forced population movements: all issues that bring space to the fore while challenging the efficiency of existing legal structures.

In order to demonstrate what I mean by an actual 'spatial' turn in law, I would like to use Doreen Massey's definition of space. In her seminal book *For Space* (2005: 10ff.), Massey describes space as a product of interrelations and embedded practices, a sphere of multiple possibilities, a ground of chance and undecidability, and, as such, always becoming, always open to the future. I would add though that this apparent openness is firmly conditioned, and not just by politics as Massey argues. Thus, multiple possibilities indicate a lack of direction and possibly destination; continuous becoming also means instability and unpredictability; interrelations denote a difficulty in pinpointing causality, origin and actors. The significance of such a conceptualization of space for the law is multiple and indeed threatening. Although law is indeed continuously *becoming* (and I mean here becoming other than itself, becoming politics or economy or technology), the rather mainstream understanding of the law is one of *being*, that is, an ontology that determines more that it is being determined. The law changes, but its change is tempered by the need to maintain the order – the emphasis here falls on 'maintain'. In its judging, the law marginalizes uncertainty; indeed, it slashes uncertainty by squeezing it out of the judgment. Law relies on a solid self-image that nothing 'liquid' can permeate: if the wordplay is permitted, the Roman Law privilege of *non-liquet*, namely the distance from judging a case because of the court's unsuitability, is not a prerogative of contemporary law. Law expects of itself (and is expected by society) to be constantly *there* even before it is called upon, to arrest the future with the solidity of knowledge of what is going to happen if one acts in a particular way. Law's function is one of fixing social expectations that law will not change from one day to the other and without (legal) justification (Luhmann 2004). But this is also the trap that the law has set up for itself. To be in some sort of denial in terms of its inherent uncertainty is a masquerade that the law often feels obliged to put on. Spatial uncertainty, the lack of direction or destination and the resistance to given measurements and spatial divisions, is precisely the kind of thing the law fears. Having to deal with multiplicities means that causality is increasingly harder to establish and (transparently) arbitrary decisions become more frequent. Finally, not having a stable (albeit constructed) temporal origin, a *Grundnorm* moment from where the law originates, that is, not having an *origin*, is a trauma for the law, for whence else does the law justify its forceful validity?

In the following section, I would like to take a closer look at how to bring spatiality in class. In order to do this, I draw from the experiences I have had with my environmental law class. The reasons I decided to 'experiment' in this way with my class should be obvious by now, and I would summarize them as follows: bringing forth the materiality of the law; making one aware of spatial legal controls; and dealing with legal and spatial uncertainty. These are of course interrelated, but separating them into the above three fields contributes to a more manageable epistemological approach. Above all, I wanted to allow for a space in which my students would feel their body moving along, between and even against lines of law, thus constructing for themselves a new awareness of identity.

Taking a Walk

I prepare my students by asking them to read some literature on law and space, as well as parts from Deleuze and Guattari's *A Thousand Plateaus* (1988). Admittedly, the latter is a demanding text, but by that point in the course (halfway through the second semester), the students are familiar with at least the struggle to master different terminologies. We have a discussion on the texts and analyse some of the issues in relation to environmental law. Once this is in place, I present them with the following text:

> walking observing thinking acting breaking flowing going against listening taking notes mapping smelling touching do not touch forgetting remembering overhearing fantasising running escaping getting lost feeling lost fearing

deviating diverting avoiding throwing yourself in manipulating never stopping moving being moved

Walking the City

Take a long walk, about 45 minutes or so, preferably alone. Try to map where you are going but without worrying too much about accuracy. Do not only take the main streets or the streets you already know. Take side streets, get tangled in places you do not know, feel a little lost (but always keep safe, use your instinct and reason to keep out of trouble, and carry with you a map so you do not *actually* get lost).

While walking:

Keep in mind three things: **yourself**, **your movement**, **your surroundings**. Try to analyse the connection between all three:

1. Does your body move differently in different situations?

2. Do you think of different things depending on where you are?

3. Do you feel constrained in your movement by anything internal (you) or external (the city)?

Think also of the way you use your **senses** while walking:

1. Do you smell?

2. Do you touch?

3. Do you ever look upwards?

4. Do you notice what other people say to each other or on their phones?

5. Can you eat/smoke/chew gum and walk? Does it bother you?

The Assemblage

Now you have an assemblage of your body/the city around you/the law around you. See whether all of it moves as one, whether you map the city you are creating, and/or whether the city determines your movement.

See how this assemblage deals with:

1. **The law**: where is the law in the city? Do you see it determining where you can walk and where not? How you walk? When you walk and when you stop? What distance you keep from things/people? What senses you can use?

2. **Hybrids**: can you see any hybrids anywhere? Human/animal/technological hybrids? Are you a hybrid? Do you use your sense in an 'animal' way – e.g., does smell stop you from doing things?

3. **Space**: what is space? What is urban space? Can you differentiate space from body – the city space you are walking and creating from your body? Is your body part of the space? Is law spatial?

I ask the students to take this text with them while taking the walk and also to map their movement on a map to the extent that it is possible and does not interfere with a spontaneous flow of movement. During the week, they upload their maps and whatever else their walk has generated (photos, audio, logs) and we discuss them in class.

The thinking behind the exercise is to make one aware of the connections between law and space through the medium of the body. This brings forth the materiality of the law both in its spatiality and its corporeality. Senses are promoted and their awareness enhanced in an attempt to enable the bodies to connect more broadly with the space and also to feel whether the law inhibits or encourages certain senses. The ultimate aim of the exercise is to show that law is spatial, corporeal and more broadly material, and that this spatiality makes the law at the same time hyperpresent and absent. One could say hypervisible and invisible, except that part of the process is to discourage the usual prioritization of the visual and allow other senses (mostly hearing and smell, and to a lesser extent touch and taste) to claim awareness of the law. The connection between the body that moves, the space in which the body moves and the way that the law determines the body's movement is what in the class we have identified as an *assemblage*, following Deleuze and Guattari's understanding of the term, namely a multiplicity that contains other multiplicities, 'human, social, and technical machines, organized molar machines; molecular machines with their particles of becoming-inhuman' (1988: 36). The idea behind the use of the term is to make sure that there are no given boundaries between the various elements (human body, technological extensions, animal qualities, the body of law with its commands, space with its particular multiple organization), but that they all form part of a moving, amoeba-like cluster. As Yolanta, a Spanish student, realizes, her moving body is part of the assemblage with the city: 'and this is the way others can see you, you are just another element in the street they are walking, in the form of yet another obstacle in their way'. An assemblage moves amongst other assemblages (in that sense, every other body, their own mapping of the city that includes other bodies, and their own perception of the law is an assemblage) and forms part of a broader, *open ecology*, namely a combination of the natural, the human, the artificial, the legal, the scientific, the political, the economic and so on, on a plane of contingency and fluid boundaries (for extensive analysis, see Philippopoulos-Mihalopoulos 2011b).

One of the basic things that most students comment on is the existence of physical boundaries that determine movement. This is not merely the distinction between the private and the public. No doubt this is immensely relevant, especially in a place like London which is characterized by a plethora of privately accessed gardens in full public view, constant construction site detours or signs that designate 'private streets' in what seems a perfectly open public area. Physical boundaries do not necessarily consist of fence-like structures. They are to be found in the distinction between buildings and open spaces (one cannot easily cross buildings unless one practises the art of parcours),[3] different functions of pavements and streets, traffic lights and other forms of signalling that channel movement. For example, Clementine, a French student, notices how the city is divided into the congestion charge area and the one without – an environmental legal measure against pollution and traffic that controls movement while relying on economics. However, the understanding of movement and its determining normativity is found to be not only geographically but also culturally determined. Elisabetta, an Italian student, comments on the fact that she cannot walk in the middle of the street as she would in an Italian city. Likewise, Lena and Armand, both Swedish, note that they do not feel obliged to wait for the green light in order to cross the road as they would do in Sweden. Jessica, a Canadian student, observes how Londoners do not have a 'joggers' culture of running to the left side of the pavement while leaving the walkers to the right. One does not notice these things until one notices them. This is not as self-evident as it sounds. It takes a differentiated observational position, a shake-up that removes one from the usual routes (both in terms of actual routes as well as the ruts of habit) for the presence of the all-permeating normativity to be rendered visible. What all students realize very quickly is that the law is everywhere, that is, it determines all the steps one does and does not take, without necessarily making its presence obvious. Rather, law's overabundant presence, especially in a tight urban environment, renders the law invisible until a spasm in the way one moves, a push (even by a teacher who wants his students to go out of the classroom and into space) out of one's normal lines of movement brings fits of legal presence centre stage.

Some students note the way their body moves in different spaces. This can be connected to social class aesthetic considerations or conditions of light/darkness. Both elements are connected to issues of safety. Walking in an affluent area is generally slower and less purposeful-looking than walking in a poorer area. Likewise, one takes one's time when moving in a well-lit area at night (yes, Shabana actually took her walk at 10 pm), whereas the rhythm becomes more hurried when in a dark, not well-lit area. In conditions of perceived safety (and this might have nothing to do with actual safety), the assemblage body/space/law spreads itself more loosely and assumes a movement that enables observation of

3 http://www.youtube.com/watch?v=eaopu5W8Ryg [accessed 22 July 2012].

such things like smells, surfaces, clothes that other people wear and so on. This does not mean that when the movement is faster and more purposeful-looking, one does not take these things into consideration. However, one is not *aware* of noticing them. In conditions of perceived lack of safety, one takes all these into account but for the instrumentality of keeping safe. When safety is not an issue, one's awareness of observation is heightened. When safety is an issue, one becomes-animal, as Deleuze and Guattari would have it: one uses one's senses instinctively and one moves about in a way that is animalistic. One does not of course start barking or miaowing. There is no representation of animal, no mimicry. Still, the process is real: 'Becomings-animal are neither dreams nor phantasies. They are perfectly real. But which reality is at issue here? For if becoming animal does not consist in playing animal or imitating an animal, it is clear that the human being does not really become an animal any more than the animal "really" becomes something else. *Becoming produces nothing other than itself*' (Deleuze and Guattari 1988: 238, emphasis added). In becoming-animal, one becomes the process of transformation itself. Becoming-animal enables simultaneous states of becoming to emerge so that one is both animal and human. When Gabriel is lost in a park, he finds that he uses his hearing more than his vision, listening out for flapping and rustling, 'at times feeling like an animal; like a predator tracking my prey'. This moment is described by some students as hybridity, namely the coexistence of animal and human characteristics in a human body (see also Latour 1993). A hybrid in that sense is an impermanent becoming that keeps on changing its form and its spatial presence. A hybrid is also a human body with a mobile phone, a cyclist, a woman walking her dog, a parking guard 'with a mysterious metallic stick' as Lilli writes, or even the students themselves: Amanee consults her electronic map while walking, whereas Lillli is suddenly aware of her 'false teeth and some artificial liquid in [her] knees'.

The students usually associate a perceived lack of safety with an absence of law, namely an absence of signs that denote law as boundary against their body. Thus, the presence of a policeman has a calming effect on Shabana. Law is seen as an enabling spatial factor of enjoyment. For another student, however, the experience is different. Armand's steps brought him to the area of the US Embassy in London, a heavily policed, barricaded area in an otherwise aesthetically pleasing square. Armand felt threatened by the presence of the law, the latter emerging from the absent presence of guarantee of order and breaking into a spatial disruption that is more forceful than the usual urban disruptions. The armed police appear threatening to Armand, who is immediately conscious of the way his body appears (posture, clothes, unshaven). The law is moving sides – no longer the thing that barricades one's body against another's but the thing that repels one's body not only from a specific space but more importantly from a specific behaviour. The law thematizes the whole square; it overcodes it by making it a space of heightened self-defence and rendering every body a potentially suspicious presence. Armand decides to dissimulate, to become absorbed in the urban fabric by taking out of his pocket the piece of paper with the walk suggestions and pretending that it is a map.

In this way, he hopes to appear as an unsuspected tourist who could not possibly pose any threat to the law. The presence of the law forces the body to see itself as a potentially criminal body and to hide behind a perceived innocent stereotype. The assemblage body/city/law in this case becomes an angular, ill-fitting jigsaw of bodies made of elbows and spaces full of potential falls. The city is no longer mapped by the freely ambling body but is forcefully squeezed into a line that precludes normal movement.

A similar presence of the law is noticed by another student, Eleanor, who is intent on using her mobile phone camera to take photographs of her walk and of the junctures where law and space affect her body. But she finds that she is stopped from doing so by various forms of other bodies, all looming high on their legal pedestal: first, a school administrator stopping her from taking pictures of a sign in a school playground (although technically not illegal, her action was seen as inimical to the particular administrator's embodiment of the law, one that is built upon the fear of children being photographed); and then an officious guard stopping her from photographing a government building (despite the fact that, as she discovered later, the building is visible on Google Images). Her encounter was with another body of the law, former Mayor of London Ken Livingstone, who was canvassing on the streets. He assured her that she had every right to take a picture of that particular building. Eleanor felt much happier in the space created between her and Ken, the city around her seeming to be transformed into something infinitely more accommodating. Needless to say, she has had her photograph taken with Ken.

Jessica had a comparable experience of spatial prohibition when taking the walk, which for her, however, translated to her daily jog. She was surprised by the fact that she was not allowed to run on the grass since cyclists and runners were supposed to use a designated lane. Gabriel has had a similar realization, this time not in the form of other people but in the form of a fence along a canal walk. Gabriel is suddenly confronted with a surprising fact, or rather with the *encounter* with the fact that the law's presence at that particular space is 'utterly pointless'. Deleuze's analysis of an encounter is telling: 'Something in the world forces us to think. This something is an object not of recognition but of a fundamental *encounter* … its primary characteristic is that it can only be sensed … it moves the soul, "perplexes" it – in other words forces it to pose a problem: as though the object of encounter, the sign, were the bearer of a problem – as though it were a problem' (1994: 139–41, emphasis added). Gabriel's realization that there is a fence along the canal walk determining very specific and limited points of entry/exit to the walk is one such encounter that brings about not just confusion and critical positing of a problem but significantly a material shift in the movement of his assemblage with space and law. He becomes aware that the spatial presence of the law inhibits him from *simply walking* aimlessly in the city. He feels constrained to have a purpose, 'to achieve an objective'. Law's spatial presence makes the *flâneurs* of today feel guilty, potentially threatening, undesired. Consider Eleanor's desire to use her camera: this is a perfectly understandable part of contemporary *flâneurie* wanting to make full use of a technological/human hybridity, yet the law stops any hybrid extension of the body from crossing the boundaries erected in the name of security.

Not being able to walk about aimlessly is a spatial triumph of an oppressive legal presence. One gets used to it: all students notice the cameras and the generalized surveillance structure that controls one's movement, but only because they have had a shake-up of the way they normally walk, a 'mission' to walk about with heightened senses. Under normal circumstances, law's presence is hyperpresent, with the effect of becoming absent. Just like breathing or putting one foot in front of the other in order to walk, after a while one stops noticing the law in the city. Only when one decides to walk aimlessly, that is, to take a walk with a teleology detached from destination and immanent to the walk itself, does one realize the law's avuncular presence. And then, most people would recognize the feeling that floods Lena, another student taking the walk and in the event failing to walk without a destination that would inform her stride: Lena was lost. This is not because she got actually lost but because, in her attempt and eventual failure to walk aimlessly, she felt lost, unable to be registered, parasitical. She tried to come out of the cocoon readily offered by cities with the hyperpresent normativity regulating space and movement, but she failed to take the risk (for this is what it is about) of letting the hand of law go. Arguably, another student, David, managed even momentarily to perform this walk without a destination and indulge the different mannerisms demanded of someone when walking on relatively unfamiliar ground: thus, he felt more careful and at the same time 'outsider' to the 'laws of the land' as he called them. He navigated himself through areas he was less familiar with and his observation was that he could notice more, even though he could integrate less.

What this walk essentially asks the students is to become nomads, to move across space, to demolish what Deleuze and Guattari (1988) call the *pillars of striation*, namely the spatial regulation of the law, the boxing up and locking in and separating and purifying, and in their place to establish a *smooth* space, a glistening surface where new lines of flight, new escape routes, new forms of normative creativity can take place. The students tried to 'free the diagonal', as Deleuze and Guattari (1988: 295) urge us. The success rate varies, but in the process, one understands that the law is not abstract and outside one's body, but very much dwelling within and amongst one's molecules. Further, one realizes that one's identity is beginning to be formed differently.

Mapping a Lawscape

The space of the city emerges full of directions, boundaries, need for destination and traceable trajectories. This is what I have elsewhere (2007) called the *lawscape*, namely the horizon of prior invitation by the one (the law/the city) to be conditioned by the other (the city/the law). In the lawscape, the two elements of law and the city coexist in a state of mutual invisibility – the law cannot be present all the time in the city, nor can the city (in the sense of geographical space) be present all the time in the law. The two traditionally take distance from each other and pretend to be otherwise. Thus, a legal city is the place where K arrives in Kafka's *The Castle*. A legal city is full of procedural labyrinths, representational nooks and crannies, loomed over by a towering sovereign in whom all originates and to whom all ends. Now, there is no doubt that most cities *are* legal cities. But they are cleverer than this. They have learned to dissimulate their legality, to make it hyperpresent, thus obliterating the possibility of any other way. *The Castle* becomes *The Truman Show*. Likewise for the law. To acknowledge the influx of spatiality in the law would render the latter powerless, horizontal, unhierarchical. Spatiality entails the right to amble aimlessly, to be able to feel ecstatically lost in wanderlust (Solnit 2000), a Lefebvrian right to the city (1996) whose mission is to dig holes in the urban texture and to make the city what Deleuze and Guattari (1988: 415) call a 'holey space', namely a space like a sponge, consisting more of air than earth that moves between striated and smooth space while communicating with both. A spatial law is a law whose boundaries are lifted for a flow of bodies to move independently of property lines. This does not mean that one has roamers through one's kitchen, but it does mean that what is still called public space is safeguarded against private homogenization and moral panic. A spatial law would preserve public space as an uninterrupted line of flight in the middle of the city, as an opportunity for creative normativity where the law guarantees the conditions for the spontaneous movement of bodies and where one can, even briefly, fancy oneself a nomad, a trailing presence that belongs to the earth and not to the high street shops (Bottomley 2007; Laylard 2010).

Perhaps my ultimate hope with this walking experiment and in general with all my rather eccentric teaching methods is that my students will begin a process of a new understanding of their identity. No longer a simple given structure of I am and I am called, a recognition by oneself and by others, nor a dialectic structure of ego/alter, namely I am ego because I am not alter. Beyond these structures, Deleuze and Guattari have suggested a new form of understanding one's identity, one that they call *hacceity*, namely the understanding that one 'consists entirely of relations of movement and rest between molecules or particles, capacities to affect and be affected' (1988: 262). Hacceity is an understanding of identity as a hybrid collectivity that does not focus on the individual but on the connection of the individual with other bodies in the broader sense of the term. It is the assemblage between one's body, other bodies, the space in which one is moving and the body of law that determines one's movement: 'The street enters into composition with the horse, just as the dying rat enters into composition with the air, and the beast and the full moon enter into composition with each other' (1988: 262). But it is also the space within law that allows the uncertainty and directionless of spatiality to appear. Hacceity includes resistance to prescribed movement and an ability to go beyond the given. As Deleuze and Guattari remind us: 'Taking a walk is a hacceity.' This is indeed the guiding idea behind this chapter and the effort in the class and indeed out of it: to enable law students to create for themselves a hacceity of creative resistance to the given, as well as creative pleasure in the given. Through learning techniques such as walking, one rediscovers and reinscribes one's reality, one repositions one's body in the middle of a newly mapped city, one observes the law in both its controlling and enabling, one becomes aware of the inevitability of materiality and one eventually thinks.

References

Bell, D. and Haddour, A. (eds). 2000. *City Visions.* Harlow: Prentice Hall.
Benjamin, W. 1985. *One-Way Street and Other Writings.* London: Verso.
Blacksell, M., Watkins, C. and Economides, K. 1986. 'Human geography and law: a case of separate developments in social sciences'. *Progress in Human Geography*, 10(3), 371–96.
Blomley, N. 1994. *Law, Space and the Geographies of Power*. New York: Guilford Press.
Blomley, N., Delaney, D. and Ford, R. (eds). 2001. *The Legal Geographies Reader: Law, Power, and Space.* Malden, MA: Blackwell.
Bottomley, A. 2007. 'From walls to membranes: fortress polis and the governance of urban space in 21st century Britain'. *Law and Critique*, 18(2), 171–206.
De Certeau, M. 1984. *The Practice of Everyday Life.* Translated by S. Rendall. Berkeley: University of California Press.
Deleuze, G. 1994. *Difference and Repetition.* New York: Columbia University Press.
Deleuze, G. and Guattari, F. 1988. *A Thousand Plateaus: Capitalism and Schizophrenia.* Translated by B. Massumi. London: Athlone Press.
Douzinas, C. and Gearey, A. 2005. *Critical Jurisprudence: The Political Philosophy of Justice.* Oxford: Hart.
Edensor, T. 2000. 'Moving through the city', in D. Bell and A. Haddour (eds), *City Visions*. Harlow: Prentice Hall, 121–40.
Ellem, B. and Shields, J. 1999 'Rethinking "regional industrial relations": space, place and the social relations of work'. *Journal of Industrial Relations*, 41(4), 536–60.
Ford, R. 2001. 'Law's territory (a history of jurisdiction)', in N. Blomley, D. Delaney and R. Ford (eds), *The Legal Geographies Reader*. Oxford: Blackwell, 200–216.
Hegel, G.W.F. 1979. *Phenomenology of Spirit.* Translated by A.V. Miller. Oxford: Oxford University Press.
Husserl, E. 1970. *The Crisis of European Sciences and Transcendental Phenomenology: An Introduction to Phenomenological Philosophy.* Translated by D. Carr. Evanston: Northwestern University Press.
Koselleck, R. 1998. *Critique and Crises: Enlightenment and the Pathogenesis of Modern Society.* Cambridge, MA: MIT Press.

Latour, B. 1993. *We Have Never Been Modern*. Translated by C. Porter. Harvard: Harvard University Press.
Laylard, A. 2010. 'Shopping in the public realm: a law of place'. *Journal of Law and Society*, 37(3), 412–41.
Lefebvre, H. 1991. *The Production of Space*. Translated by D. Nicholson-Smith. Oxford: Blackwell.
Lefebvre, H. 1996. *Writings on Cities*. Translated and edited by E. Koffman and E. Lebas. Oxford: Blackwell.
Luhmann, N. 2004. *Law as a Social System*. Translated by K. Ziegert, edited by F. Kastner, R. Nobles, D. Schiff and R. Ziegert. Oxford: Oxford University Press.
Massey, D. 2005. *For Space*. London: Sage.
Philippopoulos-Mihalopoulos, A. 2007. 'In the lawscape', in *Law and the City*. London: Routledge, 1–20.
Philippopoulos-Mihalopoulos, A. 2010. 'Spatial justice: law and the geography of withdrawal'. *International Journal of Law in Context*, 6(3), 1–16.
Philippopoulos-Mihalopoulos, A. 2011a. 'Law's spatial turn: geography, justice and a certain fear of space'. *Law, Culture and Humanities*, 7(2), 1–16.
Philippopoulos-Mihalopoulos, A. 2011b '"... *the sound of a breaking string*": critical environmental law and ontological vulnerability'. *Journal of Environmental Law and Human Rights*, 2(1), 5–22.
Solnit, R. 2000. *Wanderlust: A History of Walking*. London: Penguin.

Chapter 8
The Moving Experience of Legal Education

Gary Watt[1]

> The courts are all shut up; the public offices lie in a hot sleep. Westminster Hall itself is a shady solitude where nightingales might sing, and a tenderer class of suitors than is usually found there, walk.
>
> (Charles Dickens, *Bleak House*, Chapter 19)

Legal education has a special problem at its core and the duty of legal educators is to alert learners to the problem and to join them in the task of overcoming it. The special problem of legal education is that the fundamental ideas of law are predominantly stationary or tending to the static, while the essential ideas of education are predominantly moving or tending to motion. The stationary ideas of the law include 'statute', '*stare decisis*' (i.e. case precedent), 'standing' to appear in court, 'statements', 'estate', legal 'status' and 'constitution'. The moving ideas of education include 'pedagogy' and 'motivation', while, of course, 'education' itself means to 'lead out', The law's preference for stability, orthodoxy and repetition has tended to produce teaching practices that favour 'inculcation' (which means, etymologically, to dig ones heels in) in place of true education of the sort that leads students into new territories where they can appreciate new views. To learn when walking, and to learn by walking, has a respectable pedigree. The fact that Aristotle's students acquired the label *peripatetikos* indicates that Aristotle walked as he taught, and, by the same token, that teaching took place in the covered walkway (the *peripatos* – a colonnade, literally a 'surrounding patio') (Thomson 1955: 12), which, somewhat like a medieval cloister, framed the open courtyard garden of the Lyceum. It was here that Aristotle founded his 'university'; the first true university, it has been argued (Thomson 1955: 16). In this chapter I will focus on my undergraduate Law and Literature module to demonstrate how I use movement, within enclosed spaces and in the open air, with a view to moving hearts and motivating minds. The module is concerned with law *as* literature (legal language as constitutive rhetoric, to echo the language of James Boyd White (1984)) and it examines law as literature in part by engaging with law *in* creative literary works and by enabling the students to submit creative writing

1 The author would like to thank Sophie Bennett, a student on his Law and Literature module, who conducted preliminary research for this chapter with funding from the Undergraduate Research Support Scheme at the University of Warwick.

in addition to an end-of-term examination. (Each piece of creative writing engages with an aspect of law or justice, broadly conceived, and takes the form of a poem, a drama or a short work of prose fiction such as a fable or fairy tale. It attracts up to one-fifth of the total grade marks available in the module. I have written elsewhere on the special challenges of assessing the students' creative work: Watt 2009b.)

How many law students begin their educational journey like Alice in Wonderland?:

> Alice opened the door and found that it led into a small passage, not much larger than a rathole – she knelt down and looked along the passage into the loveliest garden you ever saw. How she longed to get out of the dark hall, and wander about among those beds of bright flowers and those cool fountains, but she could not even get her head through the doorway. (Lewis Carroll, *Alice's Adventures in Wonderland*, 1865)

Let us hope that at the end of their degree courses, our students will have discovered, as Alice discovered, that in the end 'very few things indeed were really impossible'. Franz Kafka wrote a haunting fable about the inability of a citizen to gain access through a door to the law (Kafka 1916). For law students and law teachers, the problem is sometimes felt as keenly from the other side. How are we to move out once we are in? From the moment that the law school 'induction day' or 'induction week' channels us into law, our minds are shaped in such a way (if not swelled to such a size) that we find it hard to step outside the texts and terrain of law. In-duction that channels us into law's texts and law's spaces can so easily become the enemy of ex-duction (that is, 'education'), which would conduct us out into new territories and new ways of learning. A healthy society depends as much upon egress from the law as upon access to it. If lawyers do not move within and without the sanctum of the law, and move bodily and not merely mentally, we can hardly expect to achieve a meaningful practical connection between law and wider society. A movement such as this must start by stirring up our static ideas of legal education.

Walking to Law and Literature

> The central problem of an education based on experience is to select the kind of present experiences that live fruitfully and creatively in subsequent experiences. (Dewey 1938: 28)

Walking is an excellent candidate to be the kind of experience that lives fruitfully, creatively and repeatedly. Of course, not everyone has the physical capacity to walk, but everybody engages in some equivalent experience of self-motivation. We cannot all walk, but we all have our own way of going for a walk. Walking is enriching on so many levels. It is first and foremost a challenge to power – so much so that it has long been a favoured vehicle of organized political protest. Consider, for instance, the famous 'March on Washington for Jobs and Freedom' which Dr Martin Luther King led in 1963. In our car-dominated culture even a simple stroll can seem like social sedition. I normally cycle to work, but on those rare occasions when I walk to work through the rural and suburban landscape surrounding the University campus, it is a palpably empowering experience; I sense, as cars pass me by, that I am in part empowered at the direct expense of systems and institutions of power. To walk is to be free. Even in prison, to walk is one of the few freedoms which never, or very rarely, fails outright. In her book *Wanderlust*, Rebecca Solnit observes that '[t]he new millennium arrived as a dialect between secrecy and openness; between consolidation and dispersal of power; between privatization and public ownership, power and life, and walking has as ever been on the side of the latter' (Solnit 2001: xi). If we learn to walk well, that is, with the eyes of our mind wide open, we learn to live well. We become attuned to ourselves because, as Solnit says, walking 'is the intentional act closest to the unwilled rhythms of the body, to breathing and the beating of the heart' and '[w]hile walking, the body and the mind can work together, so that thinking becomes almost a physical, rhythmic act' (Solnit 2001: 5, xv).

The physical act of walking is by its nature inherently educative, and not only because it pumps a steady flow of oxygen to the brain. Walking is a primal and perennial teacher. Even in its mother's womb, the embryo learns from the law of gravity, from the regulation of the mother's heartbeat and from the andante rhythm of the mother's step – the rhythm of the walk moderates the law of gravity and the regulatory heartbeat to perform a sort of equitable music, the first harmonious variations on a code. When the child reaches the age of being able to walk on its own two feet, the educational possibilities expand exponentially – there is potential to explore, to stumble, to trip, to balance, to pace, to pause, to tip-toe, to stretch and to take great strides. Walking brings all the senses into contact with new experiences. There is also, underlying it all, an educational quality intrinsic to walking that is as inherent as gravity, pulse and the sense of footsteps *en ventre sa mere*, for the fact is that normal pedestrian progress requires us to walk by means of balanced oppositions: the left foot advances with the right hand, while the left hand advances with the right foot. This so-called 'cross-lateral motion' is said to exercise not merely the arms and legs, but also the trans-hemispherical capacity of the brain. As Carla Hannaford writes in her book *Smart Moves*:

> Cross lateral movements … work both sides of the body evenly and involve coordinated movements of both eyes, both ears, both hands and both feet as well as balanced core muscles. When both eyes, both ears, both hands and feet are being used equally, the corpus callosum orchestrating these processes between the two hemispheres becomes more fully developed. Because both hemispheres and all four lobes are activated, cognition function is heightened and ease of learning increases. (Hannaford 2005: 92; cf. Blakemore 2003)

For students in a law and literature module, the trans-hemispherical benefits of walking might have a special bearing on the processes of creative writing; for psychologists have observed that 'artistic creativity in general benefits from interhemispheric collaboration' (Bogen and Bogen 1969; see also Jarvis 1999). In his study of *Romantic Writing and Pedestrian Travel*, Robin Jarvis observes that the hypnotic rhythm of walking promotes 'introspection and concentrated creative thought' and that '[t]his enhanced mental excitation is possible because walking has a remarkable ability to purge the mind of its habitual, everyday clutter' (Jarvis 1999: 68). To such general benefits of the walking process one can add the benefits of natural light, which frequently accompany pedestrian activity – most especially when walking outside or on a sunny day. To illuminate the eye with natural light is one good way to illuminate the brain (Dunn et al. 1985; Graetz 2006). Studies have concluded that cool-white artificial light produces a correspondingly frigid atmosphere (Rosenfeld 1977: 169) and that artificial light can be in various ways biologically detrimental (Ott 1964; Seagers 1963; Wurtman 1968). One study that compared the different effects of natural light and cool-white fluorescent light on undergraduate students concluded that natural light was (somewhat paradoxically perhaps) at the same time more stimulating and more relaxing than artificial light (Kleiber et al. 1973). Then there is the spatial aspect of walking. Unless one walks on the spot, walking involves displacement. Thus, walking is highly apt to embody the educational journey from one place to another. To quote from Solnit again:

> the rhythm of walking generates a kind of rhythm of thinking, and the passage through a landscape echoes or stimulates the passage through a series of thoughts. This creates an odd consonance between internal and external passage, one that suggests that the mind is also a landscape of sorts and that walking is one way to traverse it. A new thought often seems like a feature of the landscape that was there all along, as though thinking were traveling rather than making. (Solnit 2001: 5–6; cf. Anderson 2004)

Jarvis has something similar in mind when he refers to the capacity of pedestrian travel to produce a mental set of impressions and memories which may be described as a 'progressional ordering of reality' (Jarvis 1999: 69). There is, in this sense, a legislative quality to a walk which, because it is constantly moving and stirring itself, is quite unlike the nature of a legal statute. Correspondent with this legislative quality of a walk, there is a literary quality. De Certeau, in his *Practice of Everyday Life*, observes that 'the walking of passers-by offers a series of turns (tours) and detours that can be compared to "turns of phrase" or "stylistic figures"' (De Certeau 1984: 100).

My Law and Literature module begins with a walk from the social science building, where the law school is psychically and psychologically located, to another campus, which just happens to be the site of the Department of Education. I accompany my students on a walk away from the law school, which is a way of walking from a certain sense of the institution of law. It is not, however, a move away from law; rather, it is a move to a different type of law – a move to law and literature – and the walk is an embodied metaphor for the journey. I have been able to incorporate a number of useful lessons and learning experiences into the walk from the law school to the teaching space on the other campus or, to put it better, I have been able to discover a number of lessons that were already intrinsic to the exercise and environment of the walk. For one thing, it has enabled us to explore the problematic idea of pedagogy. It has always troubled me that the modern educational ideal continues to be expressed in the language of slavery. The *paedagogus* was the household slave who in Ancient Greece, and later Rome, had responsibility for his master's children and accompanied them to and from school. On the walk from law to law *and* literature, we resist any notion that the students are to be led like children or that the tutor is to be made a beast of burden to carry them (Watt 2006). Our destination on the other campus is the 'Reinvention Centre', which is a studio-style learning space that has been recognized by the Higher Education Funding Council to be a 'Centre for Excellence in Teaching and Learning' (CETL). I must confess that, for all the benefits which the walk bestows, it was the practical contingency of *having* to travel to the Reinvention Centre that prompted me to use a collective walk as an opportunity to elucidate and explore the philosophy, ethics and aims of the Law and Literature module. The contingent, practical reality of life is the best of tutors. There is hardly a more basic fact of life than the fact that one must start *here* if one is to get *there*. If necessity is the mother of invention, then contingency is the father of imagination.

Metaphor: The Walk Home

Students come to the study of a law degree as rounded, creative, expressive beings, and many do so with a love of, and some expertise in, creative literature. However, law degrees do not always (and some do not ever) encourage students to fulfil this aspect of their characters and desires. The walk with which the Law and Literature module begins is therefore, in some sense, a walk back home. Finding one's way back home can be a testing trial. The experience of Alice in Wonderland is testimony to that. It will sometimes involve a walk on the wild side, as Little Red Riding Hood discovered on the way to her grandmother's home in the woods. Appropriately, then, the first substantial stories with which the module engages are the pre-literary stories of the oral tradition: including fairy tales, fables and myths – how many of these were tales about homecoming or tales for homecoming? The main focus of the module, though, is upon the capacity of rhetoric to constitute language and the capacity of language, in turn, to constitute thought. Central to constitutive rhetoric and core to the module is the trope – literally 'the move' – of metaphor. Etymologically, metaphor is a meta-ferry which carries us from one place to another, although I prefer to think of it as a bridge which maintains a constant connection between abstractions (for example, 'love') and tangible reality (for example, 'a red, red rose') (Watt 2009a). The vehicle of a metaphor is one that takes us from the remote, nameless and general to the contiguous, familiar and particular. Because it is a bridge to that which is concrete and that which is close, metaphor can be considered to be a route home. It is this metaphorical dimension of the poet's art which is especially brought to mind by the words of Theseus in Shakespeare's *A Midsummer Night's Dream*:

> The poet's eye, in fine frenzy rolling,
> Doth glance from heaven to earth, from earth to heaven;
> And as imagination bodies forth
> The forms of things unknown, the poet's pen
> Turns them to shapes and gives to airy nothing
> A local habitation and a name. (5.1.13)

The walk from the school of law to the space devoted to the exploration of law and literature is metaphor (and it is *a* metaphor) and it incorporates discrete opportunities for the appreciation of the rhetorical (including metaphorical) foundations of legal language and legal thought. Steven L. Winter offers insights to illuminate this particular path:

> Basic experiences common to the human organism *motivate*, that is, make sense of, the *source-path-goal* schema and the *Life is a Journey* metaphor. This concept of motivation has nothing to do with subjective intent, but rather refers to that which makes meaning possible. Because the human mind understands new input in terms of and by comparison to existing knowledge, the cognitive process begins with unmediated, directly encountered experience. Meaning is elaborated by imaginative extension of this experience to understand and conceptualize other, more abstract domains. Thus, the experience of moving through space toward a goal makes it possible to conceptualize the *source-path-goal* schema and to understand the *path* and *journey* metaphors and the more abstract domains, like *purpose* and *life*, that they structure. The concept of motivation is a central component of cognitive theory; it expresses the process by which meaning and knowledge are made possible, but not determined, by prior experience. It yields a sense of knowledge and meaning as neither arbitrary nor determinate, but rather as systematic and imaginative. (Winter 1989: 1133, emphasis in original)[2]

The student traveller has only to open his or her eyes and to open his or her mind in order to see that the world is written in signs which speak to us. For the distinctly Augustinian-Platonic theologian Giovanni di Fidanza ('St Bonaventure') (c. 1221–1274), the everyday objects of ocular attention are 'offered to us as a sign from heaven, as a means toward the discovery of God' (Bonaventure 1960).

2 Footnote in original omitted.

Jean-Jacques Rousseau read the same signs to a different end. He thought to read truth 'not in books written by your fellow-creatures, who are liars, but in nature, which never lies' (Rousseau 1913). For us, they are the signposts to a more critical understanding of law and a more concrete appreciation of law's future and our place in it.

Here, then, is a typical walk from a room in the law school, into the corridor, into the courtyard, down the path, past the tree, under the bridge, near the lamppost, past the wall, between the streams, alongside the playing field, to University House, via the car park, onto the main road, with its road signs, through the woods, until, finally, we move inside. The walk is a moving gallery of scenes and it is best presented as such here. It should be fast-paced and only briefly in focus. It should produce a shifting sequence of images in the mind. Image stimulates imagination and imagination makes the image. A similar belief formed part of John Dewey's 'pedagogic creed':

> I believe that the image is the great instrument of instruction … I believe that much of the time and attention now given to the preparation and presentation of lessons might be more wisely and profitably expended in training the [student's] power of imagery and in seeing to it that [the student] was continually forming definite, vivid, and growing images of the various subjects with which [the student] comes in contact. (Dewey 1897)

The most appropriate thing to do at this stage is to direct the reader to an uncaptioned and in that sense uncaptured slideshow of some key sites through which the walk is strung. This is one way to walk beyond the text. The reader who wants to abandon reading can view a sequence of scenes online.[3] The reader who wants to go beyond text by teasing open the textile in order to reveal the spaces within might stay here and forgive me if I describe the walk in the rambling style that it deserves. In the paragraphs which follow, I try to describe the walk in a way that does not contain it. The Law and Literature module calls for an element of creative writing, so I have included lines broken from a poem – '*Jus Spatiandi*' – which is not yet written.

The Room

> Snowed in; snowed under; sealed by salary within a cell. ('*Jus Spatiandi*')

The office – the officer, that which is official. The first sign, the first signifier of the law, is that we are sealed in our cells. The last is that we end in chambers.

3 See http://www2.warwick.ac.uk/fac/soc/law/staff/academic/watt/educationaljourney/ [accessed 24 July 2012].

The Corridor

> Galleries – long narrow rooms like corridors, though often leading nowhere. (Solnit 2001: 86)

The corridor should be the careering place, a place to run. But it is ordained that we shall not run in corridors – indeed, not run indoors at all. It is ordained that career is status. And those who run here run like rats in rabbit holes, down dead ends, blind turns and all for dreaming of *un pot d'or*.

The Door

> Shylock: What, are there masques? Hear you me, Jessica: Lock up my doors. (Shakespeare, *The Merchant of Venice* 2: v)

The door to the law school parts like opposing teeth; pearly PVC, grinning like a Cheshire cat. We recall that the imagination of Alice could open a door which the rights of Kafka's countryman could not. The door to the law school is an ambiguous portal.

Courtyard

> The enclosed garden had been, since the Song of Songs, a metaphor for the female body. (Solnit 2001: 87)

After the maze of corridors, it is a relief to feel the relative freedom of the courtyard, with its trimmed triangle of grass and strange erotic statue and a tree or two. Is it permitted to walk on the grass? We do, and we defy any regulatory spy. The walls surround us and appear to glance through many glass eyes, but they are blind and we are unchallenged. It is freedom, but in a faculty's frame.

Pathway

> What Heaven has conferred is called The Nature; an accordance with this nature is called The Path of duty; the regulation of this path is called Instruction. The path may not be left for an instant. If it could be left, it would not be the path. (Confucius)

The path of law is paved with what and passes how? Is it a straight path? Direct. Right. True. Is it superimposed upon nature? Does it bend and weave like text around the objects of everyday life? At the edges, the enthusiasm of nature is uncurbed.

The Tree

> The pave upvaults with knots and slow gymnastic torts. ('*Jus Spatiandi*')

The tree has branches like the law and it has deep roots which sustain even when they cannot be seen. The tree is for the most part dead wood, but there is a thin layer of life below its broken skin which lives to grow and to accommodate, or to destroy, as it stretches to water and light. It has smart clothes and dirty feet.

The Bridge

The bridge that links the library to the concourse of science is high. We understand and under pass. We do not cross this bridge. It crosses over us. All understanding must be a relation to a bridge or bond. In law and literature, is the bridge the 'and' or mere ampersand?

The Streetlamp

Streetlamps sleep like laws. Bright line rules lie in dormant filaments. In the dark the law radiates unnatural regulation.

The Wall

A tall wall is a great commitment of bricks. It is a foundation and dependency. It is a regulation of hard edges and soft mortar. We can scale walls. They are always perfectly balanced between this side and that, and it is always a fancy to suppose that there can be an inside or an outside to a wall. There might be an inside and an outside to a building, but the limits of the building, its walls, are always neutral and disregarding. The only inside of a wall is the gut of the mortar and the brick. This is where the door lives and it too has neither in nor out. Forgive the wall, for it keeps the possibility of a door.

The Streams

> Generally speaking, there can be no ownership or right of property in the running water of a stream. (Wisdom 1962: 11)

Here on either side of the path are the twin inducements of two straight-edged shallow channels. Artificial rivers like old law and equity streaming through different courts in different corners of Westminster Hall. And the water is justice. Ever humble, ever lowering itself to the lowest level, ever wanting to move. And, like equity, slowly, surely, melting and mollifying the strict edges of the right-angled stones.

The Playing Field

> In Hebrew … justice is associated with the sibling words for level ground and uprightness – *miyshor* and *meyshar*. (Watt 2009a: 153)

Level playing fields are always made by violence and violence ever plays there. The great edifice of law is always built on the level of some flat battlefield. In law, war becomes another sort of game.

University House

And here is an edifice of law and equity. The great abstract generality of a universe, turned into a house of work, never quite a home, and a glass house at that, potted with waxy plants and the pottering sound of heels on tiles.

The Car Park

> He entered a garden, steadied himself against a motor-car that he found in it. (E.M. Forster, *Howards End*)

Cars run as rivers do and stagnate in pools. The motor and all motivation arrests in the parking lot of law. Set out in excellent squares of bright-line rules. But we see a sign that speaks with moving irony of the law which allows 'No parking'. '"He won't move on," says the constable calmly, with a slight professional hitch of his neck' (Charles Dickens, *Bleak House*).

The Road and the Sign

> Road signs have two key features: the configuration of the network to which they belong and the freedom of its users to move about in it. (Jean 1999: 88)

The main road is as long and straight as any corridor of law. So open and yet so constraining. A very deadly stream and a gallery of warning signs. Like the law, it is a grey scale of accidents and it is paved with infinite possibilities for death and other progress.

The Woods

> O lead me to the wide-extended walks … there with th' enchanted round I walk/ The regulated wild. (James Thomson, 'The Seasons', c. 1734)

We wander off the road and path and negotiate the beautiful inconvenience of trees. We know we are near our journey's end when we have peeled back all the signs to this. Two trees: Life, and the Knowledge of Good and Evil.

Moving Inside

Finally we move inside. This is not the end of motion, but the beginning of a new movement. Inner space is open to exploration and interpretation every bit as stimulating as that which we have enjoyed in outer space. However, moving inside is, quite literally, another story for another time (see Monk et al. 2011).

Appreciating the Aesthetic

In the course of preparing this chapter, I discovered an article that, by its title, held out great promise to teach me something valuable and, as it is now said, 'on topic'. The authors of 'Moving beyond the classroom: accommodating the changing pedagogy of higher education' (Jamieson, Dane and Lippman 2005: 17) pose some essential questions:

> What is the role of the university campus environment as more active, student-centered approaches to teaching and learning are taken up? What types of 'classrooms' need to be developed to facilitate the pedagogical trends that are emerging in higher education? How can we break with traditional approaches to designing on-campus learning environments in order to enhance the quality of student learning?

The authors provide a range of insightful and stimulating answers to these questions. For example, they are surely right to suggest that: 'When the spaces outside the classroom are layered for the diverse ways in which students learn, they cease to exist as paths and become "learning spaces" in their own right' (Jamieson, Dane and Lippman 2005: 19). And yet, for all its appeal and for its many pleasant layers, it was ultimately an uncomfortable read. Perhaps I am too sensitive, like the princess who was disturbed by the pea lying at the bottom of the layers of mattresses on her bed, but it is the small signs which so often betray the big picture. The pea in this particular bed is the suggestion that 'outdoor or garden spaces that once largely served an aesthetic function might become active learning environments' (Jamieson, Dane and Lippman 2005: 21). The problem with this suggestion that is that it implicitly denigrates the aesthetic function (not least by calling it a 'function') by contrasting it with a future hoped-for utility function; at the very least, it denigrates the potential for aesthetic appreciation to be an 'active learning experience' in its own right. Consider how starkly this attitude contrasts with John Dewey's insights into the uplifting potential of an aesthetic experience:

> the aesthetic is no intruder in experience from without, whether by way of idle luxury or transcendent ideality, but ... it is the clarified and intensified development of traits that belong to every normally complete experience. (Dewey 2005: 48)

We have all let a pea slip beneath our mattresses at some point or other, and it must be acknowledged that the authors of 'Moving beyond the classroom: accommodating the changing pedagogy of higher education' are well intentioned, but if we are to open up the learning experience and motivate learners, it is crucially important that our species of language and thought is compatible with the educative enterprise in which we are involved. There is little point in moving beyond the formulaic frames of the classroom if our project is to frame and formulate the world beyond.

References

Anderson, J. 2004. 'Talking whilst walking: a geographical archaeology of knowledge'. *Area*, 36(3), 254–61.

Blakemore, C. 2003. 'Movement is essential to learning. (Physical education and academic achievement)'. *Journal of Physical Education, Recreation & Dance*, 74(9), 22–41.

Bogen, J.E. and Bogen, G.M. 1969. 'The other side of the brain III: the corpus callosum and creativity'. *Bulletin of the Los Angeles Neurological Societies*, 34, 191–217. Available at: http://www.its.caltech.edu/~jbogen/text/OSOB_3.html [accessed 24 July 2012].

Bonaventure, St., 1960. 'Mystical Opuscula', in *The Works of Bonaventure, Vol. 1*, translated by J. De Vinck. Paterson, NJ: St Anthony Guild Press.

De Certeau, M. 1984. *Practice of Everyday Life*. Berkeley: University of California Press.

Dewey, J. 1897. 'My pedagogic creed'. *School Journal*, 54 (January), 77–80. Available at: http://dewey.pragmatism.org/creed.htm [accessed 24 July 2012].

Dewey, J. 1938. *Experience and Education*. London: Macmillan.

Dewey, J. 2005. *Art as Experience*. New York: Perigee.

Dunn, R., Krimsky, J.S., Murray, J.B. and Quinn, P.J. 1985. 'Light up their lives: a review of research on the effects of lighting on children's achievement and behavior'. *The Reading Teacher*, 38(9), 863–9.

Graetz, K.A. 2006. 'The psychology of learning environments'. *EDUCAUSE Review*, 41(6), 60–75.

Hannaford, C. 2005. *Smart Moves: Why Learning is Not All in Your Head.* Marshall, NC: Great Ocean Publishers.

Jamieson, P., Dane, J. and Lippman, P.C. 2005. 'Moving beyond the classroom: accommodating the changing pedagogy of higher education'. *Refereed Proceedings of 2005 Forum of the Australasian Association for Institutional Research*, 17–23.

Jarvis, R. 1999. *Romantic Writing and Pedestrian Travel.* Basingstoke: Palgrave Macmillan.

Jean, G. 1999. *Signs, Symbols and Ciphers*, translated by S. Hawkes. London: Thames & Hudson.

Kafka, F. 1916. 'Vor dem Gesetz' ('Before the law'), in *Almanach dem Neuer Dichtung.* Leipzig: Kurt Wolff Verlag.

Kleiber, D. et al. 1973. *Environmental Illumination and Human Behaviour: The Effects of Spectrum Light Sources on Human Performance in a University Setting*. Ithaca: Cornell University Press.

Monk, N., Chillington-Rutter, C., Neelands, J. and Heron, J. 2011. *Open-Space Learning: A Study in Transdisciplinary Pedagogy*. London: Bloomsbury Academic.

Ott, J. 1964. 'Effects of unnatural light'. *New Scientist*, 25, 294–6.

Rosenfeld, L.B. 1977. 'Setting the stage for learning'. *Theory into Practice*, 16(3), 167–73.

Rousseau, J.J. 1913. Introduction to 'A Dissertation on the Origin and Foundation of the Inequality of Mankind' in *Social Contract & Discourses.* New York: E.P. Dutton & Co. Available at http://www.bartleby.com/168/602.html [accessed 24 July 2012].

Seagers, P. W. 1963. *Light, Vision and Learning.* New York: Better Light Better Sight Bureau Press.

Solnit, R. 2001. *Wanderlust: A History of Walking.* London: Verso.

Thomson, J.A.K. (trans.) 1955. *The Ethics of Aristotle*. Harmondsworth: Penguin Classics.

Watt, G. 2006. 'The soul of legal education'. *Web JCLI*, 3. Available at: http://webjcli.ncl.ac.uk/2006/issue3/watt3.html [accessed 24 July 2012].

Watt, G. 2009a. *Equity Stirring: The Story of Justice Beyond Law*. Oxford: Hart.

Watt, G. 2009b. 'Reflections on creative writing within a law and literature module'. *Law and Humanities*, 3(2), 231–55.

White, J.B. 1984. *When Words Lose their Meaning: Constitutions and Reconstitutions of Language, Characters and Community*. Chicago: University of Chicago Press.

Winter, S.L. 1989. 'Transcendental nonsense, metaphoric reasoning, and the cognitive stakes for law'. *University of Pennsylvania Law Review*, 137, 1105–238.
Wisdom, A.S. 1962. *The Law of Rivers and Watercourses*. London: Shaw & Sons.
Wurtman, R. 1968. 'Biological implications of artificial illumination'. *Illuminating Engineering Society Journal*, 63, 523–9.

Chapter 9

The Battle of the Precedents: Reforming Legal Education in Mexico Using Computer-Assisted Visualization

Panagia Voyatzis and Burkhard Schafer

Introduction

This chapter will explore problems that have been created for legal practitioners in the Mexican (civilian) legal system by the increased use of precedent-based reasoning and will indicate how a combination of innovative visualization techniques with Artificial Intelligence (AI) could create teaching tools to address them. It will argue that these problems can be predominantly attributed to the operative image of the law and legal reasoning that the Mexican legal profession holds, one that seems to be ill-suited for understanding and successfully engaging with precedent-based reasoning. The first part of the chapter presents the problems as felt by legal practitioners, the images of law that the latter seem to hold, and the inadequacy of these images for engaging with precedent-based reasoning. The second part will describe the use of visualization tools that could offer legal practitioners a more suitable image of reasoning to guide them when using legal precedents. We first give a critical overview of AI-assisted argumentation diagramming in law and then propose an extension that draws from visualization in military history.

Better a Slave to Principles than a Slave to Men

During the last decade, the role and working practice of the Mexican federal judiciary has changed dramatically. The judiciary is in the process of becoming a more confident and active precedent-giver and also precedent-user, moving away from its historical self-understanding as part of a civilian jurisdiction and orienting itself more towards the USA as the predominant economic power in the region. Integration in NAFTA and constitutional reform under the last government all played a role in a process that changes not just the use of precedents, but pushes the judicial system in its entirety towards an adversarial, common law approach that emphasizes adversarial, oral procedure in more types of proceedings than was previously possible. As a result, more federal precedents are issued, published and made available to all legal professionals. As a consequence, precedents are also being increasingly cited in the daily practice of the lower courts.[1] However, this fundamental change in 'legal style' has not been problem-free for the legal community. In 2006 the Supreme Court of Justice published the results of a comprehensive, three-year-long study of the perceived problems that judges, officials and legal practitioners in Mexico face with the administration of justice. The research conclusions and the working papers show that legal practitioners experience disorientation when dealing with precedents: they expressed doubts about the role of precedents in daily practice[2] and, specifically, they complained that often they did not know what to do with so many precedents, which are perceived as either repetitive or contradicting each other. What was intended to increase legal certainty is perceived as having the opposite effect, creating confusion and a perceived loss in legal certainty.[3] The research participants suggested that there should be clear rules for giving weight to conflicting precedents and to determine their validity, that courts should issue fewer precedents, that contradictions should be avoided by institutional incentives and that institutional efforts should be put into practice to unify precedents.[4] In short, what was asked for can be understood as no less than a 'codification of precedent-based reasoning' – defying in a sense the very reason for moving away from the traditionally used codes towards an increased use of precedents in the first place. What creates certainty in the view of these practitioners are codified abstract rules, which make precedents a 'legal irritant' (Teubner 1998), something that needs to be tamed. Psychologically, we can understand this reaction as a form of cognitive inertia or cognitive dissonance: faced with massive changes across all aspects of the legal profession (and indeed wider society and politics) in a short period of time, practitioners in Mexico cling to their learned reasoning and behaviour pattern especially strongly where it comes to the core of their self-understanding and what it means to think legally. In 2007 a public enquiry raised by the Senate of the Mexican Republic regarding the functioning and future reform agenda for the judiciary raised similar concerns and questions about precedents.[5]

Legal professionals claim that they are dealing with more legal information than they can handle, which makes them ask for less, more unified and non-

1 Suprema Corte de Justicia de la Nación. Dirección General de la Coordinación de Compilación y Sistematización de Tesis, *Libro Blanco de la Reforma Judicial: Una agenda para la justicia en México* (Mexico City: Suprema Corte de Justicia de la Nación, 2006) 166.

2 Ibid, 166–8.

3 Suprema Corte de Justicia de la Nación, *Estudio sobre la reforma judicial integral. Diagnóstico ciudadano y conclusiones de los foros. Problemario: Problema 19* (Mexico City: Suprema Corte de Justicia de la Nación).

4 Suprema Corte de Justicia de la Nación, *Libro Blanco de la Reforma Judicial*, 166–9.

5 Senado de la República, *Consulta Pública de la Reforma del Estado en México. Foro local sobre la reforma del Poder Judicial*. Monterrey, Nuevo León, 28 June 2007.

contradictory information. To put this desire into its proper context, though, we need to see beyond their *perceived* problems and solutions; we need to understand more about the objective load of information, the way this information usually 'behaves', and also the practitioners' knowledge in context. First, it is quite illuminating to find that the amount of information available to legal practitioners[6] does not seem to be excessive compared to that available in other legal systems – in fact, quite the opposite. Second, it is necessary to remember that precedents are models of decisions with variable degrees of authority, persuasiveness and 'on point-edness', and as such cannot be used in an all-or-nothing way; they usually help practitioners in building functional maps of the law and in making inferences. However, it is precisely this type of understanding, acquired when learning how to reason with legal rules, that dominates the legal-cognitive problem-solving apparatus of the Mexican legal profession.

A system of precedents provides a more or less wide range of past decisions with varying degrees of authority. Their weight can be evaluated according to a set of complex considerations, both formal and substantive – precedents of lower courts are normally trumped by precedents of higher courts, older decisions by newer decisions, tangential decisions by on-point decisions, etc. Aspects that determine the weight also include whether the case was decided by a slim majority or an unanimous decisions, and whether the specific part that is cited is core of the ratio or a mere obiter (Atiyah and Summers 1987: 115–16). Precedents are also sensitive to their relations with other precedents, i.e. precedents often form clusters to make strong 'fronts' that can be subjected to 'attacks' in different strengths from contradictory precedents. In the (civilian) German legal system, this is known as 'ständige Rechtsprechung' or 'consolidated jurisprudence' – the recognition that sometimes a consensus emerges across a variety of cases over an extended period of time. This gives the position a considerably higher weight than a single precedent and can even trump precedents from a notionally higher-ranking court.

This information is used to build stories about the legal system and to make sense about the 'location' of particular legal claims and their likely outcomes. Thus, precedents can be understood as past decisions providing context-sensitive models that point with variable force towards a certain direction, guiding future decisions. As such, precedents do not have all-or-nothing validity, but are better understood as having *degrees of authority*, *soundness* or *force*, and, as MacCormick and Summers point out, 'this is a truth already understood in some quarters within common law systems, but the partial convergence of civil law systems … requires us to face up to it frontally' (1997: 544).

6 In the Mexican legal system, only 'extracts' of resolutions selected by the Supreme Court of Justice or Collegiate Tribunals are published as precedents; that is, not all resolutions are available as precedents that do not represent overwhelming amounts of legal information.

Here we argue that the perceived information overload that legal practitioners report in the Mexican context is partly the result of their image of the law and the corresponding cognitive toolbox they have at their disposal. The image of the law circulating within this legal system is that of classical legal positivism (Cáceres 2002; Cáceres and Rodruguez 2008), i.e. one that depicts the law as a system of rules from which practitioners should identify those which *apply* to the particular case. The rules are valid or invalid and therefore are applicable or inapplicable, binding or not binding: in this model, there is no place for degree of force. As Duxbury argued: 'precedents, unlike statutes, do not bind judges in an all-or-nothing fashion, that the binding force of a precedent is best explained not in terms of its validity (this being a non-scalar concept) but in terms of its authority (of which there can be degrees)' (2008: 23). For example, if we look at the most authoritative introductory book for legal studies in Mexico, we find that only seven pages are given to the issue of precedents, the so-called *jurisprudencia*; in there the author explains the statutory law that creates the official system of precedents and comments on when precedents are binding and when they are not – for example, 'when there is normative contradiction it is not possible that the incompatible precedents are both valid' or 'determining if two contradictory precepts have or have not binding force is not a problem for logic but something that only positive law can solve' (Garcia Maynez 2000: 68–75). Maynez's language is that of (all-or-nothing) *bindingness, validity* and *applicability*, and in this account there is no room for evaluations of normative *soundness* that function as a matter of degree (on the inadequacy of classical positivism in understanding precedents, see Duxbury 2008: 58).

Legal practitioners in Mexico seem to have deeply internalized an image of the law incompatible with the way in which legal precedents work in a legal system. They seem to be expecting to find unique answers and clear signs of validity as they were taught to, while precedents seem to require a different idea of what ought to be done. The operative idea of law in this context is unsuitable for precedent-based reasoning. In order to enable lawyers to function appropriately in the new system, more than just acquiring additional information is necessary; rather, a more radical 'Gestaltswitch' that changes deeply ingrained cognitive assumptions is required.

This points us to an often overlooked topic in both comparative law and jurisprudence. In comparative law, the work of Pierre Legrand heralded a 'cognitive turn' that identified legal families and legal systems by the unique 'legal mentality' of its members (Legrand 1996). In legal theory too, certain cognitive attitudes shared by a group feature prominently in a wide variety of theoretical accounts of the notion of 'legal system', from the system theoretical account of Guenther Teubner to the 'interpretive community' of Ronald Dworkin. However, while the emphasis on shared cognitive practices is an important insight, there is little analysis or reflection on how these shared practices emerge. Rather, the legal systems under consideration are typically mature systems that have evolved over centuries and in the process have accumulated a rich stock of 'problem-solving methodologies' (Legrand and Machado 1998). Dworkin's 'Hercules' too operates in a 'data-rich environment'. What sets him apart from mere mortal lawyers is that he has full knowledge of all cases and precedents, and on this basis can calculate the optimal 'fit' for the decision at hand. The problem that his metaphor addresses is therefore one of an apparent oversupply of precedents that seem to permit a 'pick and choose approach' where every decision can be supported – just as is stated by the Mexican judiciary. However, in Dworkin's analysis, this is the result of limitations of the human mind and its memory – full knowledge reduces the scope of permissible interpretations. In this analysis, the Mexican judiciary is not confronted with too many precedents, as they believe, but just enough to permit conflicting interpretations, and yet not enough to *see* patterns emerging. It is here that we encounter a direct link to the theme of this book – the ability to see patterns in a wealth of data is a visual ability that is not easily reducible to simple rules that can be communicated textually. In the same way in which an experienced chess player will 'see' that a group of pieces is weak or strong, an experienced lawyer will have developed a 'feel' that a certain group of cases, taken together, form such a strong pattern that they allow us to blank out contradictory information as mere noise.

The problem is of course where these skills and cognitive practices come from. In Dworkin's theory, the legal system is already mature, its interpretive communities well established and benefiting from an abundance of data points. In Legrand's approach, the common lawyer and the civilian lawyer are equally already 'fully formed' and already so ingrained in the cognitive paradigm of their respective systems that they may well be 'uneducatable' in principle and unable to ever develop a true understanding of what it means to be a lawyer in the opposite system (Legrand and Machado 1998). As a consequence, their theories are not designed to analyse and understand legal systems in radical transition, to the point that Legrand at least seems to deny that such a transition is possible in principle.

The missing element, in our view, is the role of legal education. Common (civilian) lawyers are not born, they are made. Studying legal education and the way in which it imparts certain cognitive traits on its 'raw material' should therefore be, in our view, integral to both the jurisprudential question pertaining to the nature of legal knowledge and the comparative legal question regarding the most basic differences and commonalities between legal systems. From this it follows that in order to understand and to support the transition of a legal system such as Mexico from a statute-based civilian system to a precedent-based system, we need to look at the reform of legal education much more urgently than at reforms of the legal framework (for example, a statute on the use of precedents, as requested by the Mexican practitioners). It is of course here that we encounter some systemic difficulties – educators who developed their own skill sets and cognitive schemata under one system are charged with imparting radically different modes of thinking to their students. At the same time, practitioners are often outside the reach of intensive educational measures and in turn tend to hire people who display skills similar to their own. This tendency to reaffirm cognitive schemata is of course at the heart of the system theoretical account of Luhman and Teubner, their emphasis on the tendency of systems to replicate themselves and their underlying conceptual orderings (see e.g. Teubner 1989). To break this circle, we therefore need tools that: a) enable training of cognitive schemata outside the established training pathways; and b) directly address the development of cognitive skills and do not just import additional factual information. Legal AI systems meet these criteria (see e.g. Conati and van Lehn 2000; van Joolingen 1999). 'Always on', Internet-enabled and unsupervised, they in theory enable learners to learn at their own pace and in their own time, outside entrenched structures of supervision and control, and without the need to physically travel to the place of education (which should make them attractive for practitioners). At their best, they build on sound cognitive science principles and are therefore particularly suitable for the type of cognitive change discussed above (see e.g. Anderson et al. 1995; Schank 1990). One of the results of this 'designed for cognition' approach is that in recent years, particular focus has been devoted to computer-assisted visualization in legal education. In Japan, a country that faced a similar transition to the one discussed briefly for Mexico, using computer-assisted legal education was for these very reasons a prime enabler to bring about a dramatic change in legal education (see Tanaka et al. 2005; Yoshino and Sakurai 2005).

In the next section, we briefly describe one particularly influential approach in legal AI that exhibits many of the features we have identified as desirable, Kevin Ashley's Legal ARgument Graph Observer (LARGO) programme (Ashley 2009). However, our analysis will show that while it is a good starting point, the specific method of visualization, which remains within the concept of arguments as directed graphs that is popular in AI, is not optimal for our purpose. We then briefly outline a radical departure from traditional argumentation visualization techniques: the battle of the precedents. Drawing our inspiration from familiar battle and campaign maps, we argue that the semantic richness of this type of visualization, and its ability to present dynamic interaction between forces of different strength, makes it particularly suitable for our purposes. Our everyday language reflects this approach: we talk about being overwhelmed by a precedent, being compelled by its force; we feel its strength and are torn between different precedents. These metaphors hint at a visual and almost haptic way to reason with precedents that we would ideally like to represent more directly than common approaches allow.

The LARGO System

While it is not uncommon to promote legal expert systems for use in legal education, few of the existing approaches have been designed with an educational purpose in mind. Rather, they tend to start their lifecycle as decision support tools which then are assigned a secondary function as teaching or training aids. Kevin Ashley's LARGO system deviates from this pattern (Ashley 2009). For this reason, and for a number of desirable design features that will be discussed below, we take this approach here as an example of the state of the art in AI-supported argumentation visualization in law. Ultimately, this system is based on his influential HYPO expert system (Ashley 1990). However, its next incarnation, CATO, is already a dedicated teaching aid, not just a re-use of an expert system for a secondary market (Aleven 2002). As a result, it takes insights from pedagogical theory right to the heart of the development of the system. Again, unlike many other AI and law systems promoted as teaching tools, both CATO and LARGO have been subject to some empirical evaluation of their efficiency – and the fact that the picture remains ambivalent is in itself an important finding (Aleven and Ashley 1997; Ashley, Desai and Levine 2002).

LARGO focuses on one specific aspect of case-based reasoning, testing the applicability of a precedent to a given scenario by means of hypotheticals. A quick example, based on the case of *California v. Carney*,[7] can help illustrate this approach: the rule to be interpreted requires a warrant for the search of a person's dwellings. The case at hand involves a Dodge Mini Motor Home. Are motor homes dwellings for the purposes of the law? The prosecution proposes a test: if the place that is searched has wheels and is self-propelling, then no warrant is required, as it is a car. The justification for this is based on principles, which in turn are derived from a history of precedents. One principle is that rules should be clear-cut and nothing seems easier than counting wheels. The defence offers an alternative test: if the place that is searched is used as a home and has the features commonly associated with one (such as a bed), then a warrant is required, as it is a home. Again, principles derived from precedents support this view, here the principle that privacy needs protecting. At the oral presentation, the judge then queries both tests using hypotheticals. For example, he asks of the prosecution: assume a case (the hypothetical) where the motor home has wheels and a motor, but is on a permanent parking lot, has gas pipes and electricity wires permanently attached to it, and cannot move without causing damage. Would you still want to apply your test and treat it as a car? At this point, the prosecution can either stick to its guns and argue that this case also should be decided under its proposed test (and hence be deemed a car) or it can refine the test by excluding, for example, situations where the car is permanently attached to an unmovable structure and in a way becomes part of it.

This type of reasoning can be found frequently in SCOTUS hearings. In addition, it also plays a major role in US teaching practice, linked to the 'Socratic model of education' (Stuckey 2007). Ashley argues that it is a suitable tool to explain and motivate rule choice and contextual and policy analyses. Citing from the *Best Practices for Legal Education*, he supports the view that open hypotheticals are particularly suitable 'to demonstrate complexity and indeterminacy of legal analysis' (Stuckey 2007: 214).

For our purposes, reasoning with hypotheticals meets several desirable features of a computer-assisted training system for Mexican lawyers coming to

7 *California v. Carney*, 471 U.S. 386 (1985).

terms with the shift towards common law reasoning. As Stuckey argued, focusing on reasoning with hypotheticals takes the idea of complexity and indeterminacy of precedents to the heart of the enterprise to teach precedent-based reasoning skills. As we noted above, one of the misunderstandings of the Mexican judiciary is the notion that precedents ought to unequivocally support one line of reasoning over the other. Consequently, case-based reasoning systems in the HYPO-CATO-LARGO tradition allow the incorporation and formal representation of wider social and political values in the reasoning process that challenge this assumption (for technical details, see Bench-Capon and Sartor 2003). This too has been identified in the studies cited above as a desideratum for Mexico. The systems are rooted in the tradition of adversarial, oral argument – another feature Mexico is increasingly moving towards. Despite all this, hypothetical reasoning is not restricted to common law systems. MacCormick observed that 'use of hypothetical cases in academic work … is a major technique used in the United Kingdom and in the United States, and also in most civil law countries' (MacCormick and Summers 1997: 529). This creates sufficient degrees of familiarity that are conductive to learning. As possible uses, he notes the following:

1. 'the construction of clear cases to which a code section, statute or doctrine must apply if it is to have any rational application';
2. 'the construction of *reductio ad absurdum* arguments demonstrating the unsoundness of proposed applications of code sections, statutes or doctrinal formulations';
3. 'the elaboration of coherent patterns of applications of authoritative language and demonstrations of how proposed or possible applications would not be coherent';
4. 'the formulation of paradigm cases so as to display a policy rationale in its clearest application';
5. 'the articulation of distinctions between paradigm cases and borderline cases';
6. 'the creation of conceptual bridges between cases along a continuum';
7. 'use [of] a well-designed hypothetical case to help justify extending a rule';
8. use of a 'hypothetical case … to help justify rejecting the application of a rule in a precedent to the case … about to be decided'.

Of these, points 3, 7 and 8 are core skills that need to be taught by any approach to instruct students in reasoning with precedents. However, points 4, 5 and 6 are of particular interest in our case, as they focus on the essentially contested nature of reasoning with precedents, the role of policy rationales and also the absence of clear-cut, hard and fast rules and cut-off points (the 'continuum of cases'). The ability to address all these points is an important design feature in LARGO. But possibly even more important is another intrinsic feature of reasoning with hypotheticals: it increases by its very nature the number of cases, or rather case scenarios, under consideration. As we argued above, it is partly the scarcity of precedents that can cause problems in a legal system in transition, and the way in which artificial hypotheticals are generated can be seen as a partial answer to this problem. Furthermore, successful hypotheticals are for pedagogical and rhetorical reasons designed to be easier to decide than the often 'muddy' real-life cases. Their purpose is to facilitate 'line-drawing' in normative reasoning by establishing positive and negative paradigm cases, that is, cases where it is intuitively clear that a rule should or should not apply (Harris, Pritchard and Rabins 2004: 64ff.).

At the core of LARGO is the 'process model of hypothetical argument' (PMHA) that expresses in a formal structure typical expert schemes of reasoning with hypotheticals.

A graphical representation of this basis structure, annotated with the *Carney* case discussed above, can be seen in Figure 9.1.

Students are then asked to use this model to create their own diagrammatic representations of the examples of hypothetical reasoning from the oral argument. Ashley argues that by making a conceptual phenomenon visible, it can become the subject of reflection. Diagrammatic visualization of conceptual models serves as 'scaffolds' that make explicit important features of good (and bad) performance, allowing the teacher to guide the students towards mastering complex knowledge by small steps (Ashley 2009: 339). LARGO can represent the facts of the case, proposed tests and hypotheticals as basic entities.

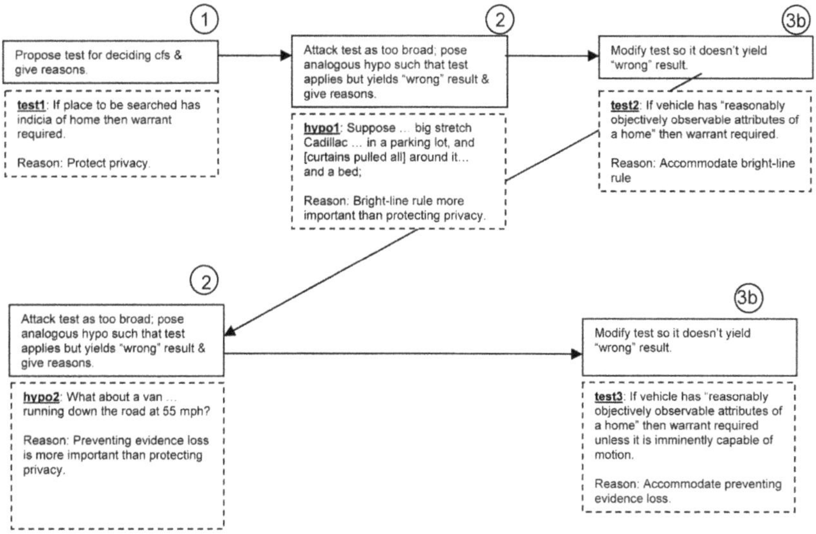

Figure 9.1 A typical HYPO reasoning diagram

Source: From Ashley 2009: 329.

These are connected by five kinds of relations among them: modifying a test, distinguishing a hypothetical, analogizing a hypothetical, a hypothetical leading to test or modification and a generic relation. Thanks to a 'graph grammar', LARGO can, through a set of predefined rules, parse the student-generated diagram, compare it to standard solutions and, on the basis of this comparison, provide feedback.

As mentioned above, LARGO (and equally so the related CATO) has been subject to some empirical evaluation. An initial small group study in 2006 showed statistically significant benefits for the group of students using LARGO in comparison to the control sample. However, a repeat with a larger sample the following year was not able to replicate this result (Pinkwart et al. 2009). In this respect, LARGO fares similarly to other approaches to computer-assisted diagrammatic reasoning software for legal education. Bart Verheij's more traditional approach, which uses Toulmin diagrams to express the support and attack relation between arguments, resulted in similarly weak evidence for an actual improvement in the learner's performance (Verheij 2007). Finally, our own experience using Wigmore charts for evidence teaching was equally inconclusive. We have given elsewhere a comprehensive analysis of these results and how they converge with research in cognitive science more generally (Schafer 2007). A summary must suffice here: there is strong evidence to suggest that visualization *can* have a strongly beneficial effect for solving analytical tasks (see Larkin and Simon 1987; Stenning 2002). But this does not mean that a diagram is *always* worth 10,000 words. Rather, as Cox argued, it depends on at least three factors (Cox 1999):

1. the properties of the representation;
2. the demands of the task;
3. user-dependent factors, such as prior knowledge and cognitive style.

The worth of a diagram – to quote Cox again – 'depends upon what kind of diagram it is, which words it represents, who produced and/or uses it, and the nature of the task' (1999: 343).

At least for our purposes, there seems therefore to be an incongruity between the properties of the representation, what the user is supposed to do with them and how both align with his or her cognitive style. If we return for the moment to the survey of the Mexican judiciary, their main problem was threefold:

1. to accept that 'bindingness' of precedents can come in degrees and that some are 'more binding' than others;
2. to accept that this requires balancing and weighting precedents;
3. to understand that despite the above two points, the outcome of this balancing process is not arbitrary.

In our subsequent analysis, we argued that for legal systems, 'phylogeny recapitulates ontogeny' so to speak. The process by which individual students in their legal education acquire certain cognitive skills is also a model for the way in which entire legal systems develop and possibly change their 'legal mentality'. The Mexican legal system, *qua* system, struggles according to this analysis with problems that are structurally similar to that of a student acquiring legal reasoning skills and vice versa. If this is the case, then the task that the learner faces is to find a way to reason with and about the various strength or 'bindingness' of precedents, to find ways to come to acceptable equilibria between conflicting precedents, and to avoid the danger, identified in the reactions of the Mexican jurists, of reducing this weighting process to a simple 'counting algorithm'.

Does LARGO address these issues? Argumentative strength is not expressed in this system, or indeed in any of the other computer-assisted diagram systems for law, which typically only represent the logical *function* of an argument (for example, to support or attack another argument) but rarely their relative weight. Case-based reasoning systems like CATO are capable of reasoning about relative strength to some degree in the background – for instance, it is able to compare the 'on-pointedness' of two cases along a range of predefined parameters. But not only is this element not expressed in the diagrammatic representation, this mode of reasoning reduces the weighting process to an ultimately rule-based calculation. This is a necessary feature of computer-based systems that aim to either solve a case or, as in LARGO, give students automated feedback to their answers. In order to be able to parse the information, ultimately some form of rule-like presentation is inevitable. Thus, not only does the system fail to address the aspect of reasoning that the learner is most likely to struggle with, it also uses exactly the (problematic) stop-gap solution that an insecure learner might crave, reducing the intuitive process of 'seeing' patterns in the precedents and 'feeling' their strength to simple, yes/no rules that promise certainty but ultimately miss their target.

This is but an expression of a broader dilemma: the more we expect the computer programme to do, the more intelligent we want it to be and the more prescriptive it is also going to be in its choice of diagrammatic representation. Mind maps allow the user almost unrestricted freedom in terms of how to arrange the information, LARGO imposes considerably more constraints in order to become 'understandable' by the computer, and CATO or Verheij's ArguMed impose more restrictions still in order to enable the computer not just to suggest feedback but also to identify and correct mistakes. From research in the pedagogical and cognitive implications of using diagrams, we know by contrast that the more the user can claim 'ownership' of his or her diagrams and construct them according to his or her liking, the greater the effect (Cox 1999).

On this basis, we will now propose an alternative to the way in which case-based reasoning is presented in LARGO. A visualization appropriate at least for our intended audience should: a) explicitly represent argumentative strength; b) represent those features of the context of an argument that influence the weighting process; c) permit 'clustering' of precedents that form coherent positions and cannot be reduced to acyclical directed graphs that express support relations between individual cases; and d) give the user sufficient flexibility to adjust the representation to his or her cognitive style.

History, and more specifically military history, has for a long time used visualizations that match all the above criteria in the form of the ubiquitous battle maps. These visualizations typically develop a semantic that is sufficiently constrained to allow a degree of standardized interpretation.

A typical example is as follows.

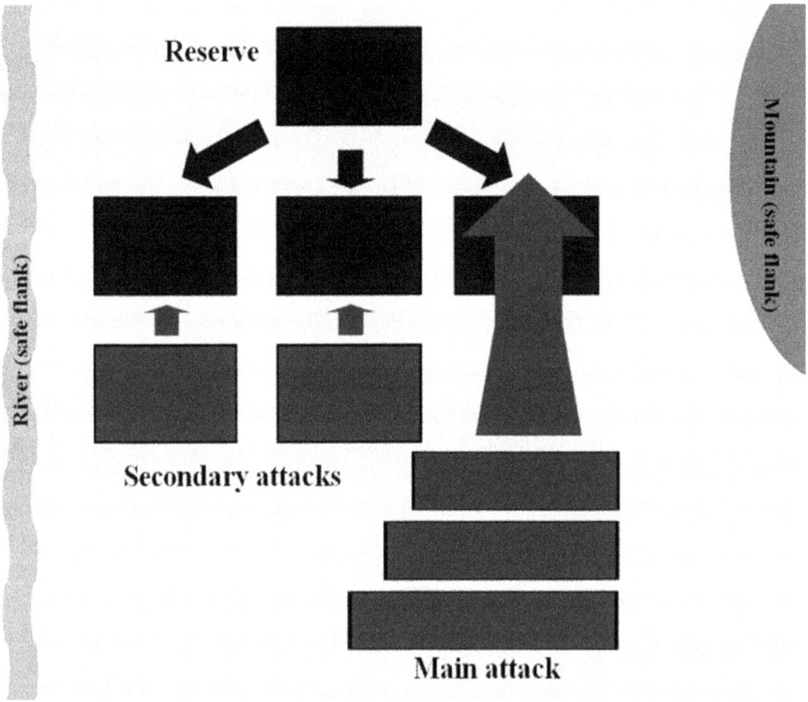

Figure 9.2 Explanation of 'attack in oblique order', from the Art of Battle website[8]

8 http://www.theartofbattle.com/tactics-tutorial [accessed 24 July 2012]. We are very grateful for the comments and support by the site's owner, Jonathan Webb. Our representation of Carney is loosely based on battles from his website; it is left to the reader to identify which one is the historical inspiration.

The different size of boxes and arrows is used to describe different strengths of a unit and different strengths of an attack respectively. This does not merely help to depict a historical battle – it is also used in the training of officers, playing a causal, explanatory role why one general defeated the other. The skill that the officer takes from this is the ability to see, immediately and without the need for complex calculations, how a combination of forces and environment creates winnable and indefensible positions and strategies. It is this causal, explanatory element aided by visualization that we are most interested in here. In a legal setting, we can now think of precedents as individual units. The difference in size would correspond to the 'objective' strength of a precedent (for example, the Supreme Court versus the Court of First Instance), whereas the size of the arrow expresses the strength of the use of the precedent in a given context – an on-point precedent will be stronger than a tangential one, for instance. In the example, we can see also how a learner would immediately identify the cluster on the right-hand side – a form of 'cohesiveness' that creates a centre of gravity and that goes beyond a simple 'support relation', so that all units support each other. Clusters of precedents are used in the same way in legal argumentation. They work not because there is an explicit linear support relation in the sense, for example, of Toulmin's warrant or support between them, but because their joint effect gives additional strength to the argument that is proposed.

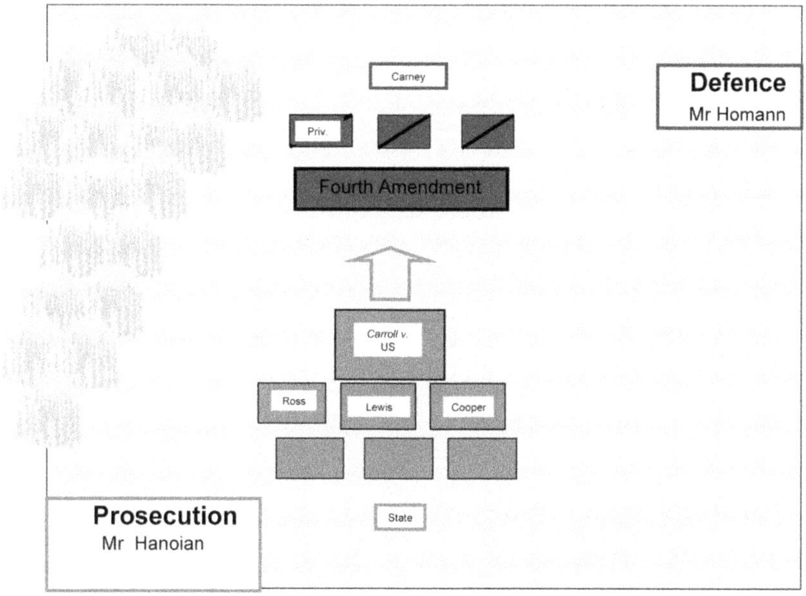

Figure 9.3 ***Carney v. US***

In battles fought between coalitions, visual markers can be used to distinguish internal subdivisions within a side – and the learner will begin to 'see' and understand them as a possible source of weakness, despite their possible utility. In the same way, persuasive but non-binding precedents from other jurisdictions can be marked up as 'auxiliary troops' within a coalition. Procedural moves at the initial stage of a hearing finally correspond to typical skirmishing attacks that do little but prepare the ground for the real issue, even if they sometimes can strike lucky.

Figure 9.3 shows how we can begin to translate the LARGO diagrams into Battle maps. Carney is 'hiding behind' the Fourth Amendment, which secures a principal value – privacy (for obvious semiotic reasons, using a battle that involves a siege, with Carney the party under siege, would have also been a possibility, the Fourth Amendment creating legal walls that correspond to the physical wall of his car). The social value underpinning the Fourth Amendment is privacy – values are indicated by the boxes with a cross bar. The prosecution is using a lead case, *Carroll v. US*, which established the vehicle exception, to pierce the Fourth Amendment protection. However, its case is supported by a whole range of other precedents, all of them mentioned, but none of them later discussed in the decision – they merely help to form the 'centre of gravity' we talked about above. These cases include *US v. Ross* and *Cardwell v. Lewis.*

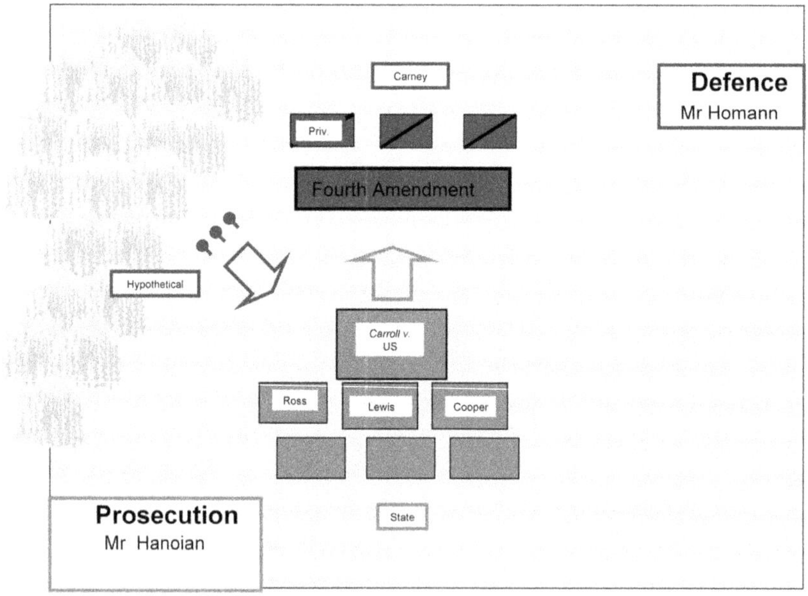

Figure 9.4 A hypothetical attacking a precedent

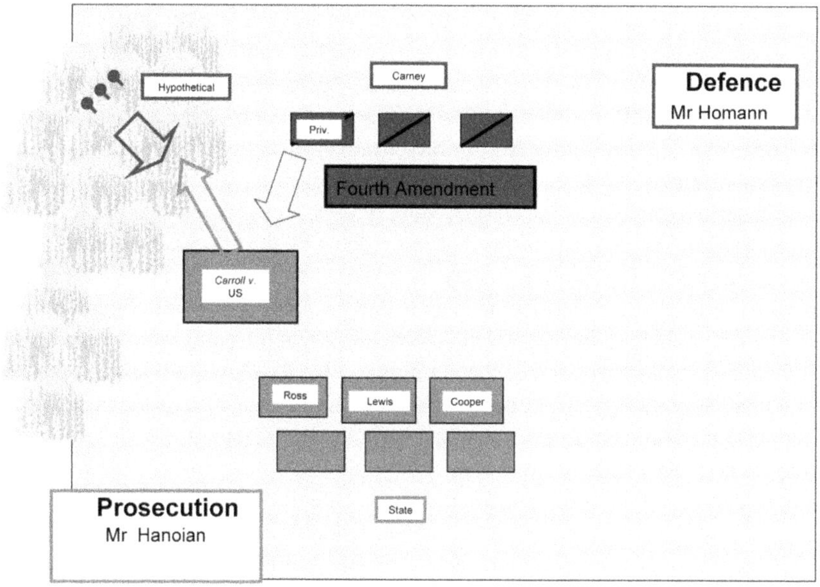

Figure 9.5 A precedent getting isolated and destroyed (restrictively distinguished)

At this point, counsel for the defence launches a counter-attack in the form of a hypothetical: what would be the case if a motor home had a tent attached to it? Would the tent be protected, but the car not?

The aim of the attack by the hypothetical, visualized as round blobs on the left (hypotheticals are not precedents, so are a symbol other than boxes), is to ‘overextend’ the precedent and lure it into territory where it can be attacked by the blue forces. By conceding, for example, that under the proposed interpretation of *Carroll v. US*, the tent too would be unprotected, the precedent is isolated from its supporting, more conservative cases. This allows it to be attacked by the privacy principle that underpins Carney’s case. Here is how a successful development would have looked like: Carroll takes the bait, overextends itself and is finally defeated by the privacy policy rationale.

Maps are potentially semantic-rich environments – depending on the graphic skills, the environment can also be used to represent relevant features. Very common are indicators of height, a natural choice given the importance of holding the high ground in battles. So important is this feature of military campaigns that it found its way into ethical discourse, and the spatial representation of maps would make it possible to graphically represent the idea of ‘holding the moral (or legal) high ground’, putting an additional (and instantaneously visible) burden on an attacker.

These representations of battles are common and predate computer animations by a considerable amount of time. What computers add in value though is their ability to incorporate them into animations. Particularly good examples can be found at the Art of Battle website[9] (which also provided the blueprint for the above illustrations), History Animated[10] or the Discovery Channel.[11] The added dynamic element will be, we hope, a particularly good teaching tool to aid the transition from the fixed, document-based procedure of the past to Mexico's embrace of oral, adversarial and dynamic hearings that coincided with the introduction of precedent-based reasoning. In addition, it may be possible to regiment the construction of maps sufficiently to make them at least in part readable by an 'intelligent' program like the one used in LARGO. Should this become feasible, automated features such as feedback generation, one of the strengths of LARGO, would become possible. As a next step, though, we hope to represent a number of interesting cases both as animated and static battle maps, using a variety of representation forms. Following this, we hope to test these on a student population, both as passive consumers and active creators of these maps. Should there indeed be a measurable benefit, the issue of balancing the demands of computer readability with the desirable freedom of the map users to develop representations that suit their personal cognitive style would have to be addressed. Jerome Frank, despairingly, characterized legal procedures as trial by combat. If this analysis is correct, and we think it is, then the techniques and methods that have been used to train new commanders should also be suitable to train new judges. Our approach hopes to make the first small contribution in this direction.

References

Aleven, V. 2003. 'Using background knowledge in case-based legal reasoning: a computational model and an intelligent learning environment'. *Artificial Intelligence*, 150, 183–238.

Aleven, V. and Ashley, K. 1997. 'Evaluating a learning environment for case-based argumentation skills', in S.A. Cerri, G. Gouardères and F. Paraguaçu (eds), *Proceedings of the 6th International Conference on Artificial Intelligence and Law, ICAIL-97, Melbourne, Australia.* New York: ACM, 170–79.

Anderson, J.R., Corbett, A.T., Koedinger, K.R. and Pelletier, R. 1995. 'Cognitive tutors: lessons learned'. *Journal of Learning Science*, 4, 167–207.

Ashley, K. 1990. *Modelling Legal Argument: Reasoning with Cases and Hypotheticals.* Cambridge, MA: MIT Press.

9 http://www.theartofbattle.com/ancient-battles [accessed 24 July 2012].

10 http://www.historyanimated.com/newhistoryanimated [accessed 24 July 2012].

11 http://dsc.discovery.com/convergence/rome/battlemaps/battlemaps.html [accessed 24 July 2012].

Ashley, K. 2009. 'Teaching a process model of legal argument with hypotheticals'. *Artificial Intelligence and Law*, 17, 321–70.

Ashley, K., Desai, R. and Levine, J.M. 2002. 'Teaching case-based argumentation concepts using dialectic arguments vs. didactic explanations', in S.A. Cerri, G. Gouardères and F. Paraguaçu (eds), *Proceedings of the 6th International Conference on Intelligent Tutoring Systems, ITS 2002*. Berlin: Springer, 585–95.

Atiyah, P.S. and Summers, R.S. 1987. *Form and Substance in Anglo-American Law: A Comparative Study in Legal Reasoning, Legal Theory and Legal Institutions.* New York: Oxford University Press.

Bench-Capon, T. and Sartor, G. 2003. 'A model of legal reasoning with cases incorporating theories and values'. *Artificial Intelligence*, 150, 97–143.

Cáceres, E. 2002. 'Psicología y Constructivismo Jurídico: apuntes para una transición paradigmática interdisciplinaria', in M. Muñoz de Alba (ed.), *Violencia Social*. Mexico City: UNAM, 335–42.

Cáceres, E. and Rodríguez, G. 2008. *Bases Psicológicas del Comportamiento Jurídico en México.* Mexico City: UNAM.

Conati, C. and van Lehn, K. 2000. 'Toward computer-based support of meta-cognitive skills: a computational framework to coach self-explanation'. *International Journal Artificial Intelligence Education*, 11, 398–415.

Cox, R. 1999. 'Representation construction, externalised cognition and individual differences'. *Learning and Instruction*, 9, 343–63.

Duxbury, N. 2008. *The Nature and Authority of Precedents.* Cambridge: Cambridge University Press.

Garcia Maynez, E. 2000. *Introduccion al Estudio del Derecho.* Mexico City: Porrua.

Harris, C., Pritchard, M. and Rabins, M. 2004. *Engineering Ethics: Concepts and Cases.* Belmont: Wordsworth.

Hurley, S. 1990. 'Coherence, hypothetical cases, and precedent'. *Oxford Journal of Legal Studies*, 10, 111–20.

Larkin, J.H. and Simon, H.A. 1987. 'Why a diagram is (sometimes) worth ten thousand words'. *Cognitive Science*, 11, 65–100.

Legrand, P. 1996. 'How to compare now'. *Legal Studies*, 16, 232–42.

Legrand, P. and Machado, A. 1998. 'Are civilians educable?' *Legal Studies*, 18, 216–30.

MacCormick, D.N. and Summers, R. 1997. *Interpreting Precedents: A Comparative Study*. Dartmouth: Ashgate.

Pinkwart, N., Lynch, C., Ashley, K. and Aleven, V. 2009. 'Assessing argument diagrams in an ill-defined domain', in V. Dimitrova, R. Mizoguchi, B. du Boulay, and A. Graesser (eds), *Proceedings of the 14th International Conference on Artificial Intelligence in Education, AIED 2009*. Amsterdam: IOS Press, 590–92.

Rissland, E. 1989. 'Dimension-based analysis of hypotheticals from Supreme Court oral argument', in *Proceedings of the Second International Conference on Artificial Intelligence and Law*. New York: ACM, 111–20.

Schafer, B. 2007. 'Can you have too much of a good thing? A comment on Bart Verheij's legal argumentation support software'. *Law, Probability and Risk*, 6, 209–25.

Schank, R.C. 1990. 'Case-based teaching: four experiences in educational software design'. *Interactive Learning Environments*, 1, 231–53.

Stenning, K. 2002. *Seeing Reason. Image and Language in Learning to Think.* Oxford: Oxford University Press.

Stuckey, R. 2007. *Best Practices for Legal Education.* New York: CLEA.

Tanaka, T., Yasumura, Y., Kaagami, D. and Nitta, K. 2005. 'Case based online training support system for ADR mediator', in *ICAIL '05 Proceedings of the 10th International Conference on Artificial Intelligence and Law.* New York: ACM, 234–5.

Teubner, G. 1989. 'How the law thinks: toward a constructivist epistemology of law'. *Law & Society Review*, 23, 727–58.

Teubner, G. 1998. 'Legal irritants: good faith in British law or how unifying law ends up in new differences'. *Modern Law Review*, 61, 11–32.

Van Joolingen, W. 1999. 'Cognitive tools for discovery learning'. *International Journal of Artificial Intelligence in Education*, 10, 385–97.

Verheij, B. 2007. 'Argumentation support software: boxes-and-arrows and beyond'. *Law, Probability & Risk*, 6, 187–208.

Yoshino, H. and Sakurai, S. 2005. 'A knowledge-based systems approach to educating creative legal minds', in H. Yoshino, K.D. Ashley and K. Nitta (eds), *AILE: Proceedings of the ICAIL-05 Workshop Artificial Intelligence and Legal Education*. Bologna: ACM, 9–13.

PART III
The Arts and Legal Professionals

Chapter 10
Is 'Beyond Text' Now Within Reach? Making a Case for Infusing the Arts into the Law Firm Experience

Valerie Fitch

Introduction

Law firms have historically shied away from change. They were, as a rule, cautious. They have tended to follow the pack in areas ranging from compensation to fees, to structure, to hiring and promotions. But these have been turbulent economic times for law firms and for the practice of law, and it may well be a time of re-invention. How, in this changing atmosphere, can law firms and legal educators seize the opportunity and infuse the legal learning culture with concepts drawn from non-textual resources? These concepts, such as trust of intuition, quiet observation and thinking beyond what we see, are not antithetical to, and in fact are vital to, the development of a truly creative legal mind.

The 'Beyond Text' project resonated with me because of my blended background of law and art. I majored in Art and Theatre in college, and had always been interested in the law tangentially, but more from the standpoint of the political process than the legal process. My first job was in advertising. This was (which came as a surprise to me) excellent training for legal writing. It taught me to write shorter sentences. It taught me that adding 'clearly' to a sentence absolutely, positively did not make anything clearer (clearly, lawyers love words ending in 'ly', but that's another issue). It taught me that economy of phrasing had more impact and that active voice was, most of the time, the only voice. It also taught me how to sell … whether an idea, a product or a service. Finally, it taught me that even the cleverest prose is rendered completely ineffective if the reader cannot remember what he or she is supposed to do (buy the product or agree with one side or the other). After graduating from law school and starting work at a firm, I came to learn that in a way, a client's legal position is not unlike a product a lawyer must sell well – whether to the trier of fact or to another lawyer on the other side of a transaction. Of course, the factual and legal precedential 'back-up' must be present as well.

As someone who had always been a student of process, who enjoyed mulling over why things were the way they were and who had an interest in history, I enjoyed law school tremendously. I became a professor of legal writing in 1991 while also practising as a litigator. I left practice a number of years ago, having found that teaching, crafting curricula and initiating change were what made me want to come to work every day. I became my firm's Director of Professional Development and I continue to teach law. As my background attests, I am, in the continuum of adult learning styles, a visual learner. This begs the following question: how could I have possibly enjoyed law school when those were three fairly non-visual years? Or were they? And if so, did they have to be?

The Challenge

The 'Beyond Text' project was an intriguing one because it sought to study legal pedagogy and practice in a new light; to examine whether the visual and movement arts could insinuate their way into the modelling of intellectual and ethical development of lawyers. It must be understood, however, that in the few years since the 'Beyond Text' project was initially proposed, seismic economic changes have taken place. The law firm business model may well be changing – forever. Business development skills and legal project management skills are being taught to attorneys to enhance client service and increase the communication of budgets and status updates in cases and deals. There are ongoing debates about the attorney billable hour, about staffing matters more efficiently, about associate compensation. Can the new law firm business model coexist with the idea of standing back, taking stock and encouraging a legal training and professional development movement that asks lawyers to learn through a different prism?

What does this mean for professional development in a law firm? What does it mean for the dissemination of knowledge and how we do it? What is needed? What will firms see as truly important for this new model? We are all trying to do more with less. Is this the ideal time for making the case for moving beyond text? Perhaps the best time for thought-provoking change is during enforced change.

But law firms tend to be cautious. There is something of a 'pack' mentality – what are other firms doing? Interestingly, one constant is that law firms all have art in their hallways and in their conference rooms, some of it quite good. There is an importance placed on having visually pleasing, stimulating artwork in the law firm environment. But it is rarely if ever discussed; no programmes are given on the artists or on why the firm chose a particular piece of art. Why is it there? What is there to see? If you look at the piece long enough, you will see more than you do when you merely glance at it while walking in the door. Can we get the creativity off the walls and into the very fabric of the legal education at law firms?

Law Firms and Training Formats

Most law firms expend a fair amount of resources on the professional development of their attorneys and, in addition, to providing mentoring, career guidance and coaching; they plan, create and deliver substantive training to all the attorneys at the firm at all levels. Their training is a blend of formal seminars (skills and knowledge-based) and hands-on training carried out in the course of a case or transaction. The typical subject matter ranges from trial and deposition skills to contract drafting and advocacy writing, to ethics and risk management, to practice group-specific training and much more.

Often, these programmes take the form of lectures, but they can also involve breakout discussions, with segments of hands-on work (drafting and editing, reading and interpreting contractual provisions). There is no doubt that for a visual learner, attending a seminar in a straight lecture format is challenging. The existence of an accompanying PowerPoint presentation does not make the experience much more visual. In fact, because presentation software is often misused and overused, a written visual presentation becomes the lecturer's script instead of a welcome visual addition. But if you have information that needs to be disseminated to a far-flung group of people in a limited amount of time, lectures (whether live or via electronic means) are perceived to be the easiest way to accomplish this task. They do not go 'beyond text' – in fact, they are highly text-based.

Is 'Beyond Text' Beyond Them?

We showed the film of the 'Beyond Text' project to a group of professional development directors and managers in New York. The film featured interviews with the participants, as well as many of the various physical and visual exercises that were part of the project's two meetings. It was fascinating to see the range of reactions. Not surprisingly, at the end of the film, when asked if their firms could replicate some of the work of the project, some just sat quietly, still processing what they had seen, and some immediately commented that their law firms 'would never go for this'. Some embraced the idea. Some assumed that the project was rigid, that it advocated the strict duplication of the exercises as opposed to the communication and incorporation of the concepts, so understandably balked at the idea of having their attorneys lie on the floor, stack chairs, wordlessly build a tableau, draw a picture, take a photograph or describe a work of art to another. These exercises were the starting place for conceiving the influences that these exercises promoted – movement, leading, following, interpretation, observation, building, tearing down, comparisons, exclusion, inclusion, teamwork, individualism, group dynamics, judgement and validation. That is where the challenge lies: in getting the firms to recognize the value that delving into these non-textual concepts can have to an attorney's creative thinking and critical analysis skills – and that they will become finer attorneys in the process.

Some Practical Takeaways from 'Beyond Text'

There are two specific exercises from the project that could be transferred *in toto* to the law firm experience. For purposes of this chapter, they are called 'Conceptual Meaning and Subtext' and 'Describe and Interpret'. Both of these can communicate and improve several key skills that attorneys need.

Conceptual Meaning and Subtext

In this exercise, the participants are asked to bring a camera and are given an envelope containing three things – which may be objects, symbols or colours. Their instructions are to take the camera, go out into the world and take a photograph that they believe is suggested, stated, implied, represented – the list is endless – by the object, symbol or colour. The direct connection to legal education here is that lawyers are often called upon to interpret facts, see beyond them, ask the unasked question, find a creative solution to the question: 'Can we do x for our client?' The more a mind is exercised and stretched, the easier those solutions will come. For example, one of the objects in the envelope is a postcard, featuring a photograph taken in the 1930s in Paris, of a group of people, recently arrested, sitting in a police station. The first problem is that it is already a photograph, so the challenge is how to take another photograph that represents this one. Think. What does the photograph show? What do you see? The subjects look furtively at the camera. What do you see? The looks on their faces project discomfort, despair and shame. How does one communicate these emotions? Go out into the street. Look. Watch. A homeless man sitting on a bench. A closed bar still reeking of the revels the night before. An empty storefront. A pigeon with one leg. Point the camera – what does the lens see and what is the person behind the lens seeing, interpreting, finding? What is the creative solution? And why did you make the choice that you did?

Describe and Interpret

In this exercise, one person faces a work of art, while the other faces away. The person facing the work of art is asked to describe it to the one who cannot see it, so that the person not looking can draw it. But there's a wrinkle – the 'describer' may be given a separate written instruction – to have the 'listener' add an element to the artwork, to take one away, to describe something completely different. It makes the describer think; retool, to have to observe one thing while adding another. Yet, the describer knows he or she has a responsibility to the 'listener', who must create a tangible representation of what the describer is saying. The describer cannot say 'it's the Mona Lisa, but my instructions are to communicate to you to make her a male and have her frown'. The describer cannot say 'draw the Mona Lisa except she's a man and isn't smiling'. He or she must use words that suggest the outcome without being specific. The listener is tasked with interpreting, in a visual way, what he or she is hearing from the describer. Both have to be very cognizant of the effect of their actions. They have to cooperate, yet act alone. There is truth and there are addenda. Lawyers need to be able to sift through information, see it for what it is and to communicate clearly with others. They may not have to draw, but it helps to be able to spell it out, especially when thrown unexpected or incomplete information.

In addition to the two exercises directly from the project, there are other ways in which law firms can enhance the professional development of their attorneys by including the visual and conceptual arts.

If They See It, They Will Learn It: Use Film

There are a number of courses that law schools and law firms teach that lend themselves to role-playing or filmed scenarios. In fact, none come to mind where at least some facet of the subject could not be more effectively communicated on film. Examples are: negotiations skills, client development, substantive topics, ethics, elimination of bias, feedback and review skills, deal and case management, etc. In a programme on Legal Ethics, film can show sticky situations between lawyers, between lawyers and clients – it's up to the audience to spot the issues and make their own judgements and, in discussions, voice their reactions and present alternatives to what they see on film. A lecture format could communicate the desired information to the attendees, but the use of film prompts interaction and increases retention because it suggests rather than tells, and it is up to the audience to mull over and accept or discard what they have seen.

If They Read It and Discuss It, They Will Learn It: Use Non-legal Sources

This may be a bit 'within text' as opposed to beyond it, but set aside that there is text involved and concentrate on the concepts that are being discussed. A successful Legal Ethics programme involves the study of moral and policy-based dilemmas that appear in works of fiction. The person who buys a lottery ticket saying he will share it, then wins; the youths who blow up an old man's house; the child who tells a lie that changes countless lives and so on. All of these involve a moment where a choice is made and the ramifications of that choice become more far-reaching than the actors imagined. The effect of this programme crept up on people and several noted that they did not 'get' how the issues related to their legal lives until several days later, when the 'aha' moment arrived. Lawyers make decisions and choices every day, as do their clients – the decision whether or not to pursue a claim, a line of questioning, etc., while consciously abiding by the ethical rules that govern a lawyer's relationship with a client. Looking at other sources for examples of influences and outcomes, good and bad, can help broaden the base of experience.

After 'Beyond Text'

The 'Beyond Text' project has an overriding theme: that we should always remember to strive to inspire others to think creatively. I tell my students that they should be creative when crafting a solution to a client's problem. What does that mean, really? Read the cases and the statutes, apply them to the facts and there you go? Yes and no. They should bring to the process their experience, their gut feeling, let the light bulb go on and create a solution, because without that creative process, nothing would ever be solved; we would simply have hills of problems. The more open lawyers' minds are to this process, the better equipped they will be to serve their clients. Law firms are client service businesses. They do not manufacture widgets; they solve problems. Firms are drafting formal Client Service Plans, populating the plans with client service initiatives and client service standards. When these are carefully read, the words used in them are thrilling – they describe actions, feelings and emotions that are non-textually based. Words like help, needs, intuitively, share, collaborate, trust, communicate and celebrate. These are skills, thoughts, efforts and feelings that cannot be taught solely in a traditional textual way. It is a time of great change.

The challenge for a law firm is to ensure that its lawyers never lose sight of the fact that, although text is key to crafting the questions, text alone can never provide all the answers. There is always context, wrinkles, unexpected rogue facts that appear throughout the process of delving into the issues. It is this muddy middle between problem and solution that has to be filled with creative thinking and powerful observation. By making an effort to communicate information and concepts in an inventive way, a law firm can better equip its attorneys to figure out, visualize, interpret, move forward, step backward, build, tear down, compare, work together, work alone, recognize what has come before while looking to the future and, most importantly, trust what they truly see.

Chapter 11
Were You with Me? Creativity, Dialogue and Self-Expression in Legal Process Narratives

Miriam Aziz[1]

Introduction

Is our imagination defined through verbal language alone? Or are we beyond words? What does it mean to feel speechless? How do we communicate *sans mots*? What does it mean to say: 'I have no idea?' In a letter to Marc-André Souchay dated 15 October 1842, Felix Mendelssohn wrote: 'What the music I love expresses to me, is not thought too *indefinite* to put into words, but on the contrary, too *definite*' (Mendelssohn 1864: 276, emphasis in original). To what extent, if at all, are words the most appropriate vehicles to convey human emotion? Do they compress communication at the expense of other communicative 'frequencies', so to speak? In his book *Ways of Seeing*, John Berger describes a 'new language of images' within which he argues that we can communicate our experiences with more precision (1973: 33). Berger's prevailing assumption is that 'Seeing comes before words' and, furthermore, that we make sense of what we see through language. I suggest that the definition of a speech act as part of legal narratives must be expanded to incorporate other forms of expression in order to expand our collective imagination of human experience. If, as Wittgenstein suggested, 'Uttering a word is like striking a note on the keyboard of the imagination' (Wittgenstein 2009: § 6), then we must explore the extent to which we may extend this precept to incorporating other forms of communication that we are trained to recognize. If, as Aristotle maintained, art forms such as painting and poetry represent examples of *mimesis* or imitation as a means to acquire knowledge (Aristotle 1996: 3), then artistic endeavour, as well as artistic appreciation thereof, may constitute a way to school our understanding of self-expression.

1 I am grateful to the editors of this collection for their feedback. I would also like to thank all of the members of Artist(s) at Large and the Baryshnikov Arts Center, as well as Giuliano Amato, Steven Battaglia, Galya Benarieh-Ruffer, Kevin Clermont, Huong Huang, Mattias Kumm, Joseph Weiler and Tracy Williams for their comments concerning earlier drafts of this chapter. Special thanks to Zenon Bańkowski for his support and encouragement. The usual disclaimer applies.

Musicians who work in recording studios often complain about the loss of frequencies when having to save their music in computer files which are easier to store.[2] Imagine going to listen to the Vienna Philharmonic perform Beethoven's *Symphony No. 9* and being able to hear only the melody and a few accompanying instruments instead of the whole orchestra – that is what listening to a compressed musical file (MP4) sounds like. Of course, you might be able to pinpoint the instruments that you are unable to hear at a concert, as you can see the instruments that you cannot hear. This is not the case if you are listening to an MP4 file, where as a listener, what you do not hear does not exist. To put it in other words: 'The limits of my language are the limits of my world' (Wittgenstein 2001: § 5.6). To what extent, if at all, does this apply to the norms and rules that govern legal discourse?

In my doctoral thesis on the regulation of human experimentation (Aziz 1997), for example, I argued that an adversarial model of regulation as articulated through the law of negligence, which is fault-based, was unduly restrictive at the expense of a complementary regulatory model based on responsibility and public participation. Victims of medical negligence are often left with doubts as to the veracity of the claims made of what actually happened; moreover, they often express the need for an apology – whatever the outcome of litigation – which is often absent. Indeed, the Truth and Reconciliation Commissions provide a useful case in point regarding alternative methods of justice. There, the testimonies being gathered are also part of a healing process where storytelling helps to bridge understanding. In my opinion, the wider the definition of expression (i.e. not solely restricted to words), the greater likelihood for truth and reconciliation if the context is one of responsibility rather than blame.

In *The Problems of Philosophy*, Bertrand Russell (1978: 6) asks whether we have any means of knowing whether there is any reality at all and wonders whether we have any means of finding out what it is like. One way by which we make sense of our experience – and that which we have acquired through hearsay – is through storytelling, which may be mediated in a variety of ways. The rise of multimedia art is no doubt a testament to the many ways by which human emotion is curated for artistic intent and purpose.

I suggest that a multi-sensory exploration of the dynamics of storytelling may be applied to teaching professional skills as part of legal education (advocacy and judgement drafting, and the rule of evidence, particularly regarding witness statements and testimony). My experience as a law teacher and as an artist has instilled me with a holistic sense of communication, particularly when words fail; human expression is multi-dimensional and multi-faceted. Art provides us with a way to engage with this complexity. For example, we readily understand the inarticulacy of a musician when being interviewed and his command of language once performing. My suggestion is that this applies to all human beings, who have

2 The metaphor is drawn from the capacity to compress files of music for digital distribution (e.g. from WAV files to MP4 files).

their own ways of learning and their own ways of communicating. My current work as an artist and as a legal scholar is dedicated to a project entitled 'Creative Thinking for Lawyers' (CTL) of which a music/dance/theatre piece that I have composed called *Were you with me?* is a useful case study.

I have been invited to outline the CTL project in more detail for this volume of chapters published for 'Beyond Text in Legal Education'. I propose the following; first, to give a brief history of the project; second, the project's aims; third, methodology and *modus vivendi*; and, finally, implications for future best practice initiatives and research agendas. Allow me to make the following observations: first, I concede from the outset that I have taken the liberty of including some personal observations about my experience of teaching law and working with artists. This may detract from my argument somewhat; however, I believe that such anecdotal evidence may in fact inform and shape a debate about best practices regarding pedagogical initiatives that arise in the context of 'Beyond Text in Legal Education'. Second, I have drawn from the writings of Ludwig Wittgenstein to the extent that his ideas regarding the theory of the mind offer valuable insights in addressing aesthetic perception in the context of legal narratives.

History

My approach to teaching law is inspired by the case method and aims to foster creative thinking through improvisation in order to explore ways of understanding the law as well as its mediation. Students are encouraged to integrate how they learn and in so doing, how to integrate that within a broad spectrum of diverse approaches to legal reasoning.

My experience of European Union (EU) law as an academic and as a practising lawyer was framed by the challenge of a *sui generis* legal order, superimposed over differing, centralized legal systems and cultures in EU Member States, that was predicated on the principle of subsidiarity whereby Member States are bound to EU institutions in a relationship built on cooperation regarding implementation of the *acquis de l'Union* (Aziz 2004). Member States struggle to retain a sense of statehood in the face of a supranational legal order which reconfigures and recalibrates national laws; at times, it may override or set aside national laws. EU law presents challenges to lawyers and public authority officials of Member States, who are ordinarily trained in a domestic legal system that not only commands loyalty but the norms of which are permeated by their own 'rule of reason and etiquette', so to speak. These lawyers and public authority officials must, however, not only be aware of the *aquis de l'Union* but must also cooperate with EU institutions and each other. Language is not the only barrier. Legal and bureaucratic etiquette or 'ways of doing things' is also a factor. Add that to the globalization of financial markets and services and the emergence of transnational or global law and governance, and lawyers are faced with challenges for which domestic legal education does not necessarily equip them.

The Internet is also a factor as it has sped up the way we work and live. Thus, the challenge is underwritten by both complexity and speed, which are separate yet related. Law students are trained to analyse treaties, legislation, case law and academic articles, and how to write essays and exam papers; does this equip them for the world beyond the law school, namely, to deal with complex, diverse legal systems and cultures and the speed with which they will be called upon as professionals to reflect, react and respond?

My teaching career began at the School of Law at the University of Edinburgh, where I was a PhD candidate; it was a mixture of lectures, the case method, and the tutorial method (Duxbury 1995). After obtaining my PhD, I taught at the *Otto Suhr Institut* at the Free University of Berlin; I was struck by the need to adapt my teaching – in terms of style and content – not only to my 'audience' but also to the realities of the German legal system and culture. Years later, when I taught at the School of Law at the University of Siena, Italy, I had to adapt once again. There I was particularly struck by the consequences of the classical approach to teaching, which was primarily in the form of lectures. My students in Siena were initially uncomfortable with being called upon to participate in class. I say initially, as they soon got used to my interactive style of teaching which was both formalist (text analysis, legal drafting, moot court) and 'supra-formalist', that is, I framed a classical approach to legal education, drawing on the case method, within the context of role play, improvisation and composition, which I had been exposed to as an artist interested in dance and theatre. I gradually began to observe how a more creative or playful approach to law teaching was able to engender a form of trust amongst the students who began to gain confidence through participation which stressed the need for basic technique as well as improvisation; teaching became a collaborative endeavour and, as is so often the case, I learned that whether I was teaching or researching law or whether I was rehearsing for a musical performance, it was a case of lifelong learning, with no comfort zone in sight! One exercise was comprised of asking four students to write out their own summary of a European Community law case on the blackboard. The class was then asked to vote on the summary that they preferred. I was struck by how unexpected the outcome was and I was reminded of the need to put myself in my students' position – of dealing with complex legal concepts for the first time, and not by force of habit of years of research and teaching.

My time at the European University Institute (EUI) exposed me to academics and practitioners trained in different EU Member States and disciplines – I began to see the need for improvisation and innovation needed to engage with one another. Good communication, the need to be clear, concise and coherent, is key. This is easier said than done. During multi-disciplinary discussions at the EUI, I would sometimes feel uneasy about the likelihood that in the absence of specific skills, analysis might become cursory, superficial or non-existent, particularly in cases where the subject matter was of a highly technical nature. I was not, for example, trained to analyse data sets or study conclusions based on economics – and it took a lot to gather the courage to ask questions, particularly when I was unsure about the questions to be asked. To some extent, we face this challenge in everyday life, that is to say, the presence of specialized, expert knowledge – when we consult a doctor, an architect or a plumber. I am loath to abdicate responsibility during such discussions to a doctor in the belief that the 'doctor knows best', although I also realize the limits to my understanding of complex issues that go hand in hand with specialized knowledge – and which, in my opinion, are not best dealt with by threatening professionals (medical or otherwise) with litigation should anything go wrong (Aziz 1997). I was struck by having to think 'creatively' about the information I was being given – to assimilate it so that I would understand as much as I was being told as possible. As anyone who has taught knows, we learn differently. Some people rely on texts, while others are more 'visual'. Human communication is also diverse. We often focus on what is being said at the expense of body language or omitting, for example, to pay attention to the meaning of silence.

Indeed, I sometimes make up cases when I am lecturing my students to see whether they will respond. They usually do – but it once took 45 minutes for a student to raise his hand and say that he must have prepared for next week's seminar, as he did not remember any of the cases I was speaking about! Then I confuse my students when they answer a question in class. While they are speaking, I may smile and nod, and then say that they are wrong or vice versa – I frown, and shake my head as they are giving me a correct answer and more often than not, they hesitate or simply give up and say that they may be wrong. I deliberately trick them, so that they become aware of body language and how body language can be used to deceive. Living and working as a lawyer in a variety of EU Member States, I sometimes had to rely on intuition. I had to observe facial expression, customs and tone of voice in order to gain a sense of what was being said, something for which my legal training had not prepared me.

My work as a musician, a dancer and as a film maker helped me a great deal – indeed, creativity is premised on improvisation (Cameron 1992; Tharp 2003). I would sometimes be performing with musicians I had met a few days earlier – and once I met a percussionist minutes before we were about to perform. This was not unlike walking into a room of lawyers in an international law firm for a negotiation. Taking a ballet class with teachers trained in different classical techniques taught me how to deal with different styles and 'rules of reason' of movement. Modern dance choreographers, in whose master classes I would participate, taught me how to come to terms with their way of working as well as with their approach to music and movement. I extrapolated from this experience to develop my pedagogical skills in order to encourage law students and practitioners to discover their own ways of seeing things and engage with others as part of good communication – in its diverse styles and form.

I began to think of ways that I might set up a teaching initiative in law schools and for other professions (doctors, nurses, architects, etc.) on creative thinking to inspire people to uncover, unblock and understand their capacity and potential in the face of complexity and speed in a globalized world.

Creative Thinking for Lawyers (CTL)

CTL is a teaching initiative which aims to foster imagination, innovation, improvisation and integration for lawyers and other professionals (doctors, nurses, architects, business executives, etc.) through simulation, case method analysis, role play and exercises in composition.[3] Its purpose is to focus on the development of a core of universal, transferable skills of problem solving, analysis, negotiation and decision-making, and presentation through active participation in exercises in creativity. There is a plethora of ways in which people assimilate and process information. However, legal education has tended to homogenize its mediation through the text; the narrative of case law recomposes, reinterprets and ultimately reduces conflicting accounts of human experience to the written word both as the highest and lowest common denominator. Is it possible to conceive of legal education and practice in ways that engage with the diversity of human experience and communication thereof?

The rationale of the method is as follows: are lawyers trained to respond to the challenge of globalization of law and governance? Are they able to react, reflect and respond adequately given the complexity and the speed (due to the impact of the Internet) with which global governance is evolving? The rules and the rule-making process are changing, and lawyers and other members of the profession are being called upon to improvise and innovate. Imagination is key. So too is creativity.

Legal education has tended to overemphasize learning by memory and passivity (lectures and seminars), despite efforts to introduce a case-method approach (which is participatory by drawing on the Socratic Method). How can students be encouraged to become active members of a cooperative and collaborative model of teaching and training? How can they gain a sense of themselves, thereby gaining experience and confidence? How can they retain a sense of enthusiasm for their chosen profession? Law is a vocation; it necessitates lifelong learning. How can they learn to communicate, to listen, to interact, particularly given that they are being called upon to work with colleagues who have been trained and practise in legal systems with different languages and legal and bureaucratic cultures? Given the theatricality of trials (Kadri 2005), it is easier to make a case for role play or incorporating acting as part of legal education.

The CTL method is a research and teaching agenda dedicated to integrating art appreciation and practice as a way of 'unlocking' the creativity of lawyers so that they are able to identify and realize their potential to meet the challenges of the

3 Which is being developed at Cardozo Law School, New York and Université Paris Dauphine (UPD).

workplace; so that they are able to develop a core of skills that are both universal and transferable; and so that they are able to succeed as professionals and not at the expense of their own sense of creativity and ultimately themselves. The aim of CTL is to devise pedagogical ways for unlocking creativity of law students and practitioners, which includes identifying and developing an individual's capacity for creativity through formal instruction (lecture, case-method analysis of legal texts, drafting and negotiation exercises) and 'creative' instruction (simulation, role play, composition exercises, 'storyboarding' a story, directing a scene from a play in class, drawing and design exercises, movement exercises derived from contemporary dance, voice exercises and use of audio/visual technology).

The aim is to develop a core of skills:

- Problem solving
- Decision-making
- Teamwork
- Reflection
- Participation

CTL may also be customized to meet the needs of a particular university course or organization (law firm, government agency, in-house law unit, etc.).

Introducing creative thinking as part of tertiary education is not a novel idea; businesses schools in particular have pioneered the link between executive training and creativity for some years (Hennessey and Amabile 2010).[4] The rise of the Technology, Entertainment, Design (TED) talks available online[5] has further emphasized the necessity of innovative and entrepreneurial thinking and project implementation. Given a global economy that shifts the sites of political, economic and legal authority almost in real time in both the real and parallel world of the Internet, professionals are increasingly being called upon to think quickly and 'outside of the box':

- Imagination
- Improvisation
- Innovation
- Integration

Having to think 'outside the box' has been accentuated by limited time and virtual technology; to some extent, communication has suffered, constraining and arguably undermining the 'dialogue' between legal professionals, their clients and, ultimately, society as a whole. The aim of fostering creativity amongst legal

4 See Professor Ray Michael's work at Stanford Business School: http://faculty-gsb.stanford.edu/ray/bio.html [accessed 25 July 2012]. See also Thieu Besselink at *The Learning Lab*: http://www.thelearninglab.nl [accessed 25 July 2012].

5 http://www.ted.com [accessed 25 July 2012].

professionals also aims at nurturing their capacity to listen, to empathize and to encourage a fuller sense of storytelling as part of legal process narratives.

A distinction must be drawn, however, between interpretation of existing rules and the elaboration of new legal norms. The former is sensitive to the context and the emotions of whoever expects justice to be done on the basis of those rules, while simultaneously upholding the value of precedent in favour of legal certainty. Otherwise, there is a risk that we fall prey to *Interessenjurisprudenz* (Heck 1968). Regarding the latter case and the formulation of new legal rules, it is here that creativity must be encouraged, nurtured and, indeed, expected.

A Case Study: Artist(s) at Large Roundtable/Open Rehearsal

On 11 August 2011, I convened a 'Roundtable/Open Rehearsal' of artists based in New York City by outlining aims that are separate, yet related:

1. to collaborate with independent artists on specific projects;
2. to provide a 'roundtable' discussion about art, health, nutrition, finance, marketing, networking, funding applications, etc. Artists have limited resources (time, money, etc.), so I suggested a 'bartering' system whereby one artist could offer a skill in exchange for another. So, for example, an artist might give feedback to a choreographer and receive a pilates or yoga session in return, or an artist might need health advice and might receive a lesson in flamenco in return; and
3. to continue research into the effect of music and movement on people's capacity to reason, to create, to innovate and to gather a sense of themselves that is empowering so that they may thrive both within and outside professional contexts (this is the basis of CTL).

Throughout 2011/2012, a series of workshops will be organized in order to convene a group of artists and law students and practitioners from different disciplines so that the 'roundtable' community can continue to experiment, exchange, innovate and ultimately thrive.

On 11 August 2011, three dancers, including myself, a musician, a photographer and a videographer met in Studio 6B of the Baryshnikov Arts Center in New York City.[6] I had also invited a select few for the last hour of what was designed to be a three-hour session.[7] I had composed a 20-minute musical score and had written out a 'time line' for the three hours which were in effect stage directions where I

---

6 Mariliana Arvelo, Jamie Chandler, Cedric Todd (dancers); William Catanzaro (musician/percussionist); Lena Adasheva (photographer); David Orme (videographer).

7 Which included an associate research scientist from the Metropolitan Museum of Art, the general manager of the Mark Morris Dance Group and the Director of Development of the Baryshnikov Arts Center.

stated the exercises I wished to try, the themes I wished to address with the goal of performing a 20-minute piece entitled *Were you with me?* at the end of our session.

Were you with me? is a dance/theatre initiative dedicated to storytelling. The *mis-en-scène* addresses the need for witnesses of our lives, both others and ourselves. New technologies have increasingly laid claim to our attention – it is more and more difficult to focus on one task at a time. *Were you with me?* is designed around the need to concentrate – to listen – to be responsive to oneself and towards others. Improvisation is a good way to achieve that – as long as it is directed and managed.

At the beginning of the three-hour session, I asked each dancer to write a sentence on a piece of paper, which I then set aside. The dancers then did their warm-up exercises as the videographer and photographer set up their materials. As there was a showcase performance going on next door, we did not use music and we whispered amongst ourselves. I had worked with each dancer individually, but they had never met beforehand. After an hour, I used a playlist of music that I had selected and set out some exercises: one dancer had to dance to the voice of another, who would tell a story; one dancer would hold up a sentence another had written and another would improvise; one dancer would be asked to dance a different rhythm than the one they heard being played; one dancer would be asked to interpret 10 different ways of expressing the same movement; dancers were asked to interpret a word that I would give them and then a sentence which became an idea for a story. By this time, the photographer and the videographer were taking pictures; I encouraged them to move with us around the studio space instead of limiting themselves to the 'sidelines' so that they would become part of the experience and that I might also, on seeing the pictures/film later on, learn a little more about the choices they were making on how they witnessed the rehearsal. These exercises were designed to create a 'distraction' to ensure that all involved remained sincere in what they were being asked to do and were not falling back on ready-made ideas and habits. Moreover, the exercises were designed to raise awareness of the various ways in which stories might be told – or withheld. This approach would also be adaptable to training legal professionals to the extent that they would be asked to engage with the dynamics of communication from different media, objects and mode or manner.

After an hour had passed, a musician called William Catanzaro arrived. He often accompanies dancers at the Alvin Ailey School and the Martha Graham School in New York. As he set up his instruments (mostly percussion), I started to experiment with whether the dancers could 'follow' and 'become' my voice, as part of an attempt to tell stories. William then joined us, using percussion, and the dancers were encouraged to dance with, against and beyond what he was doing, interspersed with a recorded soundtrack of the score I had composed. During the last hour, we had an audience of four people, who witnessed an open rehearsal which became a performance, based on the work we had been doing that afternoon. We used sentences that the dancers had written at the beginning of the session, such as 'I feel like I am in a cage'. We also asked the audience to give us a sentence which we could interpret.

By exploring how their sentences resonate through music and movement, we addressed different ways that their meaning could be interpreted, raising awareness to tensions between subjective and objective sensory data that underpins not language per se, but the way that it is used. One of our dancers stepped into a role as a director/editor as we attempted to render the sentence visible (for example, do you mean …?). Both success and failure in doing so, to my mind, are useful ways of searching for a process to understand the gap between language and meaning. I say to my mind, as this is an impression that I hope to develop further during subsequent rehearsals as I try to find a way to extrapolate this experience for the purposes of teaching law. According to Wittgenstein (2001: § 5.47), 'Logic takes care of itself; all we have to do is to look and see how it does it.' Stressing the visual component of human communication allows us to discern the logic or the 'organising principle' of a narrative or, let's say, to use a legal example, a witness statement so that as lawyers we are able to engage with the nuance of what is being said and try to gain an overall context. When a witness is asked to tell a court what he or she saw 'in his or her own words', lawyers as well as members of the public must be sensitive to the multi-faceted nuance of the content of a story and how it is told. Lawyer's intuition must be schooled to be able to engage with communication of emotion that may be 'beyond words' or may leave the storyteller speechless. For example, those who suffer from Post-Traumatic Stress Disorder (PTSD) after having suffered or witnessed atrocities are often unable to speak of what they have seen; their bodies speak in ways that are louder than words. How often have we felt that a poet has expressed an emotion that we feel but which we have been unable to express; how often have we seen a film in which we recognized ourselves or which resonated with our own experience? Art is also a vehicle; it is a mouthpiece or a *portavoce* which deserves to be included as part of legal education as well as part of legal narratives of justice.

Working with three dancers, a musician, a videographer and a photographer, while being attentive to the body language of the audience, was challenging. I both performed and directed music and movement in a way that enabled us to structure the enquiry *are you, were you with me?* Improvisation is both sensitive and susceptible to concentration lapses. As performance artists know only too well, a concentration gap due to tiredness, preoccupations and so on is immediately visible – though I played and drew from that not only as a source of inspiration but as an organizing principle. Furthermore, whereas I suggested dance phrases and themes, I did not interfere with the dancers', the musician's, the photographer's and the videographer's vocabulary – what emerged was freedom of expression which was underwritten by themes that were tied to the concept of the art of listening: are you with me? Listening is not only a skill or ability but is also an art. This is the case for lawyers as well – being able to engage not only with what is said but how it is said. Moreover, there is a need to address the absence of words as people also communicate through silence.

I have avoided focusing my attention on the intercultural context of communication as I believe that this is a separate yet related avenue of enquiry. However, it is submitted that engaging with the cultural context of legal discourse as part of teaching enables students to be aware of human communication that is diverse, even within the same cultural context (avoiding the pitfalls of attaching too much significance to clichés). Furthermore, through movement research, I believe that law students and practitioners could become sensitive to body language. The artistic director of a dance company based in New York relayed a comment by a member of the public who had watched a site-specific piece that he had choreographed at Battery Park in Manhattan and said that after the performance, she returned home on the subway and she started to see choreography everywhere. My model of CTL goes one step further to the extent that I wish to draw attention not only to the fact that the body speaks (Wittgenstein 1980: 23) but also that it is a duty of a lawyer to intuit, to interpret and to undertake to carry a client's words, for instance, as a *portavoce* who is aware of the variety of human communication.[8]

My model for a pedagogical approach to law training draws from ostensive teaching (Baker and Hacker 2005: 43), which provides that meaning is not in a word or an object but is part of how both it is used and how we use it, as a society and as an individual. It is used to generate associative habits regarding legal narratives as part of what Wittgenstein referred to as the '*Hinweisende Erklaerung*' or ostensive explanation (Wittgenstein 2009). To understand the 'complete dialogue' (Arnheim 1957: 208) inherent to human communication is to commit to the art of listening to the other, both within and outside the remit of words not only as a value per se but also as a fundamental organizing principle. Testimony may be mediated through words, silence, music, images and so on. In effect, this necessitates engaging with testimony as expression, communication and expression as well as the art of analysing derivative narratives (witness testimony – expert witness statements/reports – cross-examination technique – information gathering – procedural discovery). It is difficult at this stage to pinpoint a model as it is very much a work in progress. Moreover, given that improvisation underlines the approach to training and that it is relational and context-dependent, it is situation-specific, so to speak.

---

8 'What I give is the morphology of the use of an expression. I show that it has kinds of uses of which you had not dreamed. In philosophy one feels *forced* to look at a concept in a certain way. What I do is suggest, or even invent, other ways of looking at it. I suggest possibilities of which you had not previously thought. You thought that there was one possibility, or only two at most. But I made you think of others. Furthermore, I made you see that it was absurd to expect the concept to conform to those narrow possibilities. Thus your mental cramp is relieved, and you are free to look around the field of use of the expression and to describe the different kinds of uses of it.' Lectures of 1946–1947 (Malcolm 2001: 43).

Future Implications

The experience of the open rehearsal/roundtable was interesting, intriguing and intense. As one of the spectators wrote to me in an email the following day: 'I thought you were convening a workshop, instead I saw an improvisation performance. The energy in that studio was palpitating.' I posted a slideshow of photographs which archive the experience on the Internet.[9] Film footage of the open rehearsal/roundtable will be released as part of a short film documentary in order to archive the process of opening up the concept of storytelling through creativity.

The conclusions which were drawn were mainly twofold; first, that we wished to continue to work on *Were you with me?* collaborating with other artists as *Artist(s) at Large*; and, second, the initiative could be used to research ways of storytelling through music, movement and film, which could be adapted to the education of legal professionals (CTL) as well as truth and reconciliation initiatives.

Conclusion

The aim of my model of teaching which emphasizes creative thinking for lawyers is to explore legal narratives that are both particular and universal, underwritten by the inherent tension between the constructed self and the self that appears out of nowhere. It is a way of engaging with the world by drawing inspiration from and collaborating with artists and lawyers from a variety of disciplines.

The aim of this approach is to coordinate the CTL pedagogical initiative in universities and law firms. These aims are separate yet related ways of fostering imagination, improvisation and innovation not only as values in their own right but as a way of promoting communication amongst society as a whole in order to embrace the diversity of human experience so that we may address the following question: how do we understand what the limits of language are? How do we communicate about that or factor that limitation into legal discourse? How do we engage with discernible and indiscernible and understand the rule of relevance, both exogenous and endogenous? My approach to law teaching and to art is not to resolve such questions. Rather, it is to learn how to address the many ways in which we seek to answer them within the context of legal discourse.

9 http://vimeo.com/29714861 [accessed 25 July 2012].

References

Aristotle. 1996. *Poetics.* London: Penguin.
Arnheim, R. 1957. *Film as Art.* Berkeley, CA: University of California Press.
Aziz, M. 1997. 'The regulation of medical research involving human subjects: a comparative study (UK–USA–Germany)'. Unpublished thesis. Edinburgh: University of Edinburgh.
Aziz, M. 2004. *The Impact of European Rights on National Legal Cultures.* Oxford: Hart Publishing.
Baker, G. and Hacker, P.M.S. 2005. *Wittgenstein: Understanding and Meaning.* Oxford: Wiley-Blackwell.
Berger, J. 1973. *Ways of Seeing.* London: Penguin.
Cameron, J. 1992. *The Artist's Way: A Spiritual Path to Higher Creativity.* Los Angeles: Tarcher.
Duxbury, N. 1995. *Patterns of American Jurisprudence.* Oxford: Oxford University Press.
Heck, P. 1968. *Das Problem der Rechtsgewinnung: Gesetzesauslegung und Interessenjurisprudenz. Begriffsbildung und Interessenjurisprudenz.* Berlin: Gehlen.
Hennessey, B.A. and Amabile, T.M. 2010. 'Creativity'. *Annual Review of Psychology*, 61, 569–98.
Kadri, S. 2005. *The Trial: A History, from Socrates to O.J. Simpson.* New York: Random House.
Malcolm, N. 2001. *Ludwig Wittgenstein: A Memoir.* Oxford: Oxford University Press.
Mendelssohn, F. 1864. *Letters of Felix Mendelssohn Bartholdy from 1833–1847.* Edited by Paul Mendelssohn Bartholdy and Carl Mendelssohn Bartholdy, with a Catalogue of All His Musical Compositions Compiled by Julius Rietz. Translated by Lady Wallace. London: Longman, Roberts & Green.
Russell, B. 1978. *The Problems of Philosophy.* Oxford: Oxford University Press.
Tharp, T. 2003. *The Creative Habit.* London: Simon & Schuster.
Wittgenstein, L. 1979. 'Letters to Ludwig von Ficker', in C.G. Luckhardt (ed.), *Wittgenstein: Sources and Perspectives*. Ithaca, NY: Cornell University Press.
Wittgenstein, L. 1980. *Culture and Value*, translated by P. Winch. Chicago: Chicago University Press.
Wittgenstein, L. 2001. *Tractatus Logico-Philosophicus*, 2nd edn. London: Routledge.
Wittgenstein, L. 2009. *Philosophical Investigations.* Oxford: Wiley-Blackwell.

Links

Miriam Aziz: http://miriamaziz.wordpress.com [accessed 15 October 2012].

Chapter 12
'You Are Here': Learning Law, Practice and Professionalism in the Academy

Karen Barton, John Garvey and Paul Maharg

Introduction

Text is one representation of meaning in the world. There are many others, involving senses other than sight, which is the predominant (though not the only) sense used in reading and writing. This chapter considers two approaches to legal education that use forms of awareness in simulations that extend beyond text to interactions with people, communication technologies and – looking to the future – maps and GIS technologies fused with arts education.

Simulation is an ancient form of learning used in military academies and rhetoric schools for millennia, and in many contemporary professions and occupations. It forms a fundamental heuristic in the learning of many arts – music, acting, sculpture and painting, to name only a few – and is used by a number of professions (notably civil airline pilot training, business, and medical education). In spite of this rich context, the discipline of law has relatively ignored it until recently. The simulations discussed briefly in this chapter are being developed and used in an international initiative involving the Universities of Strathclyde and Northumbria in the UK, and the University of New Hampshire (UNH) School of Law. We use two forms of simulation heuristic in order to enhance student learning of professionalism and legal practice, namely Standardized Clients (lay people taught to simulate clients), and a digital simulation environment called SIMulated Professional Learning Environment (SIMPLE). To our knowledge, only a few law schools in the USA have ever used Standardized Clients and no other law school uses SIMPLE, but it is the convergence of the two that makes this initiative unique and of interest to legal educators in any jurisdiction. The initiative takes place within an innovative capstone programme at UNH Law School called the Daniel Webster Scholar Honours Program, which we shall describe briefly before outlining the simulation initiatives.

The Daniel Webster Scholar Honors Program (DWS)

The stated mission of DWS is 'Making law students client-ready'.[1] Although the programme does not presume to graduate new lawyers who are ready to take on all levels of complexity and recognizes that legal education is a continuing process, it does seek to provide a practice-based, client-oriented education, which prepares law students for the responsibility of representing others. As recommended by the MacCrate Report, the programme is a collaborative effort, which includes the New Hampshire Supreme Court, the New Hampshire Board of Bar Examiners, the New Hampshire Bar Association and UNH School of Law. Students apply to the programme in March of their first year of law school and are selected in the June following their first year. Selection is based upon overall ability to succeed in the programme, which includes evaluation of academic, professional and interpersonal skills.

Programme participants must meet all of the law school's requirements for graduation, as well as requirements that are specific to DWS. During each semester, in addition to electives, scholars must take specifically designed DWS courses, which generally involve substantial simulation, including: Pre-trial Advocacy; Trial Advocacy; Negotiations; a mini-series that exposes them to Family Law, Law Office Management, Commercial Paper (Articles 3 and 9) and Conflicts of Law; Business Transactions; and a capstone course that integrates and builds upon the skills they have already learned through the programme. Each student must also take four additional courses that ordinarily would be elective: Business Associations; Evidence; Wills, Trusts & Estates; and Personal Taxation. Moreover, each student must have at least six credit hours of clinical and/or externship experience. Following the mini-series exposure to Family Law, all students are trained to be DOVE (Domestic Violence Emergency) attorneys and they work with supervising attorneys and real clients during their 3L year. Students must obtain at least a B- in all DWS courses and at least a 3.0 cumulative school transcript grade point average on a 4.0 scale. Scholars who successfully complete the two-year programme and who pass the Multi-State Professional Responsibility Exam and the character and fitness check are then certified by the Board of Bar Examiners as having passed the New Hampshire Bar exam and are admitted to the New Hampshire Bar upon graduation (Garvey and Zinkin 2009; Garvey 2010).

1 For further information on the Program, see http://law.unh.edu/academics/jd-degree/daniel-webster-scholars [accessed 25 July 2012].

Standardized Clients (SCs)

SCs are laypeople who are trained to act as if they are clients for the purposes of enabling students to learn legal communication and client-centred skills. SCs can also be used in high-stakes assessment of such skills and capabilities. The methodology creates powerful simulations of client contact that enable students to practise and improve a range of skills, values and attitudes, as well as their knowledge of substantive law. Deriving from medical education initially but now used in a wide range of disciplines and professions, the SC approach also introduces to the legal curriculum a unique client-centred assessment instrument.

Careful training of SCs is essential to the success of the method. In the Glasgow Graduate School of Law (GGSL) at Strathclyde, which piloted the introduction of the technique in law in the UK, a training programme was designed to train SCs in how to deliver a scenario in an interview. SCs were also trained to assess a lawyer's client-facing skills. In a statistical study of the method, we proved that SCs could assess students as accurately as staff tutors, and SCs are now used at Strathclyde in high-stakes assessment of student performance at interview (Barton et al. 2006).[2] A version of this programme was used with SCs in UNH School of Law.

It may appear that SCs are simply acting to a loosely defined script and that the technique is really a form of acting; however, the reality is more complex. The ability to inhabit a role is central, but a key element of the training of SCs concerns the ability to think on several levels simultaneously. SCs need to be able to monitor their affective performance, their cognitive performance (for example, what information can be released, what questions do I want to ask as a client), and their improvisatory skills (when to lead the interview, how to deal with puzzlement, etc.). They also need to practise their ability to switch fast from in-role thinking to assessment thinking, with students being assessed on an eight-point global Likert scale.[3] Finally, they need to be trained on giving feedback

2 This international pilot (involving Clark Cunningham and Greg Jones from the Georgia State College of Law, and Karen Barton and Paul Maharg from Strathclyde) was designed by an interdisciplinary team (Dr Jean Kerr, Clinical Skills Unit, Medical Faculty, University of Dundee, joined us to advise on the project), which was also internationally funded – the W. Lee Burge Fund, from the College of Law, Georgia State University, the GGSL and the College of Law in England and Wales contributed funds to the project. For further information on the medical context of standardized patients, see Wallace (1997), and for a related initiative in SCs, see Grosberg (2001).

3 Training on each of the points on the Likert scale (40 in total) minimized unreliability and bias (Tamblyn et al. 1991). Among the extensive research carried out by medical educationalists on the approach is a body of articles analysing SC experiences. In one study on inter-doctor variation on managing headaches, conducted in Germany, SCs were used with real GPs, unannounced. In post-consultation discussion of their experiences, the SCs were 'very dissatisfied with the majority of GPs visited' and their confidence in

out of role, while referring back to the experience of being in-role (Bokken et al. 2009).

SIMPLE (SIMulated Professional Learning Environment)

SIMPLE is at the same time simulation software and a hitherto relatively unregarded method of simulating legal practice. Using the software tools, staff create in the software the simulation that they wish students to work upon. These sim tools are highly flexible, enabling staff to create quite open simulations of legal practice (for instance, where students may engage in extensive fact-gathering) or highly bounded or procedural transactions (for instance, the purchase and sale of real estate, or litigation). Such simulations enable students to focus upon client-centred skills and issues. Within them, students learn about the detail of legal practice and can begin to grasp the complexities of dealing with clients and practise ethical lawyering.

The software has been in use in a number of law schools throughout England, Scotland and Wales, and in the School of Architecture and the School of Management Science at the University of Strathclyde. They range in duration from one week to two semesters, from undergraduate first-year projects to postgraduate professional legal education transactions. The transactional method has, with the guidance of the GGSL at University of Strathclyde, been developed in different directions by others, most notably the RechtenOnline Foundation in the Netherlands, which was recently awarded a grant of 2.4 million euros to continue its work with a similar simulation system, Cyberdam. Transactional learning, based upon principles and approaches to learning, epistemology and social practice outlined by John Dewey and others, is a way of learning substantive law as well as the skills and values associated with its practice in society.[4] It is a heuristic that therefore involves students not just in knowledge application but also in knowledge formation. As many educationalists have pointed out, professional knowledge has a complex relationship with academic knowledge and we need to provide porous zones in both the academy and in practice where students can move between the two domains. SIMPLE enables students to do this.[5]

---

primary care was shaken by their experiences (Sielk et al. 2006). See also the meta-review of Rethans et al. (2007).

4 For further information on transactional learning, see Barton, McKellar and Maharg 2007; Maharg 2007; Maharg and Owen 2007.

5 The application itself has received several awards – in May 2009, SIMPLE was designated the best simulation toolkit in the IMS 2009 Global Learning Impact Awards and in September 2009, it received the Innovation in E-Assessment award at the Scottish E-Assessment Awards: http://www.e-assessment-scotland.org/?page_id=1109 [accessed 25 July 2012].

Convergence

Perhaps what is most interesting about this initiative is the extent to which the two hitherto separate methods of simulating practice – SCs and SIMPLE – will be used in complex simulations on the DWS at UNH School of Law. Strathclyde and Northumbria (Karen Barton and Paul Maharg) have been working directly with staff to create simulations where SCs are the clients not just at first interview but also throughout a transaction, and Northumbria is also involved in a technical capacity. The Center for Computer-Assisted Legal Instruction in the USA (CALI) is funding the provision of technical support to the project through Northumbria University as well as funding the second iteration of the simulation toolset for SIMPLE.[6] The result is a form of experiential legal learning that is cost-effective and sustainable, resulting in increased learning of substantive law and increased learning of client-facing skills. Above all, we believe that the professionalism of the students at UNH School of Law will be deepened, as will their understanding of the ethical basis to legal practice.

Progress to Date

Standardized Clients

UNH Law School has six trained clients. They have been used for an empirical study comparing Webster scholars with newly admitted bar members. The Law School now uses them twice per year for SC interviews with the Webster scholars. SCs also serve as clients and witnesses in the pre-trial ad simulation. The School has a training review session lasting about four hours before each evaluative session. There are currently four review sessions, two empirical study interview sessions and two Webster scholar sessions per year. UNH is looking to expand the use of SCs, as they can easily handle more students. Presently, the Law School is considering a SC component for all third-year students – at least on a voluntary basis to start with.

We have begun a study of their use within the DWS, and while the statistics have yet to be fully analysed, there seems to be a strong correlation in the initial data between DWS client interview training with SCs and significant improvement in elicitation of factual information in the case fact patterns. Future plans could include the development of interprofessional use of SCs and law students along the lines described by Westberg et al. (2006).

---

6 We are currently working with CALI on further developing SIMPLE, largely the software tools (simulation toolset and the simulation platform) and the development of a community of practice. See http://simplecommunity.org for updates.

SIMPLE

There are two SIMPLE sims under construction: one, with a significant amount of resources, will be used on the capstone project with SCs. The other, a fairly brief and lightweight sim, will be used to accustom staff and students to using the SIMPLE environment. Both simulations have been designed and implemented, and will bc run with students in the next academic year. We are also currently planning the convergence of the SCs within the SIMPLE sims.

In the next sections we shall examine in more detail issues of cost, feasibility and impact on student learning.

Cost It is a commonly held view that experiential learning – indeed, much interdisciplinary learning involving the arts – is expensive to design, run and maintain. We do not think that this is always the case: good learning design need not be expensive. We will show in some detail how high-quality experiences in simulation need not involve costly curriculum designs. High costs usually associated with this form of learning include:

1. high staff–student ratios;
2. the need for extensive teaching support materials;
3. the need to create multiple assessments for high-stakes assessment in order to prevent plagiarism;
4. the requirement to minimize assessor variation by standardizing assessor marking through the production of examples;
5. post-assessment scrutiny of assessor performance.

Standardized Clients

The following table is a brief general response to these issues.

Table 12.1 Costs of SC training and use

	Costs	SCs
1	High staff–student ratios	Academic staff train SCs, administrators organize their use with academics. SCs can be used for formative as well as summative or high-stakes assessment. They are paid daily or half-day rates for training and for practise as an SC. Staff–student ratios can be substantially lowered by their use in a curriculum.
2	The need for extensive teaching support materials	Specialist SC training materials may need to be developed (though some of these can be used for students too). Already-existing materials can be used to support student learning outside of the encounter with the SC. No need for resources to be developed for the SC–student encounter itself, since this is dependent upon experiential learning.
3	The need to create multiple assessments for high-stakes assessment in order to prevent plagiarism	No need when developing SC scenarios. As long as there is a range of scenarios, which is cycled regularly, there is very little opportunity for cheating.
4	The requirement to minimize assessor variation by standardizing assessor marking through the production of examples	SC assessment is calibrated during training, with occasional refresher training. SCs are cheaper than full-time faculty and, as we have proven in our correlation study, are as good at assessing students as faculty.
5	Post-assessment scrutiny of variation in assessor performance	No need. We do, though, as a matter of Quality Assessment, double-assess all failed interviews. The quality of assessment, in our experience, tends to be very high: in the vast majority of cases, we agree SC assessment of student performances.

The training of SCs is a cost factor – they are paid for the time they spend in training, and resources need to be collected that can be used in training – but we found in Scotland that the costs of training and refreshing this training were significantly lower than the costs of the conventional method of assessing student interviewing performance, namely videotaping students interviewing actors (the actors were paid, of course, for their time), requiring staff to assess the videotape and then sampling the results for variation, and standard-setting accordingly. Even using adjunct staff on a daily rate (often lower than higher-cost full-time academic faculty), the cost of using SCs in high-stakes assessment was lower than the costs associated with the conventional model.

SCs could also be used to give valuable formative feedback to students on their performance. In our experience in Scotland, students benefited significantly from the experience of interviewing a SC, then receiving immediate feedback on that performance (which could of course be videotaped so that students could review their performance later in the light of the SC feedback).

All these cost points were replicated in the UNH study. The SCs interview about 30 newly admitted lawyers per session and they interview 20 Webster scholars per session. This is a total of about 90 interviews per year. SCs are paid $18.00 per hour. $18 x six people x four sessions x four hours = $1,728 per year. This works out at around $19.20 per interview, including the cost of SC training. UNH also spent a total of about $300 using them in the various simulation roles, including during depositions.

Costs and SIMPLE

Once again, the following table is a brief response to the general issue of costs.

Table 12.2 Costs of setting up and running a simulation in SIMPLE

	Costs	SIMPLE
1	High staff–student ratios	Properly designed, SIMPLE can reduce staff–student ratios substantially.
2	The need for extensive teaching support materials	Once created, they can support multiple transactions and other forms of learning and teaching.
3	The need to create multiple assessments for high-stakes assessment in order to prevent plagiarism	No need. Documents in the SIMPLE environment can be variablized so that each document set is unique in legally significant ways.
4	The requirement to minimize assessor variation by standardizing assessor marking through the production of examples	Useful, but generally not necessary – see point 5.
5	Post-assessment scrutiny of variation in assessor performance	Depends on form of assessment process. Generally speaking, the more detailed the assessment (e.g. specific drafting clauses), the easier it is to assess without significant variation. Larger assessment tasks, such as assessment of whole files, will require some form of variation control.

As with most significant curricular reforms, the capital costs lie largely in the creation and set-up of new processes, new resources and training. Academics, administrators and technical staff need to plan the embedding of simulations within the curriculum and the effect this will have on other aspects of the legal curriculum. Simulation resources need to be created and set up within SIMPLE using the SIMPLE toolset. Staff and students need basic training on SIMPLE, using what we call 'sandpit' sims (the equivalent of learning how to do things in online environments such as *World of Warcraft*). Much labour can be saved if staff within a law school and indeed law schools themselves collaborate on the production of resources. For example, there are sample sandpit sims posted up on the Simshare website (www.simshare.org.uk) that can be used and adapted for almost any academic or professional curriculum.

Once these costs have been met, simulations can be a surprisingly efficient form of teaching, learning and assessment. We can, for instance, compare the delivery of a conventional Personal Injury syllabus within the Diploma in Legal Practice to a simulated transaction delivered using SIMPLE.[7] In the conventional syllabus, there might be a mini-lecture series, supported by 10 x two-hour seminars, multiplied by the number of students in the cohort (for example, 264), each seminar with no more than 12 students per group – adjunct faculty costs per hour for teaching alone would work out, roughly, at £18–19,000. There would also be the costs of setting an examination and marking and second-marking the results of the examination. Costs could rise, in the Scottish model, to beyond £20,000 for adjunct staff costs alone. These costs recur each year, increasing according to levels of staff remuneration.

In the alternative simulation model, much of the initial costs are sunk into resource planning and creation. Once the syllabus resources are online to support learning (for example, project information, transactional flowcharts (who does what when why how), webcasts and set-up of discussion forums for students), these only need to be updated each year, according to changes in the law or on account of student feedback. The ongoing costs of this are fairly minimal. The design of the simulated transaction itself can be resource-heavy; however, it should be pointed out that the software, SIMPLE, is cost-free, being an OER (Open Education Resource), and there are many simulation resources that can be downloaded for free and adapted (under Creative Commons licenses) from the OER Simshare site.[8] Staff need to be trained, both academic or adjunct staff need to be involved directly in the simulation and administrators will need to be informed about their roles in administering this relatively new heuristic. Students need to be informed about the syllabus changes, the background to the innovation and what expectations will be of their performance.

In the first year of design and implementation, then, the costs of the alternative simulation syllabus may be as high as for a conventional syllabus. Thereafter, the costs drop dramatically. The Personal Injury transaction was run by one academic as part of his teaching allocation, along with a visiting adjunct professor. Students wrote letters, memos, formal legal documents and the like to fictional characters,

---

7 Clearly, costs would vary according to the practices required by regulators in a jurisdiction as well as the local curriculum design in a law school.

8 For more information on SIMPLE, see http://simplecommunity.org [accessed 25 July 2012]; for more information on Simshare, see http://www.simshare.org.uk [accessed 25 July 2012].

played by adjunct staff – normally postgraduates, trainees and newly qualified lawyers – who answered student mail in character, using template documents or freestyle letters (called 'PI mentors'). They also acted as staff supervisors for the transaction. If they encountered any problems they could not solve, they contacted either Paul Maharg or the Visiting Professor, via a passworded forum. After the first year of set-up (and stripping out the capital costs of the software, which were considerable, since the software is now free, and Paul Maharg's teaching allocation), the annual staff costs for the new syllabus were around £9–11,000 – a significant saving, slightly less than 50%, on the staff costs of the conventional model of learning, teaching and assessment. When the main simulation scenario is changed, costs will spike, but not as much as in the first transitional year of shifting from conventional to experiential curriculum, and thereafter will fall to around half again.

The resources can also be designed to build, year on year, so that they are used efficiently by students and staff. The discussion forums, for example, are a valuable resource for students. In the GGSL we ran two passworded forums (one for plaintiffs and one for defendants) and archived the forums at each year's end so that students could search the forums for answers to questions they might have had. Over the course of a decade, hundreds of questions and answers were available for students – a remarkable resource for them, answering precisely the type and level of issues that they found difficulty with on the transaction. The same design that students used was also used by our adjunct staff. The PI mentors' forum was layered, year on year, so that the mentors could search the archive for issues that had been raised in previous years.

We would expect that the cost issues discussed above would be resolvable in a broadly similar pattern in the UNH SIMPLE transactions. What is unique about simulation used in this way is that the learning zone is not separated from the assessment zone, which is the norm in academic assessment. The two can use the same environment, such that assessment of work arises from the learning that students evidence in their case files. Where an academic syllabus has two main cost columns – teaching and learning resourcing, and assessment resourcing – SIMPLE has only one: the transactional case file.

Feasibility

SCs and SIMPLE Convergence

Using resources available such as SIMPLE and Simshare, and the experience that has built up around the use of simulation, it is entirely feasible to build transactions that will enable us to dovetail the two methods of learning and assessment. The shape is flexible and adaptable to a degree that is difficult to appreciate unless one takes part in simulation learning and assessment. Take, for instance, the following narrative.

The client (the SC) is injured at work. The client visits the law student and is interviewed. The law student opens a file and proceeds to investigate the factual and legal background to the case. The law student keeps in touch with the client by mobile phone, also reporting through SIMPLE on case progress, possibly taking instruction in another interview. After pre-litigation negotiation, the law student settles the case according to the client's instructions and winds up the file.

In this convergence, the face-to-face reality of client communications is underpinned by the communications with virtual characters in SIMPLE. The file comes to life, uniquely and entirely, under the hand of the student firm. Students learn not just fact-finding but also how to integrate client communications with communications addressed to other professionals, witnesses and others – and they learn experientially not just how to conduct legal business efficiently but also ethically.[9] Use of SCs also adds another dimension to the assessment of student capability. To date, we have used SIMPLE to assess students on the basis of whole-file, part-file or single documents. With the addition of SCs, we can now factor in the client experience as a literal actor (that is, someone who acts within the drama of legal practice) and use SCs to assess student client-facing skills and attitudes.

Flexibility

The use of SCs is not just applicable to capstone projects: they can be used at any point in legal education and assessment. They are being used, as described above, on the Diploma in Legal Practice in Scotland. They are also used on a course called the Professional Competence Course (PCC) in Scotland, which is taken by trainees 6–18 months into a 24-month mandatory traineeship. At Strathclyde, the interviewing module begins with an initial interview with a client, at the end of which trainees are given feedback by the client on their performance. Trainees then investigate the case and research the possible options open to the client, discussing these with supervisory staff if required. They then meet the client for a second interview at which they outline the work they have undertaken on the client's behalf, and begin to seek instructions from their client. Again, trainees are given feedback on their performance.[10]

SCs are also used in Scotland, in a modified form, for specialty accreditation of qualified lawyers, in the WS Society, Edinburgh.[11] They are currently being adapted by the SRA (Solicitors Regulation Authority) for use as part of an OSCE (Objective Structured Clinical Examination) within the newly redesigned Qualifying Lawyers Transfer Scheme (QLTS) – an assessment scheme for lawyers from other jurisdictions outside the UK wishing to practise in England

9 For examples of this, see Maharg 2007: Chapter 7; and Maharg 2011.

10 It should be noted that this programme has been phased out by the Law Society of Scotland and replaced by PEAT 2 (Professional Education & Training, phase 2).

11 For information about the Signet Accreditation, see http://www.thewssociety.co.uk/accreditation/index.asp [accessed 25 July 2012].

and Wales.[12] The use of SCs is also being designed for third-level undergraduate students in the University of Northumbria Law School as a preparation for the mandatory clinic work that all undergraduate students undertake at level four. There are plans to use the heuristic in other jurisdictions as well.

If simulation (either SCs or SIMPLE) were to be used on its own to replace a conventional syllabus, it would be a poor substitute for the variety of learning forms in the conventional syllabus – lectures, seminars and individual study, for instance. It might be argued that simulation should be adapted to suit a conventional curriculum. We would argue the opposite: experiential learning's power is best leveraged where conventional curricula are modeled around the student experience of the simulation as the focus of the curriculum. An example of this from Strathclyde is our use of 'surgeries'. These are used in place of seminars or workshops, but they use very little of the conventional discourse of seminars. Based on the model of medical consultation, this voluntary form of learning is available for students who want more intensive learning than is available from either the supervisor, discussion forums or online information. Students sign up for a brief time slot, normally 15 minutes or so. They do so because they have a specific issue that they need to discuss and resolve. In the surgery they outline their issue and a tutor enables them to resolve it. The learning is focused, tightly organized, intensive and brief. It can be face-to-face or online (for example, using Skype video). On one level, learning happens from the ground-up within the transaction: tutors will facilitate students in coming to a resolution of the problem that is the core of the surgery and may take this further in the direction of either policy or theory discussion, but the focus is on the practical issue at stake. On another level, though, the surgery model is an example of the out-of-role discussion that happens in many forms of radical theatre – Augusto Boal's *Theatre of the Oppressed* is one instance (Boal 1998).

The SIMPLE environment, which has been redesigned in its second iteration, offers flexibility through customizable widgets. For example, calendars and communications forums can be added to the environment.

Design and Set-up of Simulations

This is one of the most problematic elements of the whole approach for staff. It is a difficulty that applies to both SCs and SIMPLE. Detailed scenarios need to be set up for SCs upon which they are trained, and the detail should be sufficient for them to be able to improvise in 'safe' areas (that is, areas of the narrative that do not significantly affect the legal validity of the scenario) – but not so detailed that they become lost and confused in the detail that they are expected to recall during the interview. Practice and rehearsal by SCs is essential of course, but so is good scenario design.

12 For information about QLTS, see http://www.sra.org.uk/solicitors/qlts.page [accessed 25 July 2012].

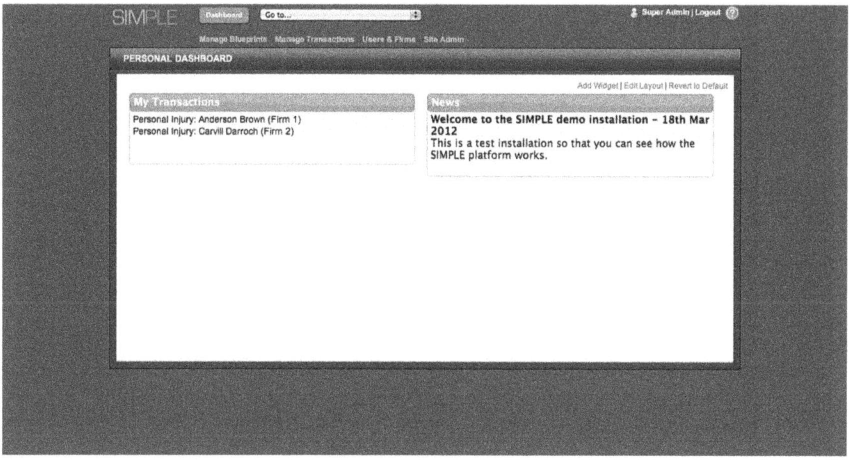

Figure 12.1 Generic dashboard

The same is true of SIMPLE. Often straightforward case designs are the most successful simulations, as they allow students the space to develop their own novice understandings of a case structure. Look at the following example of a Narrative Event Diagram (NED) for the Personal Injury sim.

The NED is shown in the Staff Tools view of the environment and illustrates the string of events that will happen in the simulated transaction. Documents can be 'triggered' or released by staff – here, the critical event that begins the narrative – and the narrative of the transaction proceeds from this. 'Player characters' are those who are actually playing the simulation, that is, students, unlike the virtual characters, who are 'Non-Player Characters'. The NED is a complex tool for creating sophisticated simulations, but much of the sophistication should remain in the background – for example, the variablizing of documents – while the scenario itself remains relatively straightforward. The skill that is required to create sophisticated yet straightforward simulations should not be underestimated. It is borne out of experience, but can be easily learned from others who have gone through the same process. It is entirely feasible that faculty can learn this design skill – experientially, of course.

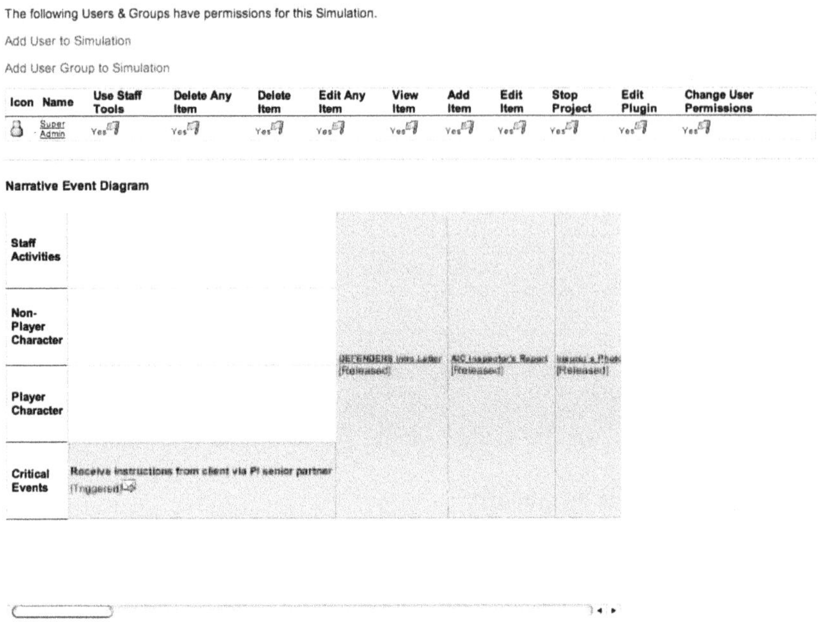

Figure 12.2 NED, Pursuer's sim

Possible Futures: Maps, Simulation and Legal Learning

There are many directions in which these implementations can be taken, and this final section of the chapter describes one where the digital arts can play a part. An element of the simulation functionality of SIMPLE is the creation of a simworld based not upon a multi-user virtual environment (MUVE) such as *Second Life*, but a map. In the GGSL, all transactions in the Diploma and the PCC took place in a typical Scottish west-coast provincial town, on the south bank of the River Clyde and to the west of Glasgow, called Ardcalloch. In 1999 the first sense of an online space given to students was a webpage consisting of a photo-montage, later developed as a rather crude schematic map with no interactive features (Figure 12.3). The following year (2000–2001), the map was redrawn so that it was graphically more sophisticated and included website links built into the map. Zoom links were added to the top-level district names, such as Alba Industrial Estate. These resources were gradually increased – in 2001–2002, a directory was added as the number of characters, businesses and institutions grew in size.

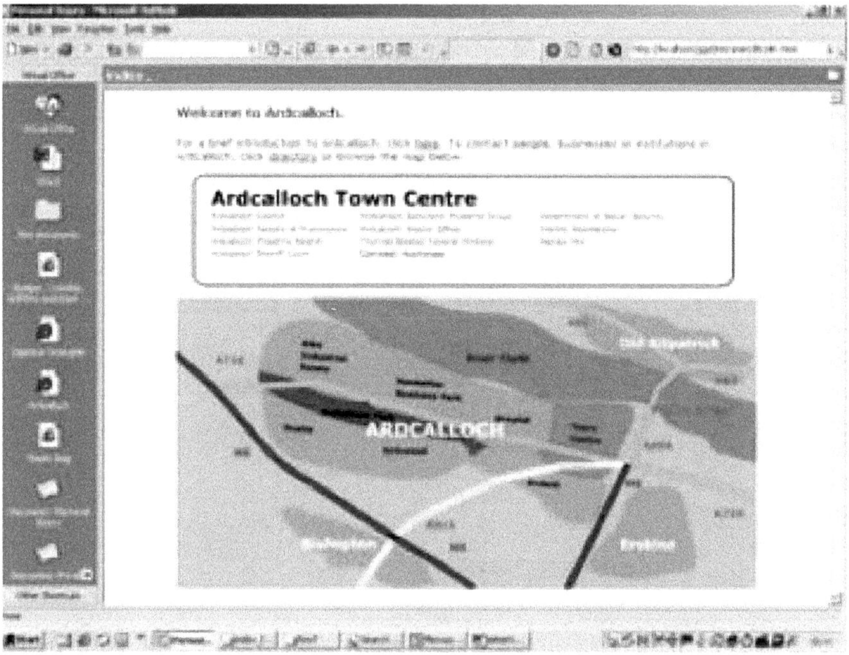

Figure 12.3 Early map overview of Ardcalloch

The map was redesigned as a Flash application, zoomable, with many small photographs attached to streets to give a sense of an actual place (Figure 12.4).[13]

The following graphic (Figure 12.5) shows the most recent iteration of the town. The photographs have been hidden, but the zoom is much more finely granular.

As the number of websites grew, it became important to manage their development as mini-projects and to consider the interface with users of the virtual environment. It was not possible for us to create a generic web template for our town sites. In reality, commercial and institutional website design is really only limited by the funds available, the creative flair and, it might be added, the bad taste of the designers. It was necessary for us to create sites that gave a presence of a business or an institution to the viewer, without importing into the site all the actual functionality of a real commercial site – and so many of our sites are 'brochure' sites. Some have more extensive and complex text than others – in part, this is due to the enthusiasm of particular designers, and we were happy to give them relatively free rein on this.

13 The photographs were taken of local urban centres in Refrewshire and Ayrshire that would approximate the look and feel of Ardcalloch. Care was taken to ensure that the photographs matched the street locale.

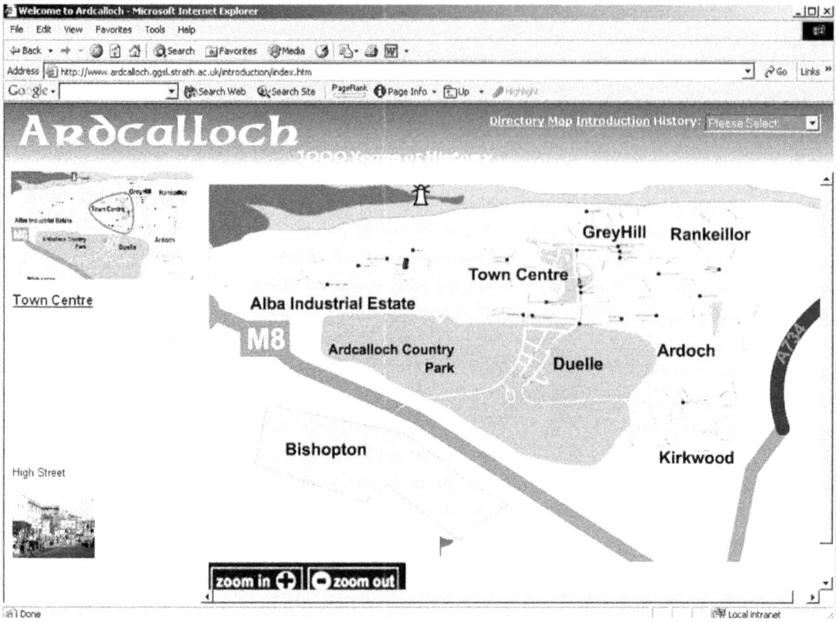

Figure 12.4 Zoomable map of Ardcalloch, overview, showing town centre by default. Note the street photographs at the bottom-left

After all, if the websites in the town all had a similar look and feel or simply dealt with matters relating to the projects, there would be no sense of realia, of the sheer randomness of reality, about the town.

The town was the function of its creation, much as islands in *Second Life* look less like real islands and are more the function of the creator. Alba Industrial Estate, for instance, was used by the PCC at the GGSL. Sited there was a multinational company called Global. This company, with headquarters in California, entered the Scottish economy in the wave of the NASDAQ Confidence in the mid-1990s to produce products for the European market and to take advantage of local research and development (R&D) expertise in the universities in Glasgow, as well as government and EU grants. The global downturn has required them to withdraw from Ardcalloch and this has created a range of legal problems, which form the basis of many of the modules within the course – for example, criminal law (a break-in at the warehouse), intellectual property (IP) rights (who owns which rights when Global retrenches) and family law (a director wishes to divorce his wife). Some of these problems are the focus of several modules, so that trainees are able to work on the same legal problem from a variety of different perspectives.

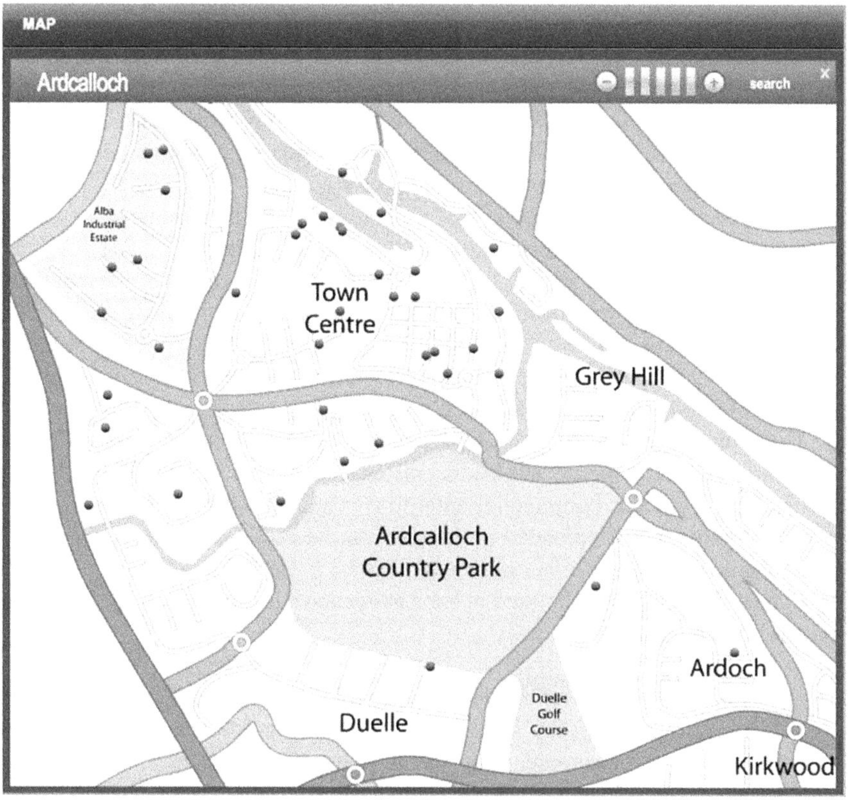

Figure 12.5 Latest iteration of Ardcalloch map

Though the first of its kind, our use of mapping in legal education had deficiences, which had little to do with its fictionality and more to do with its interactivity, or lack of it. Our map was really a paper map on the web; it gave some contextual information but little else. Students would typically visit, be interested and then would use the Directory for the addresses that were required for their projects. Occasionally they would visit a company or institutional website to find a name or contact not in the Directory. The map itself was relatively ignored because it was irrelevant to most of their document-based work. There was almost no functionality that would be useful to their working lives. There is no reason why such data should not be useful, though – all that was lacking was imagination and analysis. Place, after all, is a contextual tool for work, as a number of online workflow and task managers point out.[14]

---

14 *Omnifocus*, for example, based closely on the popular work of David Allan, defines tasks partly in terms of context, and context is defined as closely related to tool,

At the same time as we were developing a map of Ardcalloch, of course, Internet commerce, and Google in particular, was mapping the real world, and the technologies of digital cartography were fast developing in the commercial and public spheres. In addition, bodies of theory and practice grew up around these technologies, focusing on the tendency for data to converge and become geospatial, where places and bodies intersect with technology and data to give an enhanced understanding not just of embodiment and topography but also of contextual culture, history, geography and much else (Abrams and Hall 2006). Harmon (2004) explored all this through a remarkable collection of personal and data maps, based upon the locative function of maps: they tell us where we are. She subverts this idea of maps by producing subversive maps that tell us quite different narratives about ourselves – approaches also developed in different domains by Turchi (2009) and Bhagat and Mogel (2008).

There are many practical examples of this in our everyday lives. Google Maps and Earth incorporate Wikipedia entries. Global positioning satellite (GPS) applications are major commercial enterprises (satnav and marine shipping, for instance); photographs uploaded to the web can be geotagged; and our journeys with GPS-aware devices in our possession can be tracked and recorded.

Can such technologies be used in legal education? They can, and the following are three examples:

1. *Visualizing conversations*. In Maharg (2011), I analyse a conversation fragment generated by a student firm on a firm-specific forum, where it is discussing its project. One of the points I make is that the rhetorical space of the forum is significantly different from any other form of dialogic or multi-logic communication, not least because the resulting discussion fed in from at least seven different media (landline phone, mobile phone, voicemail, phone text, Instant Messenger, email and forum text). One of the problems for students was to converge these media to ensure that no important communication was lost. If this is to be designed, then it could be argued that participants might want to see the temporal, locative, personal and semantic patterns created by their communications (Donath 2002). A map of tagged communications with a record of where in-firm communications are generated might also help students to understand work patterns.
2. *Synchronous updating*. This is described in detail in the Conclusion to Maharg (2007: 283–6). If a website is used in a simulation, it could be updated synchronously when an action is triggered or completed in a simulation, and this could include the insertion, deletion or emendation of data in a map.

person or location, for example, phone, work colleague or specific locale with which the task is associated.

3. *Participatory and annotative mapping* (Tripodi 2008; see also Eckardt 2008). This is an example of user cartography, where the detail of a map is added to not by the cartographer but by map users, often in peer production. Since the widespread introduction of geographic information systems (GIS), these mapping projects have been significant examples of peer productions (Benkler 2006). Recently Google announced that for users in the USA, it was launching a tool called *Map Maker* (http://www.google.com/mapmaker) that allowed users to correct (for example, place markers) and add data to Google's map of the USA. In addition, users could upload much more personal data, including favourite coffee houses, detailed maps of a campus, streetview photographs, etc.[15]

While Google is certainly not creating an open source resource, it is clear that it is leveraging the participative power underlying other initiatives such as Wikipedia. In truth, Google was only following in the footsteps of other, more radical projects – the *Urban Tapestries* project, for instance, in 2004–2007, which, by embedding narratives and data such as photographs, video and audio with GIS, created a contemporary form of Mass Observation archive based upon digital maps (http://urbantapestries.net/). A related project was *34n 118w* (http://34n118w.net/), set in a locale in Los Angeles called the Freight Depot that, through fictional first-person narratives and texts, explores the modalities of speed, time and the power of earlier technologies (specifically telegraph and railways). An annotative project such as this is not fictionally based as is Ardcalloch, but it uses fiction to retell a scripted narrative about the past of a specific locale – a past that inevitably involves law as well as technology.

Such annotative and participative projects have obvious applications in legal education. Law is part of the distributed system of regulation and is enacted within networks and local cultures (Castells 2004). Students could for instance become involved in historical data-mapping projects (the Holocaust Initiative, at http://www.ushmm.org/museum/exhibit/focus/maps/googleearth.php, is one example) or contemporary projects that track human rights abuses (such as Eyes on Darfur, http://www.eyesondarfur.org/), engage in multi-disciplinary socio-legal projects that map indices of socio-economic status against crime, or volunteer to help use GIS applications in global emergencies (the Hurricane Katrina map provides an excellent example of this).[16]

15 There is an extensive literature on the Internet. See, for example, blogs such as Frank Jacobs' *Strange Maps*: http://bigthink.com/blogs/strange-maps [accessed 25 July 2012].

16 http://gregstoll.dyndns.org/scipionus/katrina.html [accessed 25 July 2012]. For more information on the Darfur project, see Martin 2007.

Impact on Student Learning

Lawyer Feedback on SCs

What do students tell us about the experience of learning experientially with these approaches? Their feedback is remarkably positive about the experience. On the GGSL Diploma, for instance, although formative feedback sessions with SCs were voluntary, we found that, annually, over 90% of the student cohort signed up for them. The PCC Interviewing module was consistently rated as one of the best on the course by trainees. When interviewed on whether they felt that the experience of working with and being assessed by SCs was useful for future practice experience, the newly qualified lawyers from the DWS gave similarly positive feedback:

> 'When I reflect on my law school tenure, the standardized client experience was the most educational aspect of my legal training. It set a foundation for me to begin the practice of law. As a new lawyer, I feel confident meeting with a client because I know I can rely on the interviewing and counseling skills I learned through the process.'

> 'Learning client interviewing skills by actually interviewing standardized clients was excellent preparation for practice. As a practicing attorney, I have found that interviewing and counseling clients are the most important tasks I perform. An attorney cannot satisfy clients unless she has a good understanding of client goals. To learn these goals, an attorney must build rapport with a client, ask probing questions, and convert legal knowledge into roadmaps that help clients understand their options. Such skills cannot be learned from textbooks, but only through practice. Interviewing standardized clients was an opportunity to develop these skills which are critical to my law practice.'

> 'I've been practicing now for almost a year and on a daily basis I receive a call from one of my clients, usually a school district superintendent, who has a legal problem and needs my advice. Because of my training using standardized clients in the Daniel Webster Scholars program, I am able to place myself in the right mindset and really listen to my client. I rarely feel intimidated or nervous; rather, I remain calm, ask questions, and elicit the information I need. The standardized client process taught me about the importance of building rapport with my clients, and as a result of my training, my clients trust my advice, feel confident in my abilities, and call me back frequently when they have a new legal question.'

Student Feedback on SIMPLE Sims

As described above, the SIMPLE sims are still in the process of being assembled and have yet to be implemented. In lieu of feedback from UNH students, here is feedback from students at the GGSL (extracted with permission from reflective reports):

> 'I felt that one of the things we could have improved on was the checking of our correspondence before sending. On at least two occasions we had to send letters apologising for previous inaccuracies, or for mistakes to people we had sent letters to. In practice this would suggest a lack of professionalism, and would be unforgivable. It also led to inefficiency in the long run, wasting time on extra letters.'

> 'If we had thought a little harder we could have minimized the number of letters we sent, by requesting all relevant information form a person in one go, rather than having to continually request further details. This was particularly true of our correspondence with [the client], and in real life I suspect that a client would get a bit impatient if he was constantly harassed for more evidence. I did feel that we all lacked a little bit of experience in such matters; knowing what to ask for and from whom, and I am confident that this exercise has helped us in that regard.'

> 'I found the whole experience to be extremely worthwhile. I believe it was a close as students will get to experiencing the 'real thing' before we commence our traineeships. It certainly taught us the importance of fact-gathering before jumping in and trying to find a solution.'

> 'The negotiation project certainly helped focus attention on letter writing skills and general IT skills ... Furthermore, where most projects/essays in the undergraduate degree have concentrated on testing your legal research skills the negotiation project was probably the first assignment that I have done that has highlighted the importance of fact-gathering. Finally the negotiation project gave you the opportunity to participate in the whole transaction from start to finish and take pride in the final settlement that you helped to achieve.'[17]

17 For a discussion of how simulation in SIMPLE enhances ethical learning in conflict situations, see Maharg 2007: Chapter 7.

Conclusion

Many features of simulation learning, whether face-to-face as with SCs or in virtual sims as with SIMPLE, actually derive from arts-based activities and often can be subversive in ways that we do not expect, precisely because they focus less on the acquisition of knowledge and more on how such knowledge changes social relations as it is applied in professional practice.[18] The theme is an ancient one in art, and simulation merely draws upon that power to engage and reveal situation, character, power relations and much else.

Many of the points raised by students in feedback here are supported by the literature on simulation and other forms of experiential learning. Above all, they show that simulation has an important role to play in how students learn professionalism. It is a role that deserves to have a much more prominent role in our law schools than it has had hitherto. From John Dewey onwards, there have been alternatives available to us that challenge current hegemonic forms of legal learning – the first step is to recognize that things can be different and better, and then follow up with action.

But knowing where we are is a necessary precondition to knowing how to get to where we want to go. 'You are here', states the pin-tag in many online maps – we need to orient ourselves to position, altitude and direction before we decide where and how to travel. Simulation and role play can give us that sense of where *we* are as teachers and can also give learners the opportunity to ask profound questions relating to social contexts and identity: am I really here? Is this who I am? Who thinks that of me? Simulation does more, though. Through practice, feedback and the opportunity to engage in practice thinking, it can also point us in directions that we had not considered we might want to go in: it is replete with future possibilities for change in social relations. In this sense, like many arts-based approaches to legal education of which it is one example, it can effect transformational change.

References

Abrams, J. and Hall, P. 2006. *Else/where: Mapping New Cartographies of Networks and Territories*. Minnesota: University of Minnesota Design Institute.

Barton, K., Cunningham, C., Jones, G. and Maharg, P. 2006. 'Valuing what clients think: standardized clients and the assessment of communicative competence'. *Clinical Law Review*, 3, 1–60.

Barton, K., McKellar, P. and Maharg, P. 2007. 'Authentic fictions: simulation, professionalism and legal learning'. *Clinical Law Review*, 14(1), 143–93.

18 In our Ardcalloch maps and associated documents, for instance, we had students writing for the newspaper, and in one article they noted there were more lawyers than nurses in Ardcalloch, and wondered if this was good for the town.

Benkler, Y. 2006. *The Wealth of Networks*. New Haven, CT: Yale University Press.

Bhagat, A. and Mogel, L. 2008. *An Atlas of Radical Cartography*. New York: Journal of Aesthetics and Protest Press.

Boal, A. 1998. *Theatre of the Oppressed*. New York: TCG Publishers.

Bokken, L., Linssen, T., Scherpbier, A., van der Vleuten, C. and Rethans, J.J. 2009. 'Feedback by simulated patients in undergraduate medical education: a systematic review of the literature'. *Medical Education*, 43(3), 202–10.

Castells, M. 2004. *The Power of Identity, The Information Age: Economy, Society and Culture*, vol. II, 2nd edn. Cambridge, MA: Blackwell.

Donath, J. 2002. 'A semantic approach to visualizing online conversations'. *Communications of the ACM*, 45(4), 45–9.

Eckardt, F. (ed.). 2008. *Media and Urban Space: Understanding, Investigating and Approaching Mediacity*. Berlin: Frank & Timme GmbH.

Garvey, J.B. 2010. 'New Hampshire's performance-based variant of the Bar Examination: the Daniel Webster Scholar Honors Programme moves beyond the pilot phase'. *The Bar Examiner*, 14, 13–22.

Garvey, J.B. and Zinkin, A.F. 2009. 'Making law students client-ready: a new model in legal education'. *Duke Forum for Law & Social Change*, 1, 101–29.

Grosberg, L.M. 2001. 'Medical education again provides a model for law schools: the Standardized Patient becomes the Standardized Client'. *Journal of Legal Education*, 51, 212–34.

Harmon, K.A. 2004. *You Are Here: Personal Geographies and Other Maps of the Imagination*. Princeton: Princeton Architectural Press.

Maharg, P. 2007. *Transforming Legal Education. Learning and Teaching the Law in the Early Twenty-first Century*. Aldershot: Ashgate Publishing.

Maharg, P. 2011. 'Space, absence, silence: the intimate dimensions of legal learning', in P. Maharg and C. Maughan (eds), *Affect and Legal Education: Emotion in Learning and Teaching the Law*. Aldershot: Ashgate Publishing, 283–306.

Maharg, P. and Owen, M. 2007. 'Simulations, learning and the metaverse: changing cultures in legal education'. *Journal of Information, Law, Technology*. Special Issue on law, education, technology, 1. Available at: http://www2.warwick.ac.uk/fac/soc/law/elj/jilt/2007_1/maharg_owen [accessed 25 July 2012].

Martin, M. 2007. 'Satellite tracks human rights abuses'. *Tell Me More,* National Public Radio News, interview transcript, 11 June. Available at: http://www.npr.org/templates/story/story.php?storyId=10935094 [accessed 25 July 2012].

Rethans, J.J., Gorter, S., Bokken, L. and Morrison, L. 2007. 'Unannounced standardized patients in real practice: a systematic literature review'. *Medical Education*, 41(6), 537–49.

Sielk, M., Brockmann, S., Spannaus-Sakic, C. and Wilm, S. 2006. 'Do standardized patients lose their confidence in primary medical care? Personal experiences of standardized patients with GPs'. *British Journal of General Practice*, 56(531), 802–4.

Tamblyn, R.M., Klass, D.J., Schnabi, G. and Murray, L. 1991. 'Sources of unreliability and bias in standardized-patient rating'. *Teaching and Learning in Medicine*, 3(2), 74–85.

Tripodi, L. 2008. 'Cartografia resistente: an experience of participatory mapping implementing open source technology', in F. Eckardt, J. Geelhaar, L. Colini, K.S. Willis, K. Chorianopoulos and R. Hennig (eds), *Mediacity. Situations, Practices and Encounters*. Berlin: Frank & Timme GmbH.

Turchi, P. 2009. *Maps of the Imagination: The Writer as Cartographer.* San Antonio: Trinity University Press.

Wallace, P. 1997. 'Following the threads of an innovation: the history of standardized patients in medical education'. *Caduceus, A Humanities Journal for Medicine and the Health Sciences*, Southern Illinois University School of Medicine, 13(2), 5–28.

Westberg, S.M., Adams, J., Thiede, K., Stratton, T.P. and Bumgardner, M.A. 2006. 'An interprofessional activity using standardized patients'. *American Journal of Pharmaceutical Education*, 70(20), 34–41.

Chapter 13

Beyond the Text: Critique and Creativity

Bruce Anderson and Kim Morgan

Legal Texts

Law students, lawyers, judges and legal scholars love their texts. Statutes and judicial decisions are dutifully collected, lovingly stored, carefully protected and proudly displayed in special libraries. These texts are discovered, scrutinized, interpreted, compiled, cited, quoted, compared, distinguished, applied, defended and, above all, revered. For the legal profession the text is the law. Law teachers collect and organize these texts in their casebooks and textbooks. Law students learn to read and dissect them. Lawyers construct their opinions and arguments based on legal texts. And judges are the arbiters of texts. Rules and principles are discovered in texts. The solutions to problems are in texts. And a 'great legal mind' is one who can manoeuvre effortlessly through and around, in and out of legal texts. To state it simply, legal education and practice begin and end with texts.

Contemporary legal theory reflects this obsession. In Jurisprudence classes we are drawn into the great debates among legal positivists about how we should distinguish legal from non-legal texts and about what we should do when we run out of legal rules. We also learn about the literal, golden and purposive rules for interpreting texts. We even read that law is an interpretive practice. Other legal theorists focus on legal discourse, rhetoric and the language of law. And legal reasoning is portrayed as deriving outcomes from texts and facts, and then making those outcomes consistent and coherent with other legal texts. To put it another way, the world of legal theorists is also a world of texts.

Placing legal texts at the centre of law has led to a slavish reliance on the written word. Legal education comes to stress the technical skills of the profession. Law students graduate with neither the interest in nor the capacity for reflecting on the methods and values of their profession. Disciplines beyond their legal texts are relevant to lawyers only to the extent that they can be used to bolster their side of the argument. This fixity in thinking can become manifest in simple-minded judicial decisions when intelligence is needed, conventional decisions when creativity is called for and legally correct decisions when justice is demanded. And the danger for legal scholarship is that it becomes focused on ironing out doctrinal inconsistencies or calculating the legal tactics best suited to promoting progressive politics.

By contrast, visual artists are primarily interested in images and objects, not texts. Further, they are widely acknowledged to be imaginative and creative people. As such, it makes sense to ask whether visual artists can help law students, lawyers and judges get beyond their texts to engage in more thoughtful and critically reflective practices. In the following two sections of this chapter I we will explore this challenge.

Beyond the Text

Although we take it for granted that visual artists are creative types, few people seem to know what it is that artists actually do. For instance, we have probably all seen the sorts of weird objects and things sculptors make and exhibit in galleries or in the street, but what exactly is their art about? Why do they make such things? It seems worthwhile to briefly consider these questions before going on to see if lawyers can benefit from visual art in any way.

Let's turn to Kim Morgan, a Canadian public art and installation artist, talking about the work of a few of her favourite contemporary artists. For Morgan, Anselm Kiefer's monumental work *Next Year in Jerusalem*[1] activates people's consciousness around the impact and debris of war through his use of materials and found objects. Materials such as lead, cement and charcoal, juxtaposed on dirty bodiless clothing, are displayed in vitrines. They suggest artefacts, but of what? The mood created with these materials is sombre, horrific. It addresses history in a profound way and unsettles us.

Kiki Smith's portrayals of women are poignant, poetic and real with all of their beautiful defects and functions. She uses the female body as a space of investigation.

Bruce Nauman takes complex philosophical ideas and texts, and turns them into visual one-liners that punch you in the gut. Even if you don't know the reference, you feel a physical discomfort that persists beyond the gallery space. Words cannot actually convey the impact of his pieces.

Art, then, is about experiencing. This experience does not necessarily translate into words, but can be emotional, visceral, sensual. As a matter of fact, most art experiences are subjective, contextual, and the exact meaning elusive. Art is about exposing. It exposes us to alternative views of the world. A successful artwork should reveal things. It should lead us unknowingly to places we normally wouldn't go without the work. Art embraces discomfort, the unknown and the invisible through an aesthetic experience. It encourages the breaking of rules under the guise of innovation. Art is about ideas without text.

1 http://www.gagosian.com/exhibitions/november-06-2010--anselm-kiefer/exhibition-video [accessed 25 July 2012].

Figure 13.1 ***The Acts of Nova Scotia 2009–2010***

Materials used in unpredictable ways transcend language and the resulting ambiguity opens up a space for subjective contemplation. Anish Kapoor builds forms covered in pigment to create a deep void of colour. Words cannot describe these works, but the experience of them borders on spiritual, an experience which eludes definition.

Ann Hamilton is an installation artist who creates sensual works which explore important social issues about class, labour and knowledge. *Myein*,[2] at the 1999 Venice Biennale, addressed the topic of slavery and oppression in American society. This stunningly beautiful wall of Braille with fuchsia pigment raining down reveals the contradictions of governments and the stains of history in a sensual way. Here sensory experience bypasses the intellectual and we have another kind of realization – a surprise where ugliness is revealed through beauty.

But our question is can art expose, reveal, uncover anything about law? What can lawyers learn from visual artists about texts? Can visual art critique law? What can visual artists offer that legal theorists cannot? These questions prompted me to create two works – a paper sculpture titled *The Acts of Nova Scotia 2009–2010* and a wood carving called *The Crest of the Nova Scotia Supreme Court*.

The Acts of Nova Scotia 2009–2010 is a representative sample of the legislation passed by the Nova Scotia House of Assembly (the provincial legislature) over a 10-year period. Each paper column is comprised of the legislation covering

2 http://www.youtube.com/watch?v=usy48VQPiDs [accessed 25 July 2012].

a particular area of law – business, government operations, taxation, the administration of justice, the protection of natural resources, the exploitation of natural resources, pensions of government employees, education, health, the declaration of provincial birds and gems and so on. The height of each column is proportional to the number of pages of legislation devoted to a particular category of law. For instance, business and government operations were the two highest columns. The column representing the exploitation of natural resources was taller than the column for their protection. In a province where very few people have pension plans, the column depicting government pensions was the same height as the education column. The column for human rights is just a little taller than the column composed of the legislation stipulating that the Duck Tolling Retriever is the official dog of Nova Scotia and that agate is the official gemstone of Nova Scotia. What is important in Nova Scotia becomes manifest. The tallest columns – business and government operations – look ready to topple over, unable to support themselves. The fragility of a democracy dependent on texts is evoked. The columns also point to failed government interventions in business and government attention turning in on itself.

The room filled with the columns of text provides a physical measure of how much law we are presumed to know. The columns of law are overwhelming. Law is omnipresent rather than understood, visceral rather than intellectual. These columns also bring to mind architectural ruins, reminding us of neglect and decay, obsolescence and irrelevance.

Figure 13.2 ***The Crest of the Nova Scotia Supreme Court*, 2009**

The 'official' version of *The Crest of the Nova Scotia Supreme Court* hangs in the courtroom used by the judges of the Nova Scotia Appeal Court. I am told these judges are protectively proud of their brand. My piece is a modification of their crest. It is a wood carving made in the Nova Scotia folk art tradition: characterized by gouge marks, crude figures and bright colours, a kind of Nova Scotia down-home kitsch essentialism. My intention was to associate these elements with the Nova Scotia Appeal Court. The modification I made was to translate the Latin text on the crest into English. The English reads: *Evil to him who evil thinks*. I did not think it was necessary to translate the French text: *Dieu et mon droit* into *God and my right*, but was mistaken because few people could read French.

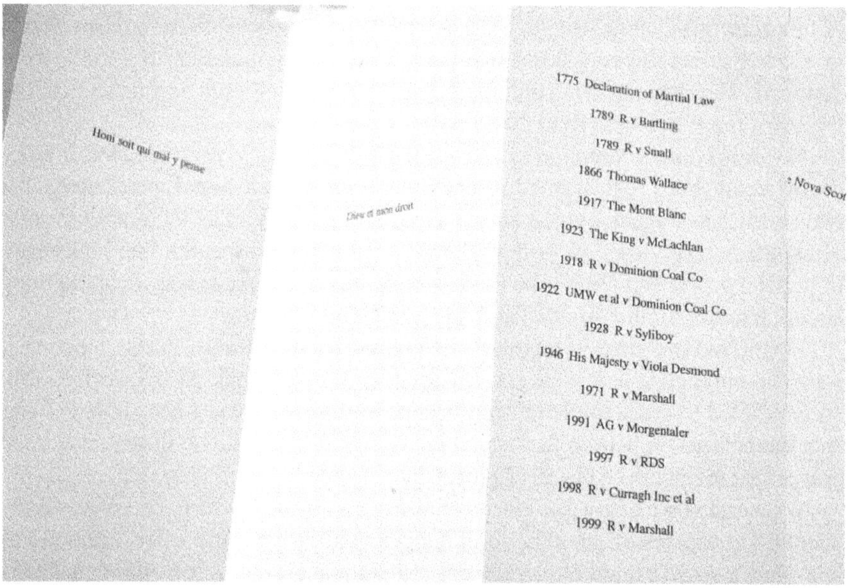

Figure 13.3 The Brochure

The Brochure

I also made a brochure listing some of the most notorious decisions this court has made (for information on these cases, see Girard, Phillips and Cahill 2004). For instance, in *R v. Donald Marshall*, one judge said that Donald Marshall, a 17-year-old Mi'kwaq man who was wrongfully convicted of murder and spent 11 years in jail, was 'the author of his own misfortune'. Evidence indicated that his conviction was due to the misconduct of the police and the prosecution, and a public inquiry later connected the wrongful conviction to systematic racism in the provincial justice system (Hickman 1989). In another case, *The King v. Desmond* (1947) (Barkhouse 1999: 226–71), a black woman who was jailed and fined for sitting in the 'white section' of a cinema lost her case in this court. Fifty-four years later, she was pardoned by the Nova Scotia government. Further, the Chief Justice of this court proclaimed the legislation expelling the Acadians from Nova Scotia in 1755. By December 1755, 7,000 people out of a population of 14,000 were deported. The deportations continued until 1762 leaving only 1,500 Acadians in the Maritime Provinces (Reid 2009: 58).

Not only was my intention to critique the high status and presumed infallibility of this court, but I also wanted to draw attention to their brand, particularly the two ridiculous slogans quoted above, slogans that we read as incredible in light of contemporary views on justice, fairness and claims respecting the legitimacy of judicial power and force. The crude kitschiness of my piece was meant to draw attention to this simple-minded and uncouth brand of justice.

I exhibited my crest in a gallery setting and, unfortunately, in this location it was incomprehensible to viewers. My artist audience dismissed the work as folk art and failed to grasp the legal significance of the crest. Had I been able to hang it in the courtroom behind the appeal court judges, my critique might have been grasped by members of the legal profession.

What do I make of my two efforts of making art about law? My two pieces draw attention to aspects of law that go unnoticed and in that sense offer a critique of law. They also give law a physical form and visceral presence, something that calls for a more immediate response than written texts. However, the challenge lurking behind these pieces and the work of others artists about law is how does an artist make art about law that is not considered trivial by legal theorists and lawyers, and at the same time is considered interesting by other artists? Nevertheless, pieces such as these offer law teachers an opportunity to expose their students to ideas about law not found in texts. In terms of critical reflection on law, such work may offer a more poignant and layered critique than 20 pages of dense text. More broadly, art-work about law that evokes feelings and provokes questions will hopefully inspire students to uncover things that lie outside their immediate horizons and beyond their legal texts.

Making art focused on law seems worthwhile, but it also seems to me that making art about law will not be enough by itself to get lawyers beyond the limited vision of their texts. Scholars have also revealed many interesting and important things about law. For instance, critical legal scholars and political scientists have successfully drawn attention to the political dimensions of law. Socio-legal scholars have uncovered gender-, race- and class-based discrimination in law. Legal historians have revealed the factors related to how particular laws have emerged and evolved. Regularly, the justice and injustice of particular rulings and judicial decisions turn into hot topics analysed and commented on by the media. Even my first-year business law students are quick to judge whether or not a judge's decision we are studying is fair.

But why have such insights had so little influence on law teaching, legal practice, judicial decision-making and law-making, particularly in North America? How can the fixation on legal texts remain immune to such penetrating criticisms? How is it that legal texts continue to hold such a mighty grip over the legal imagination? In short, how do we get beyond the legal text?

Before the Text

We take it for granted that the attitudes and work of lawyers and artists are very different. At a glance, lawyers and artists seem to be at opposite ends of a spectrum of creativity. We presume that lawyers settle for conventional solutions to problems, that their answers are in their texts. By contrast, we see visual artists as creative people devoting their lives to seeing and making things in new ways and subverting the status quo. However, the actual situation is more complicated.

On the first day that I teach my undergraduate class in business law, I tell my students that lawyers excel at a number of skills. Not only are lawyers experts at deciphering the dreadful prose of legislators and judges, they also excel at tackling complex problems, breaking them down into manageable parts and then coming up with intelligent and practical solutions. In fact, members of the legal profession with a mixture of awe and trepidation readily identify their imaginative and cunning colleagues. Even some judges are celebrated for their creative and wise decisions after they die. Occasionally, recollections of such judges resemble what Karl Llewellyn and Adamson Hoebel wrote about in their book *The Cheyenne Way*. They described the Cheyenne's abilities to solve legal problems in terms of 'utterly clean juristic intuition, individualized yet moving with singular consistency whither tribal welfare demands that it shall move' (Llewellyn and Hoebel 1941: 313). They admired 'the deftness and boldness of line with which the apt solution is marked in swift, sure strokes that fit at once justice, policy, and the given body of legal and social institutions' (1941: 313). Throughout their book are examples of 'the Cheyenne ability to deal at once with the problems of social policy presented and with the most delicate features of the particular case in hand, letting neither obscure the other' (1941: 314).

The best law students, lawyers, judges and legal scholars are recognized by their peers as people who discover the best solutions to complex problems. In fact, in order for lawyers, judges and legal scholars to do their jobs, creativity seems unavoidable. Yet the role of creative problem solving is neglected, even suppressed, in law. Consider legal reasoning. Legal reasoning for law students means learning how to 'think like a lawyer', that is, how to distinguish between issues, how to interpret legal texts, how to tease out principles from precedents, how to construct arguments and how to apply statutes to situations. Lawyers see their work as advising their clients on the application of law, not how the law should be improved. Moreover legal theorists who study legal reasoning portray it in terms of how judicial decisions are, and should be, legally justified. My point is that legal education, practice and scholarship are not explicitly concerned with recognizing, cultivating and celebrating the actual process of intelligent and creative problem solving. Why is it that the spontaneous and creative intelligence required to be a good law student, competent law teacher, effective lawyer and fair-minded judge is not encouraged by law schools?

You may not be aware of this, but visual artists are also excellent problem solvers. Art-making is one big creative problem-solving process. Artists know this; in fact, they dismiss work that is not in some way 'novel'. Such problem solving is grounded in an extensive knowledge of art history, contemporary art, art theory and criticism, cultural theory, materials, fabrication techniques, computer programs, engineering, architecture, politics, visual culture, pop culture and themselves. In this sense, visual art is a very successful form of interdisciplinary studies. Not only have visual artists worked collaboratively with architects, engineers, scientists and philosophers, but as a matter of course they research topics in any discipline that is relevant to their art practice. For an artist, no subject is off limits and disciplinary boundaries are generally ignored.

The crux of the difference between lawyers and artists noticed above is that lawyers operate within a more or less unacknowledged and spontaneous culture of problem solving that is shaped and bounded by legal rules, principles and texts, whereas visual artists are engaged in an open and deliberate problem-solving process which they judge to be one of the most important aspects of their identities.

A further important difference between lawyers and artists pivots on methodology. Most lawyers are not seriously interested in their methods. Legal research courses in Canadian law schools, for instance, are concerned with teaching students how to find and cite cases and statutes. The methodological concerns of most lawyers are limited to how best to persuade an adversary or judge to accept their side of the story. For lawyers, their key aim is to win their argument. They are not interested in things that are not immediately practical. Even for legal theorists, studies of legal method are dominated by the role of argumentation in justifying legal decisions.

By contrast, one of the most striking features of visual art is the massive effort and care taken by artists to critically reflect on, and assess, their own work and the work of other artists. Visual artists openly and critically reflect on what they do and why they do it, what makes one media different from another, what makes good art different from bad art. Anything and everything is open to scrutiny and evaluation.

At its root, visual art is about ideas. This orientation is characterized by relentless questioning of artists' intentions, the choice and use of their materials, the effects of their work on audiences, the nature of art-making processes, the connections between one artist's work and that of past and contemporary artists, how art-work is exhibited and the influence, for instance, of economics, politics, pop culture and personal experience on an artist's work. Any type of question about any subject is asked and artists expect thoughtful answers. More than any other discipline, artists investigate the nature of their methods and want to locate their work and themselves in a historical context. In fact, in this pursuit, visual artists seem to have become one of the most important voices of cultural critique.

Such talk of visual artists as 'imaginative and creative problem solvers devoted to critical reflection' easily provokes the following question: is there something here that lawyers can learn from visual artists? If lawyers were to take the creative attitude of artists as their inspiration, a very different culture of legal reasoning might emerge. Perhaps, like artists, lawyers would recognize and cultivate the driving force of curiosity and questioning in law. They might come to explicitly appreciate the messy nature of solving problems and the huge interdisciplinary efforts required to find adequate solutions to complex problems. Perhaps, like artists, lawyers would notice the importance of intuition and insight. They might even invent ways to protect and promote the full creative potential of thinking and reasoning in law. They might come to see legal reasoning primarily as a creative problem-solving activity rather than a search for solutions in legal texts. Imagine a law school where the core objective of legal education is the encouragement and development of creative problem solving and good judgement. Imagine a legal world where a 'great legal mind' is a person who is celebrated for his or her insightful grasp of complex problems and his or her successful experiments in creative problem solving.

When teaching my business law students, I stress that legal problem solving is a process of asking questions and seeking answers. My aim is to invite students to ask questions and answer them, and to become aware of themselves asking and answering questions. My students find answering their questions relatively easy. The challenge is to ask the right questions and not to stop asking questions until they have asked all the relevant questions and have satisfactory answers. They often ask whether they are permitted to give their opinions and I answer 'what else is there?'. In this way, my aim is to draw their attention to their own process of discovery – asking questions, finding answers and making judgements.

Although these undergraduate business students have little knowledge of other disciplines, they still have the advantage of people new to studying law. They are open to various points of view that are non-legal and they confidently assert their own sense of what is fair and just. They treat their legal texts as data, part of the raw materials for their inquiry, rather than as places to find solutions to 'legal' problems. In a naive way, they are beyond their texts.

Not only do I think that law teachers and students can go beyond their texts by learning from the attitudes, practices and work of visual artists, I also believe that the legal profession must develop an explanatory understanding of the problem-solving process. This would include coming to appreciate legal reasoning as essentially a process of discovery rather than the deployment and defence of sophisticated rhetorical techniques dominated by logic. To state it simply, the discovery process needs to be accepted as one of the central topics in Jurisprudence courses.

In the theory courses I have taught to law students and political science students, the decision-making process formed the core of these courses. I invited, cajoled and challenged students to appreciate that they ask questions, achieve insights and make judgements, and that such mental activities are actually conscious, deliberate, intelligent and rational. Further, I have tried to lead them to grasp that even the activity of testing insights is creative. To be more specific, I illustrate and explain the decision-making process as the operation of 13 empirically-verifiable mental activities: sensible presentations and memories, what-questions, direct insights, interpretations/definitions/explanations, is-questions, reflective insights, judgements of fact, what-can-be-done-questions, practical insights, courses of action/options/alternatives/plans, what-should-be-done-questions, practical reflective insights, judgements of value and decisions (see Anderson 1996). In this light the mental operations named above are the real ground and source of law, not legal texts. It follows that a written or oral expression of a judicial decision is something quite different from the decision-making process itself. My rationale for stressing the decision-making process is that by understanding what we do when we solve problems, we can learn to do it better. For instance, if we learn that the criteria for a judgement of value is asking all the relevant questions and being satisfied that we have asked them all and answered them satisfactorily, we may develop the confidence to move beyond legal texts in our search for adequate and suitable solutions to 'legal' problems (for further discussion, see Anderson 2008; Anderson 2013). My experience is that when students know they are questioners, they grow in their confidence to ask hard questions and are less inclined to settle for superficial answers.

In this new context, legal texts might be recognized as what they are – the expression of the discovery of intelligent solutions to recurring problems, the expression of some very serious thinking, guides not recipes to be repeated without more serious thinking. It is in this fashion that artists might point lawyers *beyond* the text by inspiring them to discover and embrace what they do *before* the text. But legal theorists must get to grips with the fact that the ground of law is questions, insights and judgements, and that what really matters is the thinking that occurs before and after texts are written. In this way lawyers might even come to earn something akin to the admiration we save for artists.

References

Anderson, B. 1996. *Discovery in Legal Decision Making.* Law and Philosophy Series, 24. London: Kluwer Academic Publishers.

Anderson, B. 2005. 'A note on the process of introspection'. *Perspectives on Jurisprudence: Scandanavian Studies in Law*, 14, 1–24.

Anderson, B. 2008. 'Business ethics versus business law: rules, more rules, and deliberation'. *Legisprudence International Journal for the Study of Legislation*, 2(3), 217–30.

Anderson, B. 2013. 'Weighing and balancing in a new context', in C. Dahlman and E. Feteris (eds), *Legal Argumentation Theory: Cross-Disciplinary Perspectives*. Law and Philosophy Series. Dordrecht: Springer, 113–23.

Barkhouse, C. 1999. *Colour-Coded: A Legal History of Racism in Canada, 1900–1950.* Toronto: University of Toronto Press.

Benton, J., Drage, A. and McShane, P. 2005. *Introducing Critical Thinking.* Halifax: Axial Press.

Girard, P., Phillips, J. and Cahill, B. 2004. *The Supreme Court of Nova Scotia, 1754–2004: From Imperial Bastion to Provincial Oracle*. Toronto: University of Toronto Press.

Hickman, T.A. 1989. *Royal Commission on the Donald Marshall, Jr. Prosecution: Digest of Findings and Recommendations*. Halifax, NS: The Commission.

Llewellyn, K.N. and Hoebel, E.A. 1941. *The Cheyenne Way*. Norman: University of Oklahoma Press.

Reid, J., 2009. *Nova Scotia: A Pocket History*. Halifax: Fernwood Publishing.

Cases

The King v. Desmond (1947) 20 MPR, 297 (NSSC).

Links

Anish Kapoor: http://www.anishkapoor.com/works [accessed 25 July 2012].

Kim Morgan: http://kimmorgan.ca [accessed 25 July 2012].

Bruce Nauman: http://www.pbs.org/art21/artists/bruce-nauman [accessed 25 July 2012].

Kiki Smith: http://www.pbs.org/art21/artists/kiki-smith [accessed 25 July 2012].

Index

Page numbers in *italics* refer to figures and tables.

For Product Safety Concerns and Information please contact our EU representative GPSR@taylorandfrancis.com
Taylor & Francis Verlag GmbH, Kaufingerstraße 24, 80331 München, Germany

www.ingramcontent.com/pod-product-compliance
Ingram Content Group UK Ltd.
Pitfield, Milton Keynes, MK11 3LW, UK
UKHW021722240926
475702UK00029BA/1781
* 9 7 8 1 1 3 8 2 7 7 2 5 0 *